BRANCHING OUT
by JAMES HALE

The Story of The Royal Canadian Legion

The Royal Canadian Legion
359 Kent Street
Ottawa, Ontario
K2P 0R7

Canadian Cataloguing in Publication Data

Hale, James

      Branching Out: The Story of The Royal Canadian Legion

      Includes bibliographical references and index
      ISBN 0-9699510-0-0

      1. Royal Canadian Legion – History
      I. Royal Canadian Legion   II. Title

      FC241.R69H35 1995   369'.271'09   C95-900338-X
      F1028.H35 1995

The Royal Canadian Legion
359 Kent Street
Ottawa, Ontario
K2P 0R7

Printed and bound in Canada by WEBCOM
9 8 7 6 5 4 3 2 1

DEDICATION

This book
is dedicated to all those who
by sea, on land and in the air
sacrificed their lives in the
service of humanity; and to
their comrades who, inspired
by their sacrifice, and with
unity of purpose, founded
The Royal Canadian Legion.

—

AUTHOR'S DEDICATION

To the memory of my grandfather,
Richard Hale, whose tireless devotion to the rights of
Canadian veterans is a constant inspiration.

His Excellency the Right Honourable Roméo LeBlanc
P.C., C.C., C.M.M., C.D.
Governor General and Commander-in-Chief of Canada

Forword

by
His Excellency the Right Honourable Roméo LeBlanc
P.C., C.C., C.M.M., C.D.
Governor General of Canada

The history of The Royal Canadian Legion is one of dedication and service to this wonderful nation by individuals who share the belief that, when the country calls, its citizens must respond. The founders first answered the call to arms in 1914, and their successors accepted the challenge once again at the outbreak of World War II, the Korean War and the War in the Persian Gulf. They also took part in countless peacekeeping missions around the world. The Legion's history is also one of change and progression within the collective agreement that is Canada.

From a society interested mainly in veteran's benefits and care, the Legion has evolved into the largest service organization in the country with more than 1,700 branches and over half a million members. While its primary aim remains the care and remembrance of those who fought for Canada when needed, the Legion's influence can be felt in all sectors of the community from its youth to the seniors who have already contributed in various ways to the development of this nation. The many charitable works the Legion has supported over the years have aided in the growth of these communities. Thus, this history is one that deserves to be told for the benefit of all Canadians.

Branching Out is a tribute to those who did not return from foreign battlefields just as the Legion's daily operations stand as a constant reminder of those who made the ultimate sacrifice in the name of their country. As Governor General and Commander-in-Cheif of the Canadian Forces, I am honoured to have been invited to provide the forword to this most fitting tribute to those who served Canada so well in times of war as well as in times of peace.

Roméo LeBlanc

The television on the wall is showing the Leafs-Boston game, and about two dozen faces in the branch lounge are turned toward it.

Jimmy has a wager riding on the Leafs. Moe has been a Canadiens fan all his life, but he can never resist a bet with Jimmy.

"Want to put another tall one on the line, Bud" asks

INTRODUCTION

Moe with a wink as the Bruins make it 3-2 late in the second.

Jimmy's still working on a comeback when their wives appear at the table.

Between periods, the talk turns to plans to visit a mutual acquaintance of the two couples — a World War I vet who's in a chronic-care facility in town. Before they finish the conversation, they're joined by the branch president and his wife.

At its last meeting, the branch agreed to purchase a new outfield fence for the local ball diamond, and the president is looking for volunteers to work next Saturday morning to put in the posts. Jimmy and Moe agree to lend a hand, but not without a few friendly jibes about the president's methods.

"Once a sergeant, always a sergeant," concludes Jimmy, nudging Moe and stiffening his back and arms into a mock form of attention. "He never has a problem with getting guys to take that step forward, even when they're sitting down."

The time is 1958... or 1988. The place... any branch of The Royal Canadian Legion from British Columbia to Newfoundland.

For 70 years, since November 1925, the Legion has been a source of camaraderie for two generations of ex-servicemen and women and their families. It has also been a source of succor for those ravaged by war, the elderly and the disadvantaged, and a major contributor to community projects of all descriptions.

In small towns — where the branch is often the social centre — and big cities, the Legion has embodied Canadian life through seven decades of the 20th century. It has evolved from the voice of social reform, to the country's moral conscience, to the leading proponent for the maintenance of traditional values.

Its history is, in many ways, the story of Canada's coming of age.

C O N T E N T S

Section 1

1920 - 1935

PULLING TOGETHER

Chapter 1

"A SPECIAL APPEAL TO THE MEN WHO SERVED..."

From a distance of almost 80 years, it is difficult to appreciate how Canadians "came home" from World War I — both in terms of their state of mind and body, and in logistical terms.

The dominant image most Canadians have — and for most of us it is a photographic image rather than a mental one — is of masses of de-mobilized soldiers, still in uniform, marching through the streets of Canadian towns and cities to a civic welcome. That image, cultivated by Canadian Corps commander Sir Arthur Currie as a means of maintaining military discipline until men were safely home, overshadows the reality of the thousands of Canadians whose war was over almost as soon as it began.

For most of the first year of the war, care of these returned men fell to private organizations like the Red Cross and St. John Ambulance, or to wealthy individuals, some of whom offered summer residences as convalescent homes. It was not until June 1915 that Prime Minister Sir Robert Borden created the Military Hospitals Commission to care for returning veterans.

As historian Desmond Morton pointed out in his book *When Your Number's Up*: "Canada had a lot to learn about veterans. The militia pension regulations in 1914 had been hurriedly improvised for the 1885 Rebellion and differed only in detail from arrangements made for the War of 1812."

Rapidly, the government struggled to establish facilities to treat the wounds of returning soldiers.

Unfortunately, no one had stopped to come to terms with what types of "wounds" Canada's veterans would have. In addition to the expected physical damage caused by implements of war, many early returnees had health ailments such as tuberculosis, or mental problems that had been little anticipated and were even less well understood by government officials.

But whether or not they understood the extent of the injuries of Canada's veterans, the government was sure it knew what was best for these men: rehabilitation and a quick return to productive labor. Leading pension experts like J.L. Todd, a former McGill University medical school professor who became one of the first three members of the Canadian Board of Pension Commissioners, and Ernest Scammell, secretary of the Military Hospitals Commission, espoused the belief that vocational training should be instituted so that men could begin to earn real wages rather than relying on pension funds. By 1916, training schemes were underway, although initial attempts proved ill-suited to men who had just returned from a war zone.

As time passed, training procedures were improved and the programs pursued a philosophy of preparing a man to return to civilian life in some type of job related to his previous occupation. While that sounded good in theory, the reality was often less rosy. Men did not adjust as quickly as the planners had hoped, and jobs were not always waiting for disabled veterans when they were fit enough to be released.

Still, the experts were convinced that they had the veterans' best interests at heart. As Morton stated: "Veterans were expected to work hard and be grateful. They had no part in planning their own re-establishment. It was experts who set pensions (and) selected appropriate re-training programs..."

In response to the government's paternalism veterans grew discontented and bitter. No one understood their concerns and their experiences save for fellow vets, so they banded together to form local associations that would provide them with a louder voice and a sense of comradeship.

On April 10, 1917, one day after Canadian troops moved out of their positions against the Germans holding Vimy Ridge, representatives of 147 of these associations came together in Winnipeg to form a national group called the Great War Veterans Association.

The first official function of the GWVA was the promotion of better hospital facilities for disabled men returning from battlefields. A new policy of treatment, pensions and rehabilitation first saw the light of day in GWVA proposals.

The GWVA's early and strong calls for better treatment might have been expected by the government. The organization's egalitarian zeal likely came as more of a surprise. Many GWVA members — ex-servicemen from other ranks — harbored a strong resentment against the officer class and the practice of preference by rank. Eschewing any type of nomenclature that implied rank, GWVA members addressed one another as "comrade."

As more and more of the 350,000 Canadians overseas began returning home, new veterans' organizations began to emerge, reflecting the concerns of members, their branch of service, or their type of disability. Among these were: the Army and Navy Veterans in Canada, which pre-dated the war and was re-organized in 1918; a GWVA splinter group, the Grand Army of United Veterans; the Tuberculous Veterans Association; the Disabled Veterans Association; the Imperial Veterans in Canada; the Amputations Association of Canada; the Naval Veterans Association; the Royal North West Mounted Police Veterans Association; the Canadian Pensioners Association; the South African Veterans Association; the Veterans Civil Service Guild; the Canadian Workers Federation of Returned Soldiers and Sailors; the Canadian National Veterans Guild; and even a Canadian Legion of Ex-Servicemen.

As the largest and most vocal of the burgeoning veterans' groups, the GWVA quickly gained the ear of the government. In 1918, with the war's end imminent, the federal cabinet summoned an advisory committee from the association for advice on how best to absorb returning soldiers back into civilian life.

GWVA secretary-treasurer Grant MacNeil had strong ideas on how Canada should treat its returning veterans. At every turn, he reminded the government that it had promised to give the veteran "the benefit of the doubt" when it came to assessing pension cases and awarding support. He met stiff opposition from the governments of Borden and Arthur Meighen, but in 1922 MacNeil managed to convince the new Liberal government of Mackenzie King that the Board of Pension Commissioners should be investigated for what he saw as a conspiracy to deprive ex-servicemen of their rights. The result was the Royal Commission on Pensions and Re-establishment headed by James Layton Ralston, former commanding officer of the 85th Battalion.

GWVA officials were also instrumental in advising the government on establishing the Soldier Settlement program, which grew out of a bill passed by Parliament in 1917. Intended to meet the dual goals of putting veterans to work and colonizing tracts of land in Western Canada, the scheme set provisions for loans to prospective farmers and disbursement of arable Crown lands. After a decade, the program proved to be a failure; rising interest rates, falling returns on agricultural outputs, and the unsuitability of many veterans to farming led one-third of the 31,000 participants to pull out. Failure though it was, the Soldier Settlement program laid the groundwork for a similar scheme that *did* work after World War II, and it went a long way in the early 1920s toward cementing the GWVA's position as a forward-looking organization.

In fact, the GWVA had been prescient enough to call for a unified voice for Canadian veterans from the very beginning. In December 1917, in the first edition of *The Veteran*, the GWVA's magazine, editor J.A. Stevenson stated: "Though making a special appeal to the men who have served in the ranks of the Army, (the GWVA) will also endeavor to serve the wider interests of the whole community and become a healthy and powerful voice in our national life…"

In July 1921, the GWVA invited representatives of Canada's diverse veterans' organizations to its annual national convention in Port Arthur, Ontario (now part of Thunder Bay). In addition to being a first, tentative step toward uniting the various factions, the Port Arthur congress is worth noting for the presence of a Frenchwoman named Guerin. She had already succeeded in convincing the nascent British Legion of the fund-raising potential in selling poppies as symbols of remembrance — an idea she borrowed from a New York YMCA canteen worker, Moina Michael — and now she did the same in Canada. On July 5, after a brief presentation from Guerin, the Dominion executive committee of the GWVA adopted the poppy as its "flower of remembrance."

The GWVA also had its eyes on international unity among veterans. Later in 1921, it sent representation — along with the Army and Navy Veterans Association — to the founding meeting of the British Empire Service League in Cape Town, South Africa. In 1923, representatives from the GWVA also attended the international conference of the League of Nations in Geneva, Switzerland, where a topic of discussion was the worldwide problem of absorbing war-disabled into industry.

The association wasted no time in importing ideas that it picked up abroad. British Empire Service League grand president Earl Haig of Bemersyde's plea for veterans' unity became the rallying cry at the GWVA's 1922 convention in Winnipeg. Citing Haig's concern that only a unified veterans' force could win rights, the association brought five other groups to the table to form the Dominion Veterans Alliance. Financed in the main by the GWVA, the alliance was intended to concentrate the attention of the various organizations on the common problems besetting all in the fields of legislation and related matters.

While the alliance gave its members an appreciation of one another, it ultimately did little to foster unity; in fact, it accentuated the differences between the groups and quickly appeared doomed to failure.

Still, the GWVA persisted in its view that veterans could be moulded into a force that could influence the greater society. At its 1923 conference in Montreal it issued a declaration of principles that stated in part: "The foundation principle upon which our association rests is national service, and we unreservedly commit ourselves to a standard of service for Canada and the British Empire in the work of national development as full, as self-sacrificing and as free from personal motives as that rendered by our army overseas. We pledge ourselves to the common service of our country, acknowledging no pre-eminence in our association except devotion in building up our national life."

A year later, in *The Veteran*, the organization stated: "Until the last veteran goes to his final resting place in the bosom of Mother Earth there will be problems arising from war service. But the major work of the GWVA in future will be nation building."

Indeed, GWVA officials seemed to have the knack for pursuing consensus, even when things seemed hopeless. Undaunted by the dissension within the Dominion Veterans Alliance, the GWVA took its hopes for Canadian veterans' unity to Haig at the British Empire Service League's 1923 convention in England. Still flushed with his success in cobbling British veterans together, he proposed that the league hold its next biennial convention in Canada, saying that if unity had not been achieved by then, an effort would be made to bring together representatives of the various organizations and factions.

In 1924, the GWVA took Haig up on his promise and extended an official invitation for the British Empire Service League council to visit Canada.

Haig's role as an itinerant champion of veterans' rights was an unlikely one. Roundly hated by his men during his time as commander-in-chief of the British Expeditionary Force for his callous use of them at Passchendaele and the Somme, he had a side he never showed them. His requests for fair treatment for wounded soldiers indicate that there was another layer to the man who once said he did not want to visit his injured charges for fear that it would affect his judgment. "I strongly urge," he wrote to the secretary of state for war on February 20, 1917, "that there should be no delay in dealing with this matter, which, if allowed to continue, will constitute a scandal of the greatest magnitude."

Two months later, just after the opening of the Battle of Arras, he wrote to Lady Haig: "As you know, I don't go out of my way to make myself popular, either by doing showy things or by being slack in the matter of discipline — I never hesitate to find fault, but I have myself a tremendous affection for those fine fellows who are ready to give their lives for the Old

✤

Country at any moment. I feel quite sad at times when I see them march past me, knowing as I do how many must pay the full penalty before we can have peace."

Even the traditional British insistence on the privilege of rank seems to have been absent in Haig. Writing in March 1922 about his vision for the British Legion, he stated: "Really, there *ought* to be no question of 'rank' in the Legion — we are all 'comrades.' That however is not possible and we must legislate to ensure that the 'other ranks' are adequately represented."

Haig's proposed visit created as many problems as it promised to solve. In order to have the visit assume the proportions and dignity of a national welcome, the GWVA sought assistance from the federal government. Many prominent government officials were opposed to the visit, claiming that conditions among the veterans' groups were too chaotic. They believed the visit should be postponed until an effort had been made to bring the groups together, and then have Haig consummate unity.

When Haig heard this viewpoint, he is reported to have said: "If that is the condition of affairs among Canadian ex-servicemen, now is the time they need me."

The GWVA scheduled its annual convention for June 1925, to coincide with Haig's arrival in Ottawa. In keeping with Haig's wishes, many of the other veterans' organizations also sent delegates to the capital.

Meeting three days before Haig arrived, the GWVA passed a resolution supporting the union of all Canadian veterans' groups, and representatives of the Tuberculous Veterans Association quickly followed suit. Both organizations offered Haig complete access to their books and records.

Upon his arrival, Haig met with representatives from the various groups, telling each that they should set aside their differences and follow the example of the British Legion. His trump card was an address to more than 3,000 veterans gathered at a rally.

Haig, a dour man with such a poor speaking style that he habitually began speeches by reminding audiences that he was no orator, delivered a self-deprecating message that put the onus for unity squarely on the veterans' shoulders: "I recognize your difficulties. We ourselves were faced with them, but, given the desire for unity, goodwill and real endeavor, they can be overcome. And if in one particular — that of distance — your difficulties are greater than were ours, that very difficulty of distance makes your need the greater, too.

"I am quite sure that if your different societies come into a single organization, the influence of that single organization for the good of ex-servicemen and of Canada will be something far more, far wider and far greater than the mere aggregate of the influence separately exerted by the existing societies.

"The whole ex-service movement will be put on a new and higher plane; its prestige will be immensely increased; its membership will grow...

"I hope that it will not be thought that I am going beyond the purpose of this meeting in giving you this advice. My excuse is that I am most desirous to see a strong representative and influential organization of ex-service officers and men in every dominion and territory of the Empire. I realize that each dominion has its special problems and its special needs, but I believe also that there is no object of common interest to them both which two men cannot achieve better by combining and co-ordinating their efforts than by working separately, disjointedly and even adversely to each other.

"I feel that the present is full of promise. Do not hesitate or delay. Let us proceed and get on with it."

Chapter 2

THE "SPONTANEOUS, ORGANIZED, MULTITUDE"

T he foresight shown by Earl Haig in his plea for unity to the veterans gathered in Ottawa in June 1925 extended beyond a view of ex-servicemen working together to improve their lot. He also foresaw an organization that would play a critical role in community service: "...the power of the Legion to help the ex-service community by its direct benevolence as well as by its advocacy will be proportional to the concern for the nation as a whole."

Appropriate to Haig's view of this new, united, Canadian veterans' organization, representation to its founding conference — scheduled for Winnipeg on November 25, 1925 — was solicited from across the country. Delegates were sought both from established organizations and from among non-affiliated veterans. In the end, 10 organizations with multiple branches and 50 independent regimental societies and clubs — 790 units and 20,000 veterans in all — answered the call.

In his absence, Haig had appointed Lt.-Gen. Sir Richard Turner VC to organize and chair the unity conference. As the date for the meeting approached, Turner set out his hopes for the attitude that delegates would bring to Winnipeg: "In the name of those who have passed on I appeal to you to forget the petty differences that have divided our ranks, to destroy the viper of suspicion and distrust which has ranged unchecked among us, to catch anew the vision which carried you to the heights of heroism and self-effacement on the battlefields, to be true to your comrades and yourselves... to unite."

The GWVA's *The Veteran* traced the path to Winnipeg all the way back to its founding conference in 1917, and viewed a successful conference as a foregone conclusion: "...a considerable amount of preliminary work has been done with a view to bringing to bear at the Winnipeg conference a great force of united opinion among veterans of the old organizations and of those who previously have had no organization affiliations. As a result, the delegates at Winnipeg have as their mandate an overwhelming verdict in favor of creating a united Canadian organization.

"The discussions of the Winnipeg conference can be confined to the structure and functions of the united body. The question of 'Shall we unite?' has been decided in the provincial gatherings and by the resolutions of existing organizations, the great majority of whom have declared unequivocally in favor of union.

"What may the veterans of Canada expect from this third conference at Winnipeg? There is only one result that will be satisfactory and that is complete unity. This jewel without price was captured by the first conference but lost, to some extent, in the turmoil of the postwar period. The halfway measure of federation failed in effectiveness. The duty of the third conference stands out as a beacon light. Failure to unite will be tantamount to failure in the trust which delegates carry with them to Winnipeg."

The Veteran set out three roles for the new organization:

- care of the war-disabled, the dependent and the needy;
- keeping alive public memory of the sacrifices of Canadians in the cause of world peace and thus provide a deterrent to future conflicts; and
- promotion of unity of thought and of effort among the peoples who make up the nation, and the consequent development of a greater national consciousness.

As fine and hopeful as these ideals were, they did not necessarily reflect the reality of all the organizations that were making their way to Winnipeg's Marlborough Hotel. The initial position statements of some of the 60 delegates indicated that consensus might not be as easy to achieve as the GWVA had assumed.

While Thomas Downing, president of the Tuberculous Veterans Association, and Lt.-Gen. Sir Percy Lake, who represented several veterans' groups on Vancouver Island, both spoke strongly in favor of total unity, Maj.-Gen. W.A. Griesbach, president of the Army and Navy Veterans of Canada, was not as positive. Although he said his organization was in favor of the principle of unity, he was not satisfied with the way delegates to the conference had been selected. He also indicated dissatisfaction with what he termed "indifferent leadership."

A.A. Palmer, delegate for the Amputations Association, said that while unity might work for the large, general-interest groups, the special-interest groups like his might do better on their own.

One of the first actions at the convention was to strike a committee under the chairmanship of the GWVA's Ontario representative Harry Bray to negotiate terms of union with the 12 organizations present.

Another early agenda item was the drafting of a resolution that summarized the purpose of the conference:

WHEREAS our comrade, Field-Marshal Earl Haig, during his recent visit to Canada carried an appeal for unity to war veterans throughout the country, declaring that by united effort we could advance with far greater facility our generally held ideal of national service;

AND WHEREAS conferences representative of organized and unorganized war veterans have been held in different provinces, and conventions of existing associations have declared themselves in favor of the principle of unity;

THEREFORE BE IT RESOLVED that this conference of delegates representative of ex-servicemen throughout Canada irrevocably pledges itself to the principle of unity towards which end all executive bodies of existing organizations shall be subordinate, and that until a united organization is completely effected there shall be no disintegration of existing organizations;

AND FURTHER, that when such unity organization is completely effected, all executive bodies of existing organizations shall be called upon to surrender their status as such, reserving only the local autonomy of branches and clubs;

FURTHER BE IT RESOLVED that this conference of duly elected delegates representative of all classes and all groups of war veterans, with this unequivocable mandate to accomplish unity, resolve itself into the first national meeting of the projected united organization and provisionally proceed to the selection of a name, the adoption of a constitution and election of provisional national officers and other necessary business.

With its mandate firmly stated, the convention next set about drawing up a constitution. Prior to the meeting, a Montreal lawyer, W.D. Lightball, had drafted a working model, based on the constitutions of several other organizations. Now, a 21-man committee led by Lake set about working through it to come up with a final document.

Other delegates turned their minds to creating a name for the new organization. Several names were suggested, but it was Turner who carried the day with The Canadian Legion of the British Empire Service League.

A financial committee under the chairmanship of Manitoba's Eli Spencer presented a report recommending that all members be assessed annual dues and that a per capita fee be levied at a rate fixed by national and provincial bodies. After some discussion, the delegates voted to set the national per capita fee at $1 for the first year, subject to revision by the first national convention, but decided to leave the issue of provincial fees to the provinces themselves.

Spencer's committee also recommended that each of the Legion's founding organizations be responsible for discharging any liabilities prior to joining.

On the question of membership cards, delegates voted that the national headquarters should maintain records of all cards issued, and that branches would be responsible for quarterly tracking of renewals and per capita payment.

Another resolution attempted to address A.A. Palmer's concern that special-interest groups would lose their purpose through amalgamation. Delegates voted that groups like the Tuberculous Veterans Association and the Imperial Veterans in Canada could continue to be represented on Dominion and provincial command executive councils.

In the pensions area, delegates passed a resolution directing the provisional executive to ensure that the Pension Board make an award or other final disposition of any application within three months; or, in the case of an appeal, render a decision within six months. In the case of a further delay, the resolution called for the applicant or appellant to be placed on pay and allowances by the Department of Soldiers' Civil Re-establishment.

The Dominion Executive Council was directed to draft a plan for obtaining and distributing poppies produced by Vetcraft shops under the control of the Civil Re-establishment Department.

Alberta delegates, led by G.E. Saunders, pushed for a motion to make November 11 — Armistice Day — a national holiday. The resolution was passed unanimously.

The convention also demonstrated unanimity in electing Lake as the Legion's first Dominion president.

In Lake, the delegates saw a president who could bring both prestige and leadership qualities to their new organization. Commissioned in 1873 in the British Army, he saw action in the Afghan War and the Sudanese expedition. He had come to Canada in 1893 as quartermaster-general of the Canadian Militia before going on to serve in staff appointments elsewhere in Canada and in England. He became chief of the general staff and then inspector-general of the Canadian Militia before going to India in 1911 as a divisional commander. In 1916 he became general officer commanding the British forces in Mesopotamia, for which he earned his knighthood. After retiring to Victoria, his quiet leadership made him a natural to represent the concerns of veterans on Vancouver Island, and he had been an early champion for unity across Canada.

Another former senior officer, Brig.-Gen. Frank Meighen, was elected to the sole vice-president post. A retired non-commissioned officer, Sgt. Jack Moore, was elected chairman, while two former lieutenant-colonels — J. Keiller MacKay and Leo LaFleche — were elected vice-chairman and treasurer respectively.

Each provincial command elected one Dominion Executive Council representative, save for Ontario, which was allotted two seats. As part of the transition process, each of the 12 participating organizations were also given seats on the council until the unity process was complete.

Turner was rewarded for his hard work by being named honorary president, along with Sir Arthur Currie. Haig was the Legion's grand president.

Lake's constitution committee reported with a document that has proven remarkably durable. It laid out principles of democracy, non-sectarianism and political non-affiliation. Among its 19 aims and objectives were the promotion of patriotism and public service among Canadians, the perpetuation of the memory of Canada's war dead, assistance to veterans and their dependants, and international co-operation with other veterans' associations. The constitution made provisions for branches to acquire and hold property, and assured provincial commands of due notice for consideration of any matter undertaken by Dominion Command.

The constitution set out three membership categories — ordinary, honorary, and associate. The latter category was created for British subjects who had served in the regular or auxiliary forces, but were not eligible for ordinary membership.

✿

Provision was also made for the formation of women's auxiliaries under the auspices of the branches and provincial commands.

On November 28, the delegates concluded their business and headed home to start the task of making the design for the Canadian Legion a reality. The year-end edition of *The Veteran* stated: "The year 1925 was great because we were able to clear the *way* for unity... 1926 should be even greater because it is the earnest hope of Canadian veterans that it shall mark the *fact* of unity.

"The real task has just begun. The co-operation and support of every veteran is needed to ensure complete success. There's a big job to be done. Let's do it!"

Another magazine editorial, this one in *The Fragment* — the house organ of the Amputations Association — indicated there were still a few potholes on the road to unity: "There is a fear that our association will be thrown into the melting pot... and the cause (we) represent is in danger of extinction... Confidence, which is all-important in matters of this kind, is lacking."

The Amputations Association decided not to bring its 1,457 members into the fold.

The 12 branches of the Army and Navy Veterans would also remain outside of the Canadian Legion.

Clearly, achieving unity was not going to be as easy as the headiness of the Winnipeg conference suggested.

The goal of the Legion's provisional leaders was to sell the notion of a united organization across the country at provincial conventions that would be convened to ratify the Winnipeg agreements. Their message was that a new organization was not being established merely for the sake of having an organization but for the sake of clearly defined objectives: assisting the widowed, the orphaned and the needy; striving for improvement in pensions; seeking re-establishment measures for the disabled; promoting harmony and loyalty among Canadians; strengthening the ties within the Empire; and fostering the spirit of peace.

In delivering this message they faced a predictable number of naysayers, including some who spread a particularly vicious rumor that the Canadian Legion was the prototype for a fascist movement.

In the face of such mounting criticism it was vital that the Legion move quickly to recapture its positive momentum. On February 17, 1926, in

Regina, Saskatchewan, veterans met to begin the cross-country ratification process. The convention opened with 128 representatives from 98 communities in attendance. In addition to a large number of delegates from the GWVA, which had a strong base in the province, there were also delegates from the Tuberculous Veterans Association, the Amputation Club, the United Services Club, the Royal North West Mounted Police Veterans Association, and various regimental associations.

The first order of business was to vote on the official creation of the Canadian Legion in Saskatchewan. The resolution received unanimous support.

Among the other motions passed at the convention were calls for proper valuation of land and stock under the Soldier Settlement program, extension of relief from the Canteen Fund for care of indigent and aged veterans, and speedier response from the federal Appeal Board in handling pension matters. The convention also urged formation of district appeal boards and the reorganization of the Board of Pension Commissioners.

James McAra, a former lieutenant-colonel from Regina who had led the GWVA in Saskatchewan for eight years, was unanimously elected president. Among the other officers elected was former Brig.-Gen. Alex Ross of Yorkton, who became the command's honorary treasurer.

In his speech to the convention, McAra encouraged delegates to work together to make the Legion a success: "I cannot appeal to you too strongly to get the broad vision — broad as our prairies, broad in the national aspect as well as broad in the particular aspect of ex-servicemen. I ask you honestly and sincerely to forget any connection you have had in the past and look to the future with a desire to accomplish the greatest good. All branches of the service, all ranks of the service, and all classes of the service should, and can, get together if they will."

In March, Manitoba followed Saskatchewan's lead in holding its first annual convention. Sixty-two units and groups were represented.

The third regional element to join the Legion was something of a surprise; later in March, a 14-member unit of the British War Veterans Association in Spokane, Washington, disbanded and reformed as the first American post of the Canadian Legion.

In May, British Columbia, Quebec and Nova Scotia held their founding conventions, followed by Ontario, Alberta, Prince Edward Island and New Brunswick in June. By July 1, 1926, the chain of provincial councils was complete, and although the goal had been reached ahead of schedule, it was decided to delay the first national convention until early 1927 to give all the founding organizations time to hold separate conventions.

Other national matters required attention as well.

Foremost was criticism that the unity process was occupying too much of the Legion's attention and resources, at the expense of veterans and their dependants.

In response, in early April, Lake convened a meeting of a special committee of the Dominion Executive Council, including vice-president Meighen, chairman Moore, vice-chairman Mackay, treasurer LaFleche, Sir Richard Turner, Tuberculous Veterans Association president Dick Hale, and Manitoba Dominion Executive Council representative Eli Spencer. This committee determined that the Legion should waste no time in assuming responsibility for veterans' pensions, and created the Dominion Command Service Bureau to take over from the legislative and adjustment bureau being operated by the GWVA in Ottawa. Although the concept of a central unit to handle service work was deemed essential, the Legion had little money to fund such an operation, so the hiring of a bureau director was deferred. In the place of a full-time director, it was decided that Thomas Lapp, editor of *The Veteran*, could oversee the operation. Three other staff members were to work within the Service Bureau: J.C.G. Herwig, adjustment officer on civil service appointments and militia claims; F.L. Barrow, pension and treatment claims; and C.P. Gilman, tuberculous pension claims (which continued under the mandate of the Tuberculous Veterans Association).

In addition, the committee decided to reorganize *The Veteran*, making it the voice of the Legion effective May 1 and renaming it *The Legionary* — a title Lake thought implied unity, strength and comradeship.

Four other decisions made by the committee helped shape the Legion's future: it determined that local units of the organization would be called "branches" and numbered consecutively within each province; branches could be given names in addition to their numbers; charters would be issued by Dominion Command upon recommendation by provincial councils; and a Dominion branch would be created for veterans who could not readily use an existing or proposed branch.

In the month following that productive meeting in Ottawa, another important decision was made, as the Dominion Executive Council selected George Inglis' design as the official Legion badge. The central element of the badge was a maple leaf surrounded by the words Canadian Legion, British Empire Service League, all of which was topped by a crown. The first copy was struck of Manitoba gold and presented to Gov. Gen. Viscount Byng on May 29, 1926.

Another official fixture of any organization — the Legion's charter — proved slightly harder to obtain.

Originally, the Legion's founders had hoped to have the organization incorporated by a special act of Parliament, but the Customs scandal and the subsequent fall of both the King government and the subsequent government formed by Arthur Meighen meant that Parliament was in turmoil throughout the early summer. Finally, on July 17, secretary of state George Perley issued letters patent under the Companies Act granting a national charter to the Legion and empowering it to organize branches, commands and women's auxiliaries. The timing of the granting of the charter meant that a formal ceremony could not be arranged, so the document was signed by LaFleche, Lapp, Herwig, Service Bureau clerk Bertha Margaret Campbell, and a barrister named Maurice Ollivier.

The Canadian Legion — described by *The Legionary* as "a spontaneous, organized multitude with a great common purpose, a perpetuation of that spirit of comradeship born of unselfish service to Canada" — was finally a reality.

Although the Legion was now a legal entity, its solvency remained in question. Until per capita payments could accrue, the Service Bureau was forced to operate on a day-to-day basis. Pleas for prompt payment of dues were published in *The Legionary*'s initial issues, and by October the organization was out of debt and had operating capital in the bank.

October 1 is also a significant date because it marked the official disbandment of the Tuberculous Veterans Association and the formation of the Tuberculous Veterans Section of the Legion. The move meant an additional 4,000 Legion members and 14 branches.

In handing over the association's members, president Hale wrote: "Many of those comrades who labored hard for us... have gone to their rest... men who sacrificed their chances of recovery in order that our work might go on... Let us carry into the Legion our traditions, our spirit of service, and continue our glorious work for the chest-disabled and their dependants..."

A key factor in the association's decision was the clause in the Legion's constitution that allowed for special-interest groups to maintain some autonomy with the greater organization and have special representation. In the specific case of the tuberculous veterans, they drafted their own interpretation of the clause and submitted it for approval to the Dominion Executive Council. The national body assured the TB veterans that the new Tuberculous Veterans Section would have representation on each command executive council, retain its own branches and have control over its own Dominion service officer.

On the heels of the Tuberculous Veterans Association's dissolution, other founding groups handed over their charters, including the Grand Army of United Veterans and the Ontario Veterans Alliance. As 1926 drew to a close, the Legion had subsumed about 97 per cent of the veterans who were affiliated with other organizations, bringing its total strength to more than 20,000 members. New members were flowing in at a rate of 4,000 per month.

Chapter 3

FEELING ITS OATS

The winter of 1927 found the Canadian Legion back in Winnipeg once again, as more than 200 of its members gathered at the Marlborough Hotel January 24-29 for the organization's first annual convention.

As if setting a convention in Canada's coldest city in the middle of winter did not ensure that business would be first and foremost on delegates' minds, the agenda was left wide open; the meetings would continue until the work was done. Dominion president Sir Percy Lake intended that this convention would be a serious stock-taking for the year-old organization, and he had requested that branches send their most capable members.

In his keynote address, Lake reminded delegates that, although unity had been achieved, the real work of the Legion had barely begun: "We must not be content with knowing that our individual interests are safeguarded, that our branches are comfortable clubs, well managed and solvent. We are bound to see that our comrades less fortunate than ourselves are helped."

The convention resolutions committee, chaired by Saskatchewan's Alex Ross, had put forward 33 proposed amendments and alterations to the federal Pension Act, along with recommendations to the federal Appeal Board and other government bodies, and it was these matters that occupied the bulk of delegates' time in Winnipeg. Suggestions were made for the extension of the scope of the Department of Soldiers Re-establishment and the Appeal Board, and problems relating to veterans in the civil service and soldier settlement were discussed.

The government's settlement policy was the source of significant debate. Delegates called on the government to reduce veterans' indebtedness to the program, to waive interest charges on loans under the program, and apply any interest payments already made to the loan principle.

There was substantial discussion on the equality between veterans and immigrants in obtaining title to federal lands. The convention went on record as endorsing encouragement of Canadian settlement by British subjects and promotion of a "spirit of Empire."

The poppy committee recommended that the Legion remain the sole distributor of poppies and that Vetcraft Industries remain the sole manufacturer. The committee also expressed its belief that poppy revenue should be shared with provincial commands to cover any unexpected shortfall.

Thomas Lapp, editor of *The Legionary* and acting head of the Service Bureau, reported on the bureau's first nine months of operation and explained a new policy for handling claims from non-members.

Not surprisingly, financial matters weighed heavily on delegates' minds. Dominion honorary treasurer Leo LaFleche reported that the Legion had a surplus of $10,000, most of it accrued through payment of the per capita fee in December 1926. The budget for the coming fiscal year was pegged at $36,000, with the ways and means committee recommending that the per capita payment remain at $1 for 1927. This motion created no little debate, as many smaller branches responded that the amount was too much for members to pay. The committee's response was that a cut in the fee at that point would mean curtailing the work that could be done on veterans' behalf. In a standing vote, the $1 fee was maintained.

As was the case at the unity conference a year earlier, the 1927 convention was responsible for adopting several policies that became synonymous with the Legion. Primary among these was a motion to adopt the Great War Veterans Association nomenclature of "comrade" for fellow Legion members. Delegates also endorsed proposals to: establish sports programs at branch level; introduce a French-language edition of *The Legionary*; and organize public relations activities that would include a speakers' bureau and a publicity liaison at Dominion headquarters.

When nominations for Dominion president closed, Sir Percy Lake's name was the only one that had been filed. The aging leader said he would accept re-election only if he could nominate LaFleche as first vice-president and delegate much of the work to him. He said that his first year as president had severely taxed his eyesight, and that he was committed to travel to England for several months in the spring.

"I realize that I am practically asking you to let me nominate the vice-president for your approval," he told delegates, "but... (LaFleche's) advice and work has helped the Legion on innumerable occasions and it has always been sound. The policy which the Legion has followed has been his as much as mine…"

Delegates had no problem with Lake's request; LaFleche, an Ottawa native who had been severely wounded as a company commander with the Van Doos in June 1916, was widely respected as a tireless worker who had firsthand knowledge of disabled veterans' concerns. The retired lieutenant-colonel was acclaimed first vice-president.

In fact, only Nova Scotia's John Roper faced any opposition before being elected to the post of vice-chairman. James McAra of Saskatchewan was acclaimed Dominion second vice-president, Jack Moore was returned as chairman — a post he would hold until his retirement in 1950 — and Ontario's J.A. MacIsaac was acclaimed honorary treasurer.

Behind the scenes at the convention, an agreement was reached with the Imperial Veterans of Canada to bring its members into the Legion. Like the former Tuberculous Veterans Association, the imperials won the right to form their own autonomous division within the Legion, governed by their own bylaws, provided the bylaws did not conflict with the parent organization's aims and objects.

The weeks immediately following the convention were spent transforming the resolutions into concrete proposals for the government's consideration. On March 7, Dominion Command delivered 50 recommendations for amendments to pension legislation, treatment and appeals procedures, and returned soldiers' insurance.

The brief placed particular emphasis on the proposed elimination of the existing time limit on applications for pension, pointing out that pensions were a right and should not be arbitrarily restricted by time limitations.

The Legion also objected to the government's requirement that unpaid pensions be returned to public funds when a pensioner died intestate. Its brief made the point that often the right to a pension was not determined until just prior to the death of the pensioner, and consequently the man had been denied the use of money to which he was entitled. The Legion proposed that, when a pensioner died without a will, the Pension Board have discretionary powers to distribute the money among immediate relatives or to those who had maintained the veteran or been maintained by him.

❋

Among the other proposals was a call for a conference of tuberculous consultants to seek consensus on questions affecting tubercular and non-pulmonary, chest-disabled veterans.

A committee of Legion officers presented the brief to J.H. King, minister of soldiers' civil re-establishment, and when they left the minister they were confident that new legislation would be introduced during the current session of Parliament. However, on March 30, King rose in the Commons to announce that no amendments to the Pension Act would be introduced in 1927. A letter from King to the Legion stated that there was insufficient time on the government's calendar to give consideration to the recommendations.

On March 31, first vice-president LaFleche wrote back to King, stating: "The number of worthy cases considered by our annual convention is too great to permit the Legion to accept without protest that nothing be done... Those we represent ask for a full measure; many die without receiving what is due them. Delay means further worry, trouble and suffering to those persons."

But the Legion's appeal did not stop there. Letters also went out to all members of Parliament, asking them to remain in session long enough to permit consideration of the legislative proposals. "The Canadian Legion appeals to you," the letter stated, "in the name of those who were disabled by war service, and the dependants of those whose breadwinners gave their lives in the service of Canada, to remain on duty..."

Branches also got involved, addressing their concerns directly to their local MPs. Newspapers were pulled into the fight, as well, and editorials around the country attacked the government's stand. Eventually, the issue came to a head during a six-hour debate in the Commons and the government was forced to back down.

With only a week to go before the House was adjourned, King introduced two amendments — one to extend by two years the time limit for applications for pension claims; the other to provide for the consideration of new evidence in the case of claims previously rejected by the federal Appeal Board. Also passed was a bill to revaluate soldier settlers' land, which, while not exactly what the Legion had asked for, did provide some relief to those affected.

In addition, King stated his intention to send the remaining recommendations to a special House committee early in the new session, and authorized the convening of a board of consultants in June to study the problem of tuberculous veterans.

The Legion had won an important battle, proving that it could get results quickly if it chose to flex its muscles.

But the government was not about to buckle on every issue. Against Legion protests, Armistice Day was set for Monday, November 7, 1927. Many branches held services on November 11 regardless.

Poppy sales continued to grow, as more Canadians came to recognize the scarlet flower as the symbol of remembrance. In Toronto that November, $40,000 was raised in the poppy campaign.

As winter settled in across Canada, news came of the sudden death of Earl Haig. Sixty-seven, he had been visiting his sister in London when a heart attack struck him in his sleep. Tributes poured in for the field marshal, whom Winston Churchill called "a man cast in a classic mould." *The Legionary* wrote: "His wise leadership of the British forces during the war earned (Canadian veterans') confidence and admiration." If others were unwilling to go that far, most conceded that his tireless work in uniting veterans on three continents had gone a long way to atone for his strategy of human attrition at the Somme and Passchendaele.

A chastened Liberal government was as good as its word, appointing a special committee to examine pensions, disability treatment, land settlement, civil service jobs for veterans, and other matters. Chairmanship of the committee went to C.G. "Chubby" Power, MP for the riding of Quebec South and a man who would become one of the veteran's best servants on Parliament Hill. The committee endorsed many of the Legion's proposals when it reported back to Parliament in the late spring.

Just weeks later, on June 11, delegates arrived in Saint John, New Brunswick, for the Legion's second annual convention.

If the 1927 congress in Winnipeg had been a stock-taking exercise, the 1928 meeting was surely a time to reflect on how quickly the Legion concept had caught on across Canada. Membership had climbed to almost 50,000, attached to 765 branches. Saskatchewan — the first command in — continued to lead the way, with 183 branches. The largest single branch — 1,308 members — was located in Edmonton. Average branch size was between 70 and 80 members.

The Dominion Service Bureau reported that it had processed an average of 562 cases a week since the previous convention, and achieved more than 70 satisfactory adjustments per week.

Debate on the convention floor revealed that many injustices relating to pensions and treatment of veterans still remained, and delegates instructed Dominion Command to continue to press for redress from the government. One problem that was becoming obvious was that the deprivations of World War I were leading to premature aging among the men who had served. In addition to the more than 48,000 veterans of the Canadian Expeditionary Force who were receiving pensions, more problems were cropping up among the remaining 270,000 vets a decade after the war. An estimated 40,000 men had already had their lives cut short by the war since 1918.

Picking up a theme from the previous year's convention, delegates in Saint John expressed their concern over the future face of Canada. Reacting to a report that showed that in the year ending March 31, 1927, the 143,891 immigrants to Canada included 83,038 people of "foreign racial origin" and 60,853 British citizens, the Legion passed a motion supporting a 50 per cent quota for non-British immigrants.

Canadian culture was also on the agenda. Delegates voted in support of a national broadcasting system owned and operated by the federal government — a resolution that would find the Legion making a strong pitch in favor of a Canadian public radio network the following year before the Royal Commission on Radio Broadcasting. In a statement of policy that seems extraordinarily prescient in light of the eventual development of both the Canadian Broadcasting Corporation and commercial radio and television, the Legion maintained that: "The development of a national culture is necessarily a long process. In the meantime, as conditions are at present, we stand in danger of our whole national life being colored by the standards that prevail in the republic to the south of us, which, however admirable, are not our own."

As much foresight as the Legion's policy on broadcasting showed, outgoing Dominion president Lake may have demonstrated an even clearer view of the future when he suggested that membership be expanded to include the sons and daughters of veterans. "We are pledged to hand down our ideals to our children," he said. "The best way to do it is to bring them into the Legion and interest them in our work." No action was taken on his suggestion.

Of more immediate concern was a way to pay respect to the men who died at Vimy Ridge, the battlefield where many consider that Canada really became a nation. In recognition of the sacrifice Canadian soldiers had made to secure the strategic position, the government had begun construction of a 42-metre high monument that was to be unveiled in 1931 or 1932.

The concept of the organized pilgrimage to visit battle sites or cemeteries was new but growing. In 1927, 30 veterans from Eastern Canada had travelled to France and Belgium for a conducted tour, and some 15,000 U.S. veterans and their families had journeyed to France under the auspices of the American Legion. In 1928, more than 11,000 members of the British Legion were set to travel to Ypres for the unveiling of the Menin Gate Memorial.

Canadian veterans felt strongly that they should be present at Vimy when the memorial was dedicated. As a result, the convention passed a resolution that Dominion Command would study the feasibility of transporting a large number of Canadians to the ceremony and would poll branches to determine the level of interest.

As the convention wound down, delegates showed continuing concern that their young organization be recognized for its prestigious leadership by electing Sir Arthur Currie, former commander of the Canadian Corps in World War I, as Dominion president.

A 52-year-old native of Montreal, Currie had been much in the news in the spring of 1928. Although well into his postwar career as principal and vice-chancellor of McGill University, he had gone to court to defend his reputation against an Ontario newspaper, the *Port Hope Guide*. In its edition of June 13, 1927, the *Guide* published an article claiming that Currie had used the Canadian Corps for self-glorification during the final days of the war. Currie was widely regarded as arrogant and self-absorbed — historian Desmond Morton has called him a "pompous fool" — but few questioned his ability as a field general. Six weeks before the Legion convention convened, a jury in Cobourg, Ontario, awarded Currie nominal damages for libel and costs against the publisher and author of the article.

LaFleche was re-elected first vice-president, and vice-chairman Roper was elected second vice-president. MacIsaac and Moore returned as honorary treasurer and chairman respectively. The position of vice-chairman was left vacant, and would remain so until 1946.

Chapter 4

SLOGGING THROUGH HARD TIMES

As legionnaires headed home from New Brunswick in the final spring days of 1928 it is likely they felt relatively secure about their organization; after all, membership was growing, the financial picture was good, and a prestigious new leader was in place. With the aid of hindsight it is clear that, like society at large, the Legion was ill-prepared for the hard times that lay ahead. The '20s had been boom years — an era of rapid growth and expanding horizons. Tough times loomed, and new strategies would be required to cope.

Looking critically at the 1928 convention, one can detect signs of discord in the discussion about the failing condition of many veterans. A growing number of men were "breaking down" — in the parlance of the day — and some Canadians were beginning to feel that the government was becoming increasingly unsympathetic to this problem. The problem affected the Legion itself. President Sir Arthur Currie fell ill before the end of his first year in office, and *The Legionary* began a regular column to report the expanding death toll of veterans. The young men who had gone to fight in 1914 were suddenly old, just 15 years later.

The statistics for 1928 showed that Canada had 58,940 war pensioners, 3,560 more than a year earlier. The cost of maintaining these pensioners was almost $40 million. Almost 4,000 new claims had been filed, and 671 pensioners had died.

A growing sense of unease was abroad in the land. In Saskatchewan, delegates to the command convention decried the number of "indigent aliens from non-preferred states" who were entering Canada. Manitoba Command unanimously endorsed a resolution to ban communist activities, and provincial president Ralph Webb, who would go on to become mayor of Winnipeg and a member of the provincial legislature, warned that children were being taught to spit on the Union Jack in Manitoba schools.

It was a gloomy group of veterans who arrived in Regina in late November for the Legion's third annual convention. The stock market crash a month earlier had signalled the end to the country's boom cycle, and uncertainty was rampant.

The mood of the convention was set by a letter written to delegates by their bed-ridden Dominion president. "Every man who experienced the hardships of war is paying some penalty," wrote Currie. The dominant theme of discussion and resolutions became the problems of veterans breaking down and "burning out," and the government's lack of interest in addressing them. It was estimated that 5,000 veterans were now disabled without recourse under existing pension legislation.

There was also more discussion about the possibility of a mass pilgrimage to the unveiling of the Vimy Memorial. Dominion Command's investigation had shown widespread interest among legionnaires across Canada, and construction on the mammoth base of the monument was now complete.

The question of bringing sons and daughters into the Legion to bolster membership was introduced again, and postponed until the next Dominion convention.

Currie's illness necessitated a change in leadership, and the task of steering the Legion into the turbulent new decade fell to first vice-president Leo LaFleche. John Roper moved from second to first vice-president, and Alex Ross of Saskatchewan Command moved onto the executive as second vice-president. J.A. MacIsaac and Jack Moore were returned as treasurer and chairman.

As it turned out, 1930 would be an election year for Prime Minister Mackenzie King's Liberals, and LaFleche would not have to wait long for a government response to the call for improvements to veterans' benefits. Immediately after the conclusion of the Regina convention, King appointed Chubby Power to head another special committee of Parliament to study the situation. Early in the new year, LaFleche went before the committee — representing not only the Legion, but also the Army and Navy Veterans in Canada, the Amputations Association, the Canadian Pensioners Association and the Sir Arthur Pearson Club of Blinded Soldiers and Sailors — to make the case for disabled vets.

On March 4, the government introduced a bill to establish allowances for veterans with disabilities not pensionable under other legislation, and put in place two vital principles: the right of applicants to have a public hearing; and the benefit of doubt in favor of the applicant. In addition, a veterans' bureau would be established within the Department of Pensions and National Health to prepare and present cases at no expense to the applicant. The bill received favorable recommendation by Power's committee, was passed unanimously by Parliament, and went into effect September 1. Seldom had the wheels of government turned so quickly.

In addition to the War Veterans Allowance Act, which would become a model for legislation in Australia and New Zealand, veterans who had participated in the Soldiers Settlement program got a break when the government cut their indebtedness by 30 per cent.

The government also established a pension appeal court to handle cases where the claimants were not satisfied with the findings of the Pension Board, or where the available evidence for a claim was insufficient to allow a favorable decision. The Dominion president was named as one of three members on the Appeal Board.

If the government was moving quickly to meet the demands of veterans, Dominion Command was also making changes in response to the needs of legionnaires. Reg Bowler, a Winnipeg veteran who had long been active at the national level, was named the Legion's first general secretary — the equivalent of the organization's chief executive officer — and M. McIntyre Hood, an Oshawa, Ontario, newspaper editor and veteran, was given the job of interpreting Legion affairs for the media.

As pressing as the needs of veterans were, Canadians of all ages and backgrounds were in dire straits by the end of 1930. Unemployment was hovering near 30 per cent of the labor force, and one in five Canadians was dependent upon government relief. In Saskatchewan, where wheat prices were the lowest in history, two-thirds of the rural population were on relief. Legion branches across the country turned their attention to lending whatever assistance they could to help ease the plight of the unemployed and homeless. Many branches operated "mulligan kitchens" throughout the winter, offering free meals to any hungry person, but funds soon began to run out.

When the fourth Dominion convention was convened in Niagara Falls, Ontario, the country's grim economic outlook was on most minds. Delegates called for the formation of a national employment council, but rejected suggestions for lotteries to raise relief funds.

Delegates also expressed their concern that, despite the new pension legislation, veterans were not getting a fair shake from the government. At the heart of their complaints was the fact that the lines of jurisdiction were blurred among the three pension bodies — the Board of Pension Commissioners, the Pension Tribunal, and the Pension Appeal Court. The commissioners maintained that they had the right to appeal tribunal rulings to the appeal court, meaning that they could challenge the overturning of any of their decisions by the tribunal.

For the second consecutive convention, delegates were faced with the resignation of a sitting Dominion president. LaFleche had stepped down in order to accept a job as deputy minister of Defence. Delegates turned to first vice-president Roper, a Halifax lawyer who had won the Military Cross as a major in the war. Second vice-president Ross was elevated to first vice-president, and Vancouver's W.W. Foster was elected second vice-president. Once again, there was no change in the positions of treasurer and chairman.

Although the Legion continued to expand — a California state command had been formed with eight posts of ex-patriates — the issue of bringing sons and daughters into the organization was raised again. Once more it was deferred — this time for what would amount to almost 40 years.

As it had following the 1929 convention, the Legion left Niagara Falls determined to argue its case with the government, in this case the Conservative administration of R.B. Bennett. Again, the Legion rallied the other major veterans' organizations behind its cause and the groups went forward united. Early in 1932, they filed a report to Murray MacLaren, minister of pensions and national health. The report claimed that 75 per cent of Pension Tribunal decisions favoring applicants had been appealed by the Pension Commission, with a 65-per-cent success rate. This was not, John Roper stated, the intention of the original legislation. The report urged closer liaison between the Pension Tribunal and the Pension Appeal Court, and suggested that the two bodies be combined into one court with an appelate division contained within it. In response, the government appointed a joint committee of politicians and veterans to study the situation.

Although Roper and the other veterans' groups had pushed their case with the minister, some veterans were dismayed by the conciliatory tone of statements like this one by Currie, who was now the Legion's grand president: "The present weakness is something which only the government of this country can remove. If the suggestion made by the veterans' organizations is not workable, then the government must find something that is. We stand ready at all times to give such helpful advice as lies within our power.

"I am sure that in this day of stress and strain for Canada there will be no attempt by the veterans or by the veterans' organizations either to embarrass the government or to impose unfair strain upon the financial resources of our country."

Reasonable as it may have been, that kind of sentiment did not sit well with veterans far removed from the power centre in Ottawa. The number of war disability pensioners had risen by more than 13,000 over the previous year, and 12,077 veterans had been admitted to hospital. A growing number of men began to chafe at what they viewed as a cozy relationship between former high-ranking officers like Currie and the government. As they had a decade earlier, many began to form splinter groups, believing they could find more success away from the Legion or any of the other established organizations.

The Legionary fired back at these groups, sparing no rhetoric: "As in all periods of stress, local disaffections are being exploited throughout the country. Mushroom organizations are springing up, prompted by the vaporings of blatherskites and oldtime barrack-room lawyers. A few have merit, others are simply rackets with sufficient ex-soldier atmosphere to get by. The first victims are the returned men who fall for that sort of thing, the next, the general public. With no record of achievement on behalf of the ex-troops behind them, and with no serious intention of getting down to the definite and concrete job of working for the ex-troops at all, the organizers of these disaffected groups devote more energy to snarling and yapping at those who are working for unity and harmony among the ex-servicemen than they ever expended against the Germans — if they ever saw a German."

The magazine might be excused its hyperbole; it was one of the main victims of the disaffection. Interest in the publication had fallen, forcing the Legion to drop the annual subscription rate for members from $1 to 80¢, and then to 75¢ a month later. The non-member subscription rate was slashed from $2 per year to 80¢. Circulation was only 11,000 copies. The number of pages began to drop as well, and the September and October issues were combined into one.

In response to this crisis, John Hundevad, a retired captain, was brought in as editor in September to replace Thomas Lapp.

The crisis faced by *The Legionary* in late 1932 proved to be only a taste of what was to come for the Legion as a whole in 1933. It was a year that would test the fabric of the seven-year-old organization.

The year began well enough, with the government's announcement that pension administration would be simplified. Bennett's solution was to abolish both the Board of Pension Commissioners and the Pension Tribunal, and replace them with a new lower court, the Canadian Pensions Commission, but there was a sticking point: Who would sit on the new body? The Legion recommended that the new commissioners should be chosen from among those who sat on the two disbanded boards. The government appointed eight former members of the Pension Board — members who were known to be hard-liners when it came to awarding disability pensions.

"(The government has) completely disregarded the wishes of the veterans for the first time," said Roper. "Is it the intention of the government in future to administer the Pension Act without regard to the wishes or suggestions of the ex-servicemen in Canada? If so, we face a serious situation."

Roper's concern was heightened by another government proposal, this one a move by Finance Minister E.N. Rhodes to force disabled veterans in the federal civil service to choose between their pension or their salary.

The internal pressure continued on Roper to speak out strongly against the government's policy on unemployment, as well. Some branches were agitating for Dominion Command to drop its non-partisan stance and take a stance against Bennett's Conservatives.

Even Armistice Day — a legal holiday on November 11 since 1931 — was being assailed. Numerous chapters of the Chamber of Commerce were lobbying to have the holiday cancelled.

It was becoming increasingly clear that the time had come to call legionnaires together for a Dominion convention. The problem was that the Legion did not have sufficient funds to convene its parliament. Roper put out an urgent call for additional money, urging members to contribute as much as they could afford in addition to their regular dues.

In a combined effort to save on costs and present the government with the reality of veterans united against its pension policies, the site of the convention was shifted to Ottawa.

Before the convention could be convened, however, the Legion received yet another blow: the sudden death of Sir Arthur Currie on November 30. His funeral on December 5, which would have been his 58th birthday, drew one of the largest contingents of military personnel ever gathered on Canadian soil. His funeral cortege stretched for miles through the streets of Montreal.

One of the late grand president's final statements — that economic conditions among veterans "should smite the conscience of the world" — was fresh in the minds of 600 delegates as they gathered in Ottawa in mid-March 1934 for the Legion's fifth Dominion convention.

The strategy of holding the convention in the nation's capital paid off in terms of attracting the attention of politicians. Among those who addressed the delegates were Gov. Gen. Bessborough, the prime minister, Opposition leader King, and CCF party Leader J.S. Woodsworth. Delegates also caught the public's eye by parading in an ice storm. Amputees in wheelchairs and on crutches were included in this group. The spectacle of massed veterans on Parliament Hill was enough to force the government to back down on its plan to make civil servants choose between pensions or salaries.

The convention's business sessions were long and trying, but there was a new spirit in the air. No one sensed it better than Alex Ross, whom delegates insisted move up from first vice-president to Dominion president. The former brigadier-general from Yorkton, Saskatchewan, was hesitant, declining the nomination at first because of the pressure of his work as a provincial judge, but the convention refused to accept his answer. Ross gave in to their wishes, but in a tactical move that would shape the future growth of the Legion, he used the moment to challenge the delegates to change their attitudes.

He told the convention that the organization had to stand on its own feet, renew its non-partisan stance, and stop relying on government support. "This is the issue," he said. "Either we continue in the rut of legislative endeavor and live on subsidies until the people of Canada become nauseated by our importunity, or we branch out boldly into a new and wider sphere where the ex-soldier will solve his own problems and make himself responsible for the care and well-being of his comrades. It is for us to decide now, and I am firmly of the opinion that we are at the parting of the ways and that our decision will have a far-reaching effect on the ultimate destiny of the ex-servicemen in Canada."

He called for a sustained and vigorous membership drive, as well, and asked branches to increase their level of funding to Dominion Command and its Service Bureau. He made it clear that, in his view, the Legion could no longer afford to devote all of its efforts to the cause of the pensioner; it must also tackle the major problem of assistance to the non-pensioner.

On the question of unemployment, delegates listened to an exhaustive report on the matter and voted to establish a special committee to conduct a survey of unemployment among ex-servicemen across Canada.

Apart from Ross' ascension to president, the elections saw W.W. Foster move from second to first vice-president, and George Drew move on to the executive as second vice-president. Victoria Cross holder Milton Gregg was elected honorary treasurer for the first time, and Jack Moore began his sixth term as chairman.

As part of the Legion's resurgence, delegates decided to resurrect the dormant plans to organize a pilgrimage to the Vimy Memorial, and the project began to take on the mantle of an event that would symbolize the unity and purpose of the organization.

There is no question that it was a re-energized Legion that adjourned its convention on March 15.

Ross wasted no time in taking his fight to the government. In late March, the Legion presented a brief that called on the Bennett administration to live up to the promises made to veterans. "It is not our desire," the Legion stated, "to impose any new burdens, or to ask for any extended benefits, but simply and solely to ensure that the benefits already conferred by Parliament shall be extended to those entitled thereto and not thwarted by the acts of those officials charged with the administration of the act."

With increased funding from branches, the Dominion Service Bureau gained a new profile, with a monthly column in *The Legionary* called "They Served Till Death — Why Not We?," and its first full-time director. After six years as pension officer responsible for tuberculous veterans, 47-year-old Dick Hale was named chief pensions officer. As a patient in the Muskoka Sanitorium north of Toronto, he had founded the Invalided Tubercular Soldiers' Welfare League in 1918 and the Tuberculous Veterans Association four years later.

Under intense pressure from Dominion Command and other parts of the Legion, the government finally gave in to demands to reorganize the Canadian Pension Commission. The sweeping changes were enough for *The Legionary* to comment: "(The government) is for the first time since the war giving a measure of real justice and satisfaction, and is working more in keeping with the manner expected by Parliament and the public."

Facing a fall election, Bennett's government also agreed to establish a royal commission under Judge J.D. Hyndman, president of the Pension Appeal Court, to investigate the unemployment problem in Canada. In

Toronto, on March 16, 1935, Ross appeared before Hyndman and his fellow commissioners, Basil Price and W.B. Woods. The thrust of the Legion's submission was that veterans should be given the opportunity to work to their maximum capacity, based on five principles:

- that a man who answered the call to duty and saw service should be entitled to employment, or adequate maintenance;

- that ample facilities should be provided to re-employ the able-bodied;

- that every pensioner who is unemployed through no personal fault should receive adequate maintenance;

- that every veteran whose physical condition prevented him from working in his usual field be cared for until he could be re-trained;

- that anyone who is unwilling to work to capacity be given little consideration.

Accompanying this statement of principles, Ross presented a detailed study that outlined the Legion's estimates of the extent of the problem and recommendations of how the program could be implemented. He suggested that the most urgent matters included the reorganization of the system of pensioners' relief, the establishment of effective agencies to supplement the assistance granted to provide for speedy absorption of as many people as possible into some type of work, the establishment of rehabilitation centres, and the extension of War Veterans Allowance benefits.

In June, the Hyndman Commission submitted its report. Noting that 38,000 veterans with overseas service were out of work, the commission recommended that "such assistance should be given those men who served overseas as may be required to alleviate the actual distress under which many of them are suffering, and to enable them and their families to exist in decency."

The commission noted that the Legion had proved its case that the unemployed veteran deserved special treatment. It recommended the establishment of a body to be known as the Veterans Assistance Commission, which would study the proposals that had been submitted.

Further recommendations included the formation of a corps of commissionaires in each of the country's major cities, the appointment of regional officers to find employment for veterans, a 15 per cent quota of veterans in any government-sponsored work, and the blocking of mortgage foreclosures.

Foremost among the recommendations and findings in the Legion's view was that the commission placed the responsibility for the care of unemployed veterans at the feet of the federal government. The organization hailed the Hyndman report as "a new charter of veterans' rights," but Parliament would not have time to study it before it adjourned for the fall election. Nevertheless, MPs voted to allot $500,000 to begin implementation of the report.

Ross was keenly aware that Legion members would be tempted to make the Hyndman findings an election issue, and he appealed to legionnaires "to do everything possible to avoid having the Legion drawn into any political controversy. We must be particularly careful to avoid any appearance of giving support or assistance to any party policy or any political party."

Campaigning on the slogan "King or Chaos" Mackenzie King's Liberals swept back into power on October 23 with a comfortable majority, and King immediately ingratiated himself to veterans by appointing three legionnaires — Chubby Power, Ian Mackenzie and Norman Rogers — to his cabinet.

By the time of the election, the Legion was already looking ahead to what would be the biggest undertaking of its first decade. Since the previous September, Ben Allen had been working full time at Dominion Command, sorting through the logistics of transporting thousands of legionnaires and their families to the former battlefields of France and Belgium. Some days, his office received as many as 800 letters seeking information or making application for the trip. By May 1935, 2,000 bookings had been registered.

Later that summer, Allen and general secretary Bowler travelled overseas to confer with British, French and Belgian authorities regarding the possible itinerary and lodging for the estimated 5,000 Canadians who would make the trip.

Finally, after years of uncertainty, the Legion had a renewed sense of purpose — and renewed strength. As 1935 ended, there were 160,000 members in 1,414 branches and auxiliaries, 349 in Ontario, 256 in Saskatchewan, 184 each in British Columbia and Manitoba, 150 in Alberta, 72 in Quebec, 56 in Nova Scotia, 52 in California, 41 in New Brunswick, 19 in Massachusetts, 11 in Prince Edward Island, two in the Yukon, and 38 elsewhere in the United States and abroad.

Chapter 5
THEM OR US?

Looking back across the years at the infancy of the Canadian Legion, and indeed at the whole of the veterans' movement in Canada, one sees a natural, almost organic, growth path that is interrupted only by external forces beyond the control of those within the movement.

There are impressive examples of leadership, some inspired vision, and no shortage of hard work. There are also mistakes, to be sure, and periods when the organization appeared to lose sight of its goals, but the first decade of the Legion's existence cleaves remarkably closely to the tenets on which it was founded. The Legion's growth from the fledgling Great War Veterans Association in 1920 to a national organization representing more than half of the veteran population is all the more remarkable when measured against government attitudes toward the men who returned from World War I.

Just how charitable you can be toward the governments of prime ministers Sir Robert Borden, Arthur Meighen, Mackenzie King and R.B. Bennett depends on how much faith you put in the original promise made to Canada's fighting men.

Addressing members of the Canadian Expeditionary Forces just prior to the Battle of Vimy Ridge in 1917, Borden made a pledge that shaped events in the 1920s and early 1930s:

"You men are about to enter one of the most serious engagements that ever faced the Canadian Corps...

"You can go into this action feeling assured of this, and as the head of the government I give you this assurance: That you need not fear that the government and the country will fail to show just appreciation of your service to the country and Empire in what you are about to do and what you have already done.

"The government and the country will consider it their first duty to see that a proper appreciation of your effort and of your courage is brought to the notice of the people at home, and it will always be our endeavor to so guide the attitude of public opinion that the country will support the government to prove to the returned man its just and due appreciation of the inestimable value of the services rendered to the country and Empire; and that no man, whether he goes back or whether he remains in Flanders, will have just cause to reproach the government for having broken faith with the men who won and the men who died."

Inherent in Borden's words was the promise that Canadians would never forget the sacrifice its veterans made, a promise that formed the basis of Canada's pension legislation and the raison d'être for the veterans' groups that came together to form the Legion. Also woven into those words, though, is a tone of paternalism that foreshadowed many of the problems veterans would face upon their return.

Given the context of the era and the background of war, it is not surprising that the government's pension bureaucrats like J.L. Todd, one of the original three members of the Canadian Board of Pension Commissioners, did not consider consulting veterans themselves to ascertain their needs and desires. Instead, Todd visited France to find out how pensions were administered there, and returned convinced that ex-servicemen should be encouraged to return to work as quickly as possible. He grafted that notion onto the British concept of basing pension rates on the income of an unskilled laborer and developed a system that was easy for his political masters to swallow. Fewer than five per cent of disabled Canadian veterans qualified for the top rate; most got less than one-quarter of the maximum.

Like the pension rates, the rehabilitation programs were designed with little or no consultation with the men who would go into them. While government programs may have been fine to re-train a veteran who had lost a leg cleanly at the knee, they did not take into account men whose personalities had been altered by the carnage they had lived through, or TB sufferers who would gasp out their final days in a sanitorium ward.

Even when the government did consult a veterans' organization, like it did the Great War Veterans Association in the early days of the Soldier Settlement program, that did not guarantee success, or ensure that the consultation would continue. Established to help populate rural Canada and provide returned men with a worthwhile trade, Soldier Settlement quickly foundered, creating as many problems as it solved. Throughout the 1920s, veterans had to fight for relief from the program itself — which promised inexpensive farms and affordable equipment but delivered crippling loan payments and foreclosures. By 1930, when the government revamped the program, more than 10,000 of the 31,324 veterans enrolled had given up their farms. Twelve per cent of those who quit did so because of recurring disabilities; 30 per cent cited lack of experience as their reason for moving off the land.

It might have been natural enough for returned men to take what their government doled out to them, but to their credit, they took Borden at his word. They had been promised "proper appreciation," and they were going to insist on being the ones who determined just what was "proper."

No one could have stirred up that feeling among veterans from coast to coast, but it took a mighty effort to harness that raw energy and turn it into a unified force. While Earl Haig must get credit for providing the impetus for uniting veterans' organizations throughout the main countries in the British Empire, Great War Veterans Association founders like J.A. Stevenson saw the necessity of pulling together the disparate veterans' groups while Haig was still at war.

Haig's role, and that of several of the Canadian Legion's early leaders, is one of the ironies of the organization's first decade. The roots of the Legion were egalitarian, as practised in the Great War Veterans Association and reflected in the term "comrade." After all, one of the forces that drove veterans toward unity was a distrust of the officer class and resentment of the privilege that accompanied it. Though they had little in common with the average legionnaire, men like Haig, Sir Richard Turner and Sir Percy Lake did provide an entrée to senior government officials, and brought an important cachet to the fledgling organization. One can argue, though, that they were not always the most effective leaders. The elevation of Sir Arthur Currie to the post of Dominion president was ill-timed given his tenuous physical condition, and while he lent status to the organization, he did little to further its cause during his tenure. Certainly, lesser-known men like Great War Veterans Association secretary-treasurer Grant MacNeil, and Leo LaFleche, Currie's successor as Dominion president, played roles that far exceeded their status among military men.

The early leadership was not always focused, either. LaFleche accomplished a great deal as Dominion honorary treasurer and first vice-president, but as Dominion president he broke the Legion's cardinal rule of non-partisanship and allowed himself to be co-opted by the government of Prime Minister R.B. Bennett. LaFleche's successor, John Roper, enmeshed himself in the fight over the makeup of the Canadian Pensions Commission at a time when most legionnaires were much more concerned with finding

❦

a job. In fact, during Roper's three-year term, Dominion Command came dangerously close to losing what had been achieved in the 1920s. It took Alex Ross' clear-headed perception and stubborn determination to set the Legion back on the right track.

With Ross, the irony surrounding the leadership of Haig, Turner, Lake and Currie turns back on itself; a retired brigadier-general with a prestigious position on Saskatchewan's judiciary, Ross had an innate understanding that the Legion's role was much broader than fighting for legislative changes in Ottawa.

Ross' vision can be traced to his prairie roots; after all, Saskatchewan was the first province to embrace the concept of the Legion and had the largest number of branches in the early years. Saskatchewan also experienced the worst of the Great Depression; its provincial income fell by 90 per cent in two years, and two-thirds of its rural population were on relief. Ross saw personally how Legion branches could work hand-in-hand with the community to improve local conditions: in 1929, Saskatoon Branch donated almost $2,000 from its poppy campaign to community relief, and found temporary work for 38 unemployed veterans; in 1932, Regina Branch put together more than 1,000 relief parcels for children in the drought-ravaged southern region of the province; and, despite the crippling Depression, Saskatchewan Command grew like topsy, increasing from 140 to 166 branches in the early '30s. Close community links bred success.

Before he issued his 1934 challenge to legionnaires to "branch out boldly into a new and wider sphere," Ross may also have reflected on the words of some early Legion builders. In his insightful 1917 editorial in the Great War Veterans Association's *The Veteran*, J.A. Stevenson had predicted that a veterans' organization would become "a healthy and powerful voice in our national life," and nine years later *The Legionary* spoke of the Legion's goal as "unselfish service to Canada."

Ross understood that what would sustain the Legion in the long run — after veterans achieved the kind of legislative protection Borden had promised — was the degree to which it became ingrained in the community. He knew that most Canadians did not see the legislative changes the Legion won on Parliament Hill for veterans; they saw legionnaires collecting vegetables for the homeless, serving soup to hungry children at a "mulligan kitchen," and running summer camps for families.

Borden was right when he told the men who were about to storm Vimy Ridge that their service would set them apart from their fellow citizens. No one could dispute the fact that veterans shared a common bond that was welded in battle, or at least in anticipation of battle. Despite that commonality, though, they were still Canadians. To view them otherwise would be to create an "us versus them" scenario that could be destructive to both the veteran and non-veteran population. There were times in the first decade of the Legion when the organization lost sight of that, and those are the times when it went astray. With Ross' speech at the Ottawa convention, however, the Legion reaffirmed its position in the larger society and never looked back.

Section 2

1936 - 1950

NEW CHALLENGES

Chapter 6

OF BATTLES PAST... AND YET TO COME

Many theories have been advanced about why veterans are drawn to return to the battlefields of their youth, when logic dictates that those killing-grounds might be the last place to which a man would willingly return. Few have explained it better than Clifford Bowering did in *Service*, the history of the Canadian Legion that was published in 1960.

He wrote: "There is far more involved here than a desire to look at a battlefield, far more than a curiosity to see what it looks like now. From time to time, men who have fought in war feel a tugging need to return to the scenes of battle, to reaffirm their unspoken but ever-present affinity to fallen comrades, to share with those who remain a re-dedication of spirit and ideals. For those who have not shared a battlefield experience it is all but impossible to understand; for those who have, it is difficult to explain, to put their feelings into words. There is about a battlefield, now mute and still but always charged by what it can say to the man who will listen, something beautiful, something attuned to the soul of the war veteran.

"To the men who fight in them, wars mean many things. They mean ugliness and hate, brutality and destruction, fear and loneliness, life and death. But they also mean compassion and comradeship, and an understanding far beyond the grasp of man's thoughts. For it is upon the battlefield that men learn the true value of themselves, of others around them and of reason. In the heat of battle there comes to all men the great moments of truth.

"Perhaps this is why men so often express the desire to reach out and return to the battlefields long after the guns have been stilled. They wish, whether by expression or subconscious thought, to rediscover the truth and the values they found so strangely in the midst of hell."

By the beginning of 1936 it was clear that far more veterans than the 5,000 originally predicted by Dominion Command wanted to make the journey of rediscovery to Vimy Ridge. Some 7,500 applications for the trip

❦

— which cost $160 per person, return from Montreal — had flowed into tour organizer Ben Allen's Ottawa office.

When the sixth Dominion convention was convened in Vancouver on March 23 the final logistical details of the pilgrimage were high on the agenda.

The veterans and their families would leave Montreal July 16 and 17 in five ships belonging to the Canadian Pacific and Cunard-White Star lines: Antonia, Ascania, Montcalm, Montrose and Duchess of Bedford. Two of the liners would land at Antwerp, Belgium, and the remainder at Le Havre, France. From there, trains and buses would transport the Canadians to battlefield ceremonies at Mons, Douai, Arras, Valenciennes, Cambrai, Ypres, Passchendaele and others before moving on to Vimy for the unveiling of Walter Allward's monument. From Vimy, the pilgrimage would cross the English Channel and move north to London, then back to France for tours of Paris and other sites. Delegates heard that construction was completed on Allward's 42-metre, twin-shaft memorial, which sat on 100 hectares of land ceded in perpetuity to Canada by five French villages. The unveiling had been set for July 26.

But there was other business to attend to as well. The Dominion Service Bureau faced ongoing funding problems. To allow it to continue its work, delegates passed a motion to establish a $250,000 endowment fund that would yield about $10,000 a year.

Delegates also voted to press the government for more assistance for disabled veterans and the unemployed.

Dominion president Alex Ross was returned unanimously. In fact, the only change in the organization's executive was at the second vice-president position, where B.W. Roscoe replaced George Drew.

Ross called the Vimy pilgrimage "a great mission... on July 26, on Vimy's ridge, we shall once more be a Canada united. On April 9, 1917, the manhood of Canada swept up these slopes; on July 26, 1936, the survivors, and the mothers, fathers, widows and children of those who fell there and elsewhere, will unite in a sacred act of remembrance... (We) hope that, by our presence on Vimy Ridge, we may have made some contribution to international understanding and world peace, so earnestly desired by us all."

As the departure date approached, the number of participants was set at 10,300 — 6,300 who would sail from Montreal, 2,000 who would travel from Canada on their own, and another 2,000 veterans and survivors who lived in Britain. Preceding the bulk of the pilgrims were two official Legion parties, one arrangements group under D.E. Macintyre, who was responsible for transportation and official ceremonies, and the Dominion president's party. Ross and his delegation landed at Boulogne, where they were greeted with a civic reception. They moved on to Paris to place wreaths on the tombs of France's Unknown Warrior and Marshal Foch, then to Cambrai. A reception by King Leopold III of Belgium followed, and then an official visit to the villages that had donated the land for the monument.

Meanwhile, the scene on Montreal's waterfront was unlike anything seen since the return of the Canadian Expeditionary Force. Crowds of well-wishers jammed the port as the five ships — escorted by two Royal Canadian Navy destroyers — steamed out into the St. Lawrence River. These scenes were repeated as the convoy passed other cities along the river. Writing in *The Epic of Vimy*, a 225-page souvenir book published by *The Legionary*, Canadian Press reporter W.W. (Jock) Murray recalled: "It was evening when the pilgrimage fleet was off Quebec City. Against a perfect background of the setting sun glinting on church spires and battlemented heights of the ancient capital, the pilgrims received a salute that will long be remembered by those privileged to be part of the scene.

"Thousands of people were gathered on Dufferin Terrace and along the waterfront; whistles blew from every vessel in the harbor; rockets glared and flared from the Citadel to fall into the river below, while a gun salute boomed out its greetings. And not to be outdone by the civilian population, the members of the Quebec City Branch of the Legion came out in the stream aboard the S.S. Lady Grey, with a band playing old martial airs."

The crowds along the bank of the St. Lawrence were just an indication of what was awaiting the Canadians in France. Everywhere the pilgrims went they were met by warm-hearted people who went out of their way to make the journey pleasant. Once in the vicinity of Vimy, the Canadians found lodgings in hotels, converted schools and private homes. Drivers from across France had been enlisted to transport the veterans and their families to the site of the monument. Joining the Canadians at the memorial were thousands of French farmers, coal miners and factory workers — a mammoth gathering estimated at 100,000 people, or approximately the same number of Canadians who had stormed the ridge 19 years earlier.

Prior to the official portion of the dedication ceremony, King Edward VIII walked down the steps of the monument to greet the Canadian delegation and inspect the veterans' guard of honor. For many, this 30-minute interlude was the highlight of the pilgrimage. The official unveiling began with the arrival of French president Albert Lebrun. Squadrons of aircraft from Britain and France flew overhead, dipping their wings in salute. After the monument, bearing the names of 11,283 Canadian dead, was consecrated, the King addressed the crowd: "Today, 3,000 miles from the shore of Canada, we are assembled around this monument — yet not on alien soil. For this glorious monument crowning the hill of Vimy is now and for all time part of Canada. Though the mortal remains of Canada's sons lie far from home, yet here where we now stand in ancient Artois their immortal memory is hallowed upon soil that is as surely Canada's as any acre within the nine provinces.

"...It is one of the consolations which time brings that the deeds of valor done on battlefields long survive the quarrels which drove the opposing hosts to conflict. Vimy will be one such name. Around us here today is peace and rebuilding of hope. And so also, in dedicating this memorial to our fallen comrades, our thoughts turn rather to the splendor of their sacrifice and to the consecration of our love for them, than to the cannonade which beat upon this ridge a score of years ago."

With those words, the King released the Union Jack shrouding the figure of Canada Mourning Her Dead and *Last Post* was played.

In his address, Lebrun pointed to the top of the twin pillars and said: "See, at the top of these two pylons — representing the Canadian and French armies — peace, justice, honor and loyalty for which they fought, sending up to them a triumphal hymn, while at their feet the Angel of Victory holds aloft in the supreme spirit the flame of sacrifice.

"To the laborer lying on the greensward resting his tired body, to the miner coming out from the entrails of the earth, the majesty and severe aspect of these stones will recall the urgent lessons which are to be learned from the past.

"It will recall to them that here several hundred thousand men from a faraway land spilled their blood to defend their hearth..."

Representing the Canadian government, Justice Minister Ernest Lapointe described the ceremony as "ancient Europe and youthful America gathered in communion..."

The next day, thousands of the Canadians found their way to Buckingham Palace in London for the King's garden party. A downpour did little to dampen their spirits, and the King did not seem to mind, either. He shouted his prepared remarks from a balcony to make himself heard over the rain, then mingled with the assembled guests.

After three days in London, more than 5,000 Canadians returned to France for ceremonies in Paris and tours of castles in Amboise, Blois, Rouen, and a little-known town that would soon hold far greater significance for Canadians: Dieppe.

The pilgrimage was, by any standards, a remarkable three weeks. Many organizations played a role – including the Department of External Affairs, which arranged to lift customs barriers and provided free passports, the federal departments of Defence and Pensions and National Health, and Canadian National and Canadian Pacific, which provided discount rail travel — but the Legion deservedly reaped most of the credit. "Even if the pilgrimage has done nothing else," stated *The Legionary*, "it has demonstrated that the Canadian Legion is equipped and manned to undertake big things and to carry them through to successful conclusions... Not a Canadian who participated in that tour left France with a feeling other than that he had taken part in a manifestation of friendship totally unprecedented in modern history."

Murray's souvenir *The Epic of Vimy* sold out quickly and went into a second printing. A filmed record of the pilgrimage, *Salute to Valor*, was also prepared (it had its premiere on July 9, 1937 at Shea's Hippodrome Theatre in Toronto with Allward in attendance).

Of course, the return to Vimy in the summer 1936 was not the only event that focused the eyes of Canadians on Europe that year. Canadian veterans were still in France when Adolph Hitler staged his Aryan show of force at the XIth Olympic Games in Berlin, and there was a growing sense that tensions in Germany were reaching a boiling point.

As early as September 1933, *The Legionary* had cautioned members that a new force was rising in Germany and treating minorities "with a savagery that has little parallel in the history of a modern civilized nation." The warning was sounded again two years later, when an editorial in *The Legionary* noted: "War clouds are darkening the international horizon." The magazine went on to decry the wretched condition of Canada's armed forces.

By the end of 1936, few could deny that Hitler was a new threat to world peace. Still, it would be a mistake to imply that the Legion did not share the widespread, but misguided, hope that Germany would be content to regain economic stability and avoid provoking a conflict. In 1937, the Dominion president led a 30-member Legion delegation to Germany at the invitation of the Union of German War Veterans Associations. Ross placed a wreath at the tomb of World War I air ace Manfred von Richthofen and took the salute from dozens of goose-stepping Nazi troops. *The Legionary*'s report on the event took an optimistic tone: "The general impression left on the Canadians was that the Germans were a friendly folk, tackling a difficult economic situation, heavily taxed to pay heavy national debts and to finance the unemployment relief works and other projects that were intended to bring about recovery."

The magazine's report ends with a sentence that is laden with irony: "As the Canadians left they were loudly cheered, and invited to return again to Germany."

Almost lost in the excitement surrounding the Vimy pilgrimage was some important work underway on the unemployment front in Canada. In response to the recommendations of the Hyndman Commission, filed in 1935 just prior to the federal election, the new federal Liberal government had appointed the Veterans Assistance Commission to study ways of putting ex-servicemen back to work. Chairing the commission was J.G. Rattray, a former army colonel who had been a president of the Legion's Ottawa Branch. Two other prominent legionnaires — H.L. de Martigny and Robert Macnicol — also sat on the commission. During 1936 and the first half of the following year, the Rattray Commission held meetings throughout Canada seeking methods of solving the unemployment crisis.

The commission made some interim reports, but it was not until December 1937 that it submitted its final recommendations to Chubby Power, minister of pensions and national health. Its principal recommendation was that unemployed veterans should be the responsibility of the federal government rather than municipalities, as had been established under the Relief Act of 1932. It proposed that unemployed veterans who were not in receipt of disability pensions should receive a monthly allowance, provided they were registered for possible employment. The recommended rates were $18.50 for single men and $30 for married men with dependent wives. The commission also recommended continuation of the probational training program to recondition former tradesmen. It also proposed that age barriers be dropped from the War Veterans Allowance Act, and that the Act be amended to permit a more liberal interpretation of legislation covering the granting of the allowance at any age to a veteran who had seen service in an actual theatre of war and who was unable to maintain himself.

Under its mandate from the government, the Rattray Commission also established the Corps of Commissionaires that had been recommended by Hyndman. Maj.-Gen. W.B.M. King of Montreal was put in charge of the corps, and its initial enrolment target was set at 2,000 veterans.

The commission also began settling unemployed veterans on small land holdings, beginning with 10 homes on 20 hectares in Brooklin, Ontario, near Toronto.

The unemployment issue topped the agenda in Fort William, Ontario, (now amalgamated into Thunder Bay) as delegates gathered in late January 1938 for the seventh Dominion convention. Power was on hand to brief the convention on Rattray's findings and recommendations, and he said that employment had been found for 10,000 veterans since the Legion had met in Vancouver two years earlier. Delegates gave their support to the commission's report, making special mention of the recommendation that Ottawa recognize its responsibility for all indigent, unemployed veterans and provide the provisional economic allowance Rattray proposed.

In its report, the Dominion Service Bureau stated that it had successfully handled 7,666 pension claims since its formation in 1926.

Membership was reported at an all-time high: more than 175,000.

First vice-president W.W. Foster, former commander of the 52nd Battalion in World War I and Vancouver's police chief, was acclaimed president. Montrealer Basil Price, who had served on the Hyndman Commission, was elected first vice-president, and Calgary's Alex Walker became second vice-president. Once again, there was no change at the positions of honorary treasurer or chairman.

If employment was foremost on the mind of most legionnaires, the worsening climate of fear in Europe was a close second. The convention passed a resolution that stated: "We believe that Canada must act... within the British Commonwealth of Nations for the maintenance of peace... In the face of conflicting philosophies all around us, the best guarantee of world peace is a strong, united British Commonwealth of Nations with its democratic principles of freedom and justice to all."

While the Legion hoped for peace, it was preparing for the possibility of war. If the experience of the returned serviceman from World War I had taught a lesson, it was that a nation at war must plan for renewed peace. Rehabilitation must begin during war and not be left for the aftermath. Reflecting this belief, delegates voted to establish a permanent Dominion Command committee on education that would take responsibility for the ongoing training of a new generation of soldiers. Chairmanship of the new committee was given to Wilfrid Bovey, president of Canadian Association for Adult Education and director of extra-mural relations at Montreal's McGill University.

In a resolution addressed to the question of mobilization in the event of war, delegates called for universal conscription.

The Legion continued its usual course of activities in 1938 – including presentation of a brief to the Rowell-Sirois Commission on Dominion-Provincial Relations that called for a strong central government and patriation of a Canadian constitution with some form of amending formula – but the threat from Europe dominated the organization's attention. *The Legionary* reported that Hitler was "jack-booting the Jews of Germany and Austria with a viciousness unparalleled in history." The organization stood against "peace at any price." During the Munich Crisis of September 1938, when Hitler threatened war unless he was given Czechoslovakia, Foster sent a telegram to Prime Minister Mackenzie King offering to put the Legion's resources at the country's disposal. In the wake of British Prime Minister Neville Chamberlain's appeasement of the Nazis, Foster fleshed out the Legion's offer with a program submitted to the Defence minister. Legionnaires not physically fit for active service would carry out essential duties, including guarding railways, bridges, factories and other important pieces of Canada's infrastructure. The plan also outlined Legion facilities that could be made available for recruiting or training purposes.

As sincere as the Legion's offer was, Foster knew the limitations of what the organization could give the country. An editorial in *The Legionary* stated: "In spite of our hopes, there is no denying the fact that we, the veterans of the Great War, are no longer young... However much we might desire to take an active part in any conflict that threatens our country, we no longer belong to the category of the fit. But there are many things we could do at home, and do infinitely better than any other group; some would be tedious and unexciting but they have got to be done."

The fact remained, though, that the Legion was the first and only Canadian organization of any description to take the Nazi threat seriously enough to offer immediate assistance. As noted Canadian military historian Charles Stacey stated in 1985: "Only gradually did the progress of events, notably Nazi aggression, alter (the isolationist) mood to the point where Canada was prepared to face taking part in another great war."

As soon as Chamberlain returned from his historic meeting with Hitler, bearing a signed promise and the news that "peace was at hand," many Canadians accepted the news that the German leader had been mollified. King publicly thanked Chamberlain for averting a war. For its part, the Legion lashed out at the complacency of the Canadian people. It described Canada's defences as inadequate and placed most of the blame on the people themselves for allowing it to happen.

Not content with offering the services of its own members, the Legion joined with the non-aligned veterans' organizations to conduct a survey of all ex-servicemen under 60 years of age to ascertain the capacity and qualifications of those who were willing to serve in a period of national emergency. More than 10,000 veterans responded in the first two weeks, and 10 times that number answered the call eventually.

Details of the survey were included in a manifesto issued by a conference of the presidents of the various veterans' groups. Addressed to all Canadian veterans, the manifesto sought "unselfish service without any vestige of compulsion or regimentation." It pointed to the lessons of the past and noted that of these "the most important is that Canada cannot in a period of international tension leave herself exposed to the perils of direct or indirect hostile action within the state, but should provide at once for our future security... Our country's protective forces should be buttressed by the services of men and women who are competent and willing to serve under the direction of the constituted authorities."

The manifesto made it clear that the organizations were not proposing to form a fighting force; the goal was to provide statistics on the men who were available to fill reserve roles. It emphasized the need to counteract any threat of sabotage that might destabilize the internal security of the country.

In April 1939, the Ontario government became the first to utilize the survey by requesting veterans be assigned to guard hydroelectric facilities at Niagara Falls, Leaside and Chats Falls, west of Ottawa. Saskatchewan followed Ontario's lead and contacted veterans to provide aid to the civil authorities. By September, 2,763 veterans were guarding vital points such as hydro plants and harbors.

Despite the Legion's harsh words concerning the attitude of the Canadian people, the organization joined in the public's fascination with the official visit of King George VI and Queen Elizabeth in the spring of 1939. On May 21, 10,000 legionnaires turned out in Ottawa for the unveiling of the National War Memorial. At the end of his tour, King George sent a message to Pensions and National Health Minister Power, saying: "One of the most notable features of my Canadian tour has been the appearance everywhere of large and well-organized detachments of veterans... I know well that the ideals that inspired them 20 years ago are still theirs, and that this fine body of men has never lost that sense of comradeship and of service to the common good which was perhaps the happiest legacy of the Great War."

As for most Canadians, the royal visit was a party that was over too soon — an interlude of national celebration and unity that was shattered by the reality of Hitler's sudden strike against Poland.

On September 13, three days after Canada declared war on Germany, Foster spoke on a national CBC radio broadcast, pledging assistance "wherever the ex-service community is required... (The) Canadian Legion has repeatedly and emphatically pledged its whole-hearted support to the government of the day."

Addressing the concerns of veterans faced with a new global conflict, he said: "We are now for the most part 45 years of age or over. We have therefore reached an age at which we must know in what sphere we can most usefully be employed, depending on physical capacity, training and experience. There will be need for the effort each and every one can make... and all will find a place. It is indeed the sole consolation of the situation that in a comparatively short time there should be left in Canada no unemployed ex-servicemen."

Chapter 7

THE "ELDER STATESMEN" MEET THE CHALLENGE

Sixteen days after Nazi stormtroopers flooded into Poland, the Legion's Dominion Executive Council met in Ottawa. Prime Minister Mackenzie King gloomily told the council: "It looks like a long, hard war."

On his national radio broadcast on September 13, Dominion president W.W. Foster had urged veterans to throw their support behind King without question, at least for the time being. "While we reserve the right of criticism (of Canada's conduct of the war)," he said, "we should withhold it until the government has had time fully to delineate its policy." For the Legion itself, this meant acceding to King's policy of voluntary enlistment, even though the last three Dominion conventions had voted in favor of universal conscription in the event of war.

Gov. Gen. Tweedsmuir told the Executive Council members: "However long and desperate the struggle may be, we are not going to flinch, and we are again going to win... You legionnaires have a most important part to play. You are the people with knowledge and experience. You have been through a war which was of a different kind from this but at the same time contained much that is similar. Just as in politics you cannot do without what we call the elder statesmen, so in defence you are the elder statesmen. You are the people who can teach the younger generation the rudiments of the business and keep the national mind balanced, the national spirit keen."

The Legion was eager to meet the challenge Tweedsmuir had outlined. Before adjourning its emergency meeting, the council proposed forming two new organizations that would become the Legion's most widely recognized contributions to the war effort.

If there was one lesson that veterans had learned from World War I it was that the boredom could be almost as dangerous as the battle. They knew that men at war should not have to worry about the well-being of their loved ones back home, and recognized that the hardships and deprivations of war could have long-lasting effects if steps were not taken to alleviate them well in advance. With these facts in mind, the Dominion Executive Council suggested to the government that the Legion be permitted to establish a new, incorporated body to administer aid to Canada's armed forces.

Within days, the government issued a charter for the Canadian Legion War Services Inc. In cooperation with other national organizations like the Salvation Army, YMCA and Knights of Columbus, it would operate as a non-profit unit of the Directorate of Auxiliary Services of the Department of National Defence, to which Foster was appointed director.

Ralph Webb of Winnipeg was named general manager of the Canadian Legion War Services and a board of directors was appointed — including several Legion stalwarts like past Dominion presidents Sir Percy Lake and Alex Ross, and honorary president Maj.-Gen. John Gunn. At the board's initial meeting, Gunn, a native of Toronto, was elected president, and seven aims and objectives were outlined:

Education — Working in collaboration with the Canadian Association for Adult Education, the Canadian Legion War Services would make it possible for members of the armed forces to continue their education while on active service. In each military district, teachers and facilities would be made available for high school courses in general studies like current events, economics, bookkeeping and stenography. Conversational and military French and German would be taught in some cases. Advanced students would be able to obtain high school diplomas or Bachelor of Arts degrees by correspondence. Similar facilities would be provided overseas by arrangement with British and French educators.

Personal services — Legion personnel, including war padres, would be made available to counsel people about problems arising from military service.

Entertainment — Troupes would be formed to entertain armed forces units in Canada and overseas. Arrangements would also be made to provide speakers, musicians and actors. Mobile movie theatres were also contemplated.

Recreation and sports — Recreation huts would be established to provide a place to read, write letters or play games. Free note paper, envelopes, books and magazines would be provided. Non-alcoholic canteens would be provided. Sports would be organized.

Overseas services — The Canadian Legion War Services would extend its full range of services to England and France, once Canadians moved overseas. Leave-centre hostels would be established to provide beds and meals at a nominal charge, along with free recreation and reading rooms. Travel bureaus would be opened to assist on-leave personnel in planning tours of historic sites.

Personnel — The organization's personnel would be highly qualified ex-servicemen with exceptional leadership skills.

Profits — Any funds remaining at the end of hostilities would be used exclusively for the benefit of veterans and their families.

"The old soldiers (of the Canadian Legion War Services) have a grave responsibility," stated an editorial in *The Legionary*. "They know the virtues and the vices which are all part of the game. They know the pitfalls into which the young soldiers can so easily tumble. It is their duty to emphasize the virtues and to caution wisely and judiciously against the pitfalls. One of the greatest teachers in life is example. Let the old soldiers be an example to the youth of today, an example in warm-hearted, generous comradeship, in unselfish devotion, in prudence and patience."

The organization opened its first recreation hut at Camp Barriefield, Ontario, in December 1939, and two months later, a residential club was established in London to entertain the troops who had already been shipped overseas. Also in February, it initiated a fund-raising campaign in Canada with a goal of $500,000. Eventually, more than $700,000 was donated.

Initially, the Canadian Legion War Services helped primarily with alleviating boredom, although more important issues were addressed, too. In some instances, in the interim between enlistment and the initial payment of dependants' allowances, War Services officers arranged for civic or social service agencies to ensure the maintenance of soldiers' families. Sometimes, direct financial aid was the only answer, and the organization helped many families avoid defaulting on mortgage payments. During the first year of operation, it dealt with 30,859 personal cases.

❦

Among the other statistics for the Canadian Legion War Services' operations in 1940:

- 3,180 movies screened;

- 2,392 concerts, dances and smokers presented;

- 4.8 million sheets of notepaper and 2.1 million envelopes distributed;

- two million cigarettes sent overseas.

By the end of 1940, the Legion was operating 25 recreation centres and canteens in Canada. Another feature of the Legion War Services in Canada was a parcel service that allowed Canadians to order a package of food to be assembled in England and shipped to a designated recipient. As Canadian troops moved into Europe, the Legion War Services went with them, providing mobile units in the field and operating clubs as cities were liberated from Nazi occupation. In other theatres of operation, the organization set up facilities in Africa, India and Burma. During the peak of the campaign, it had 35 stage shows on tour in England and on the continent, and was operating more than 1,000 canteens, both mobile and static.

In total, some 10 million pieces of stationery and nearly 125 million cigarettes were distributed. Attendance at Legion-sponsored films was in the millions. Trucks bearing the Legion crest became a familiar sight in the field, and Legion facilities were widely recognized as a place where a Canadian soldier could find a little piece of "home."

For many young Canadians overseas, these services provided a first-hand introduction to the Legion — for many, an abstract concept they related to solely as a club for old soldiers. This entrée would prove invaluable after the war. The Canadian Legion War Services yielded more immediately tangible benefits, too; more than $1.1 million was in the corporation's treasury on V-E Day. The money would be placed in trust with a government-appointed board to administer the Canteen Fund.

Another tangible benefit of the Legion's involvement in World War II was the knowledge imparted by the Canadian Legion Educational Services — an extension of the Dominion Command education committee that had been established in 1938.

Like the committee, Educational Services was placed under the leadership of Wilfrid Bovey, the director of extra-mural relations at McGill University and president of the Canadian Association for Adult Education.

A lieutenant-colonel in World War I, Bovey had become a protegé of Sir Arthur Currie while serving at Canadian Corps Headquarters and had followed Currie to McGill.

Under the auspices of the newly formed Canadian Legion War Services, Educational Services came together in late 1939 in conjunction with Bovey's adult education association. Sidney Smith, president of the University of Manitoba, chaired a committee that developed several objectives for the new Legion initiative:

- to maintain morale by stimulating the development of personal resources and inculcating reasoned social attitudes;
- to retain and cultivate aptitudes and skills;
- to make constructive use of leisure, especially during leave or convalescence, or during internment as prisoner-of-war in a neutral country;
- to facilitate the civil rehabilitation of the soldier by gearing this enterprise into a gradually evolving plan for retraining and vocational guidance which should be made available whether discharge occurs during hostilities or at their termination.

In its plan, Smith's committee emphasized technical and vocational types of training, and suggested a variety of teaching methods. High on its recommendations was the notion that Canadian soldiers' morale could be kept up by teaching them about the benefits of democracy in the form of civics and history classes. Another priority the committee stressed was the need for cooperation between the Defence Department and the civil department responsible for re-establishment so that the education process would not be interrupted when military service ended.

The plan was submitted to Defence Minister Norman Rogers, and the government acted quickly to authorize the Legion and the Canadian Association for Adult Education to proceed.

The first steps were to establish regional committees and attract leading educators to participate. Bovey realized that, given the nature of mobilization, it would be essential to establish a uniform curriculum and textbooks that could be used whether the student was an airman stationed in North Battleford, Saskatchewan, or a soldier awaiting assignment in England. To accomplish this task — no mean feat, considering the parochialism historically associated with education in Canada's nine provinces — Bovey recruited J.W. Gibson. Gibson, director of correspondence instruction for the British Columbia Department of Education, was widely regarded as the father of correspondence education in Canada. He was seconded to the Canadian Legion Educational Services for the duration of the war to supervise production and edit textbooks.

In January 1940, Educational Services appointed three permanent officials: Robert England, an economist who was director of extension for the University of British Columbia, was named director for Canadian Forces Overseas; Andrew Moore, Manitoba's inspector of secondary schools, became field secretary for Canada; and Arthur Chatwin, superintendent of a school for the deaf in Saskatoon, became chief administrative officer.

England travelled to Britain immediately to determine the needs of soldiers who were training there, and returned in the summer of 1940 to report that new methods were required. He told Bovey that "the circumstances of a year in England without engaging the enemy" demanded greater attention than necessitated by training in Canada. A survey he had conducted among 800 soldiers indicated that half of them had attained junior matriculation and required correspondence and reading courses. However, military training requirements stood in the way. Lt.-Gen. Andrew McNaughton, then commander of the 1st Canadian Division, had introduced classes in conversational French, mathematics and shorthand, but formal classroom training had been suspended because of the rigors of military preparation. England reported some reluctance on the part of military officials to press the need for education while in the field, and once back in Canada he set about clearing away the barricades.

In November, McNaughton finally accepted the Legion Educational Services' plan, but by then England had been hired away by the government to act as executive secretary of its demobilization and rehabilitation committee. In his place, McNaughton accepted the appointment of Chatwin as overseas director of education for the Canadian forces. The general announced a plan to appoint an education officer from each battalion or equivalent unit in the 1st and 2nd divisions to ensure the largest number of troops could take advantage of the services offered, stating: "...we are particularly impressed with the possibilities of the Legion's correspondence courses, the success of which will depend on the provision of adequate and competent staff."

It was clear that Chatwin and the entire Educational Services organization had won an influential ally. Agreements with the Royal Canadian Navy and the Royal Canadian Air Force to conduct educational work in those branches of the service followed shortly.

During 1941 and the early months of 1942, demand for course material was heavy. There were 56,000 applications for courses in Canada and 12,000 overseas. Nearly 800 oral courses were established in Britain and 1,300 in Canada, with enrolments of 23,000 and 60,000 respectively. Some 21,000 books were placed in British libraries and 57,000 in Canada.

After some initial problems with gaining commitment from students, the Legion's correspondence courses caught on in mid-1942. The majority of the courses men registered for were at the grades nine and 10 levels, but many men also worked on senior matriculation and university courses while they were at war. The curriculum was not limited to those in the field of battle, either; many Canadians continued their studies while prisoners of war. Through arrangements made with the International Red Cross, nearly 60,000 textbooks were sent to prison camps and depots. Almost 2,000 Canadians took university courses while they were incarcerated.

Most university studies were undertaken in more traditional surroundings. Chatwin had organized a university-leave program that operated at every college in England, as well as some in Scotland, Italy, Brussels and Denmark.

This program resulted in some interesting tales: in Florence, for example, courses were conducted just 40 kilometres from the battlefield; one young lieutenant registered for post-graduate work in engineering while he was stationed in England, and had obtained his doctorate by the time his regiment reached the Normandy beach; a pilot who had been allowed to fly from France to England to write his final exams was called back to active duty before the test was finished, but still managed to score 70 per cent.

During the course of the war, the shape of the Canadian Legion Educational Services changed considerably. One change was the increased involvement of the various branches of the armed forces; eventually all three had appointed representatives to sit alongside the Legion Educational Services and the Canadian Association for Adult Education on their various organizing committees. Another change was the extension of educational programs to the Royal Air Force, Newfoundland forces, Merchant Navy, Royal Canadian Mounted Police, Canadian firefighters and others. The services also received approval by the Army Institute of the United States and were used by a large number of U.S. Coast Guardsmen and army and navy personnel.

Altogether, the Legion Educational Services had set up 60 elementary, high school and technical courses, and distributed more than two million textbooks. By VE-Day, servicemen and women were registering for correspondence courses at a rate of 3,500 a month in Canada and 1,500 a month overseas. During its final year of operation, Educational Services had more active students than all of Canada's universities combined. Its total expenditure was $6.25 million.

As with the umbrella War Services organization, the Canadian Legion Educational Services provided many Canadians with a positive introduction to the Canadian Legion; what's more, it gave many a leg up on careers and further education that was not available to men returning from World War I.

Chapter 8

A CALL FOR
TOTAL WAR

W hen war erupted in Europe in 1939, the average legionnaire was 49 years old. As Dominion president W.W. Foster had stated in his radio address to the nation on September 13, that meant most veterans would be too old for the new fight, but there were some obvious exceptions in the organization's top ranks. By early 1940, the war had already depleted the Legion's leadership.

Foster stayed on to finish his term as president, although he had begun his duties with the Defence Department's auxiliary services. Basil Price, who held the rank of brigadier, resigned his position as first vice-president to become a brigade commander. Lt.-Col. Milton Gregg left the post of honorary treasurer to take command of the West Nova Scotia Highlanders.

Others began to answer the call as well. Jock Murray, known to readers of *The Legionary* by his pseudonym, The Orderly Sergeant, left journalism to become chief cable censor on the Canadian general staff.

Across the country, Legion branches opened their doors and became transformed into recruiting and training facilities, as needed. They turned their fund-raising energies toward the war effort. The pall of the Depression that had hung over the country for a decade was replaced by the urgency of the plight of European refugees and evacuated British children.

Members also turned their energy to criticism of the government's response to the crisis. Measured against the speed of the Legion's call to arms, many veterans found the King administration's reaction time wanting. By early summer, when almost 900 legionnaires gathered in Montreal for the eighth Dominion convention, the mood was feisty.

Reporting on the convention in *The Legionary*, editor John Hundevad acknowledged what he called "fifth column activities on the convention floor," but summarized the outcome in a positive light: "...the principal things that stand out, now that the heat of the verbal battles has cooled off, are the intense patriotism and loyalty of every man-jack present, the over-powering desire of every delegate to have Canada contribute her very utmost to help the Mother Country and our gallant allies, and the burning wish of all to create opportunities for sailors, soldiers and airmen of the First Great War to again do their bit."

Aside from confirming the programs already undertaken by Canadian Legion War Services Inc. and the Canadian Legion Educational Services, the primary means of assisting the war effort for the average delegate was expressed in support for formation of the Veterans Guard of Canada.

Delegates voted overwhelmingly in favor of demanding that the government act immediately to bring the country's war machine up to full strength by conscripting Canadians.

The tone of the delegates' anger toward the King government was softened somewhat by the reassurances the convention received by Defence Minister Norman Rogers and newly appointed Air Minister Chubby Power. Any possible backlash against Rogers' call for calm in the face of Hitler's fury was blunted by his death in a plane crash just days after his speech.

With three vacancies among the elected officers, delegates faced more choices than ever before, and made Alex Walker of Calgary the first non-commissioned officer to become Dominion president. A sergeant in the 50th Battalion, Walker had been seriously wounded in France. William Nicholson, a lieutenant-colonel who lost an arm at Amiens in March 1918, was elected first vice-president. J.D. Winslow became second vice-president. Gordon Rochester of Ottawa, who had been handling the honorary treasurer's duties since Gregg's re-enlistment, was confirmed in the position. The venerable Jack Moore returned for his ninth term of office.

Less than a week after the convention closed on May 30, Walker met for two days with Prime Minister King and his ministers of justice, defence and air. He pressed the Legion's case for conscription, echoing his words from the convention: "The Canadian Legion calls for complete and unrestricted mobilization. Every man, every dollar, every industry must be placed immediately at the service of the country. Our war effort must be speeded up to the maximum and then strained to the breaking point, for if we frolic today we shall die tomorrow."

He also recommended that the government take advantage of the 1938 national veterans' survey to fill the ranks of the Veterans Guard because of what he termed "the entire inadequacy of existing military provisions for the defence of vital and strategic areas within the Dominion."

Walker came away from the meetings guardedly optimistic, and said that "the Legion intends to watch developments closely and will not hesitate, if necessary, to make further representations."

The formation of the Veterans Guard gave ex-servicemen the opportunity to serve their country and decreased the likelihood of sabotage against Canada's essential infrastructure installations. Members had to be 50 or under and physically fit. Initially, 12 companies of 250 men each were formed, but by year's end the number had expanded to 29 companies and their duties had been extended to include the guarding of internment camps. Three other civilian guard organizations were formed independently: the Saskatchewan Veterans Civil Security Corps under former Dominion president Alex Ross; the Civil Protection Corps of Quebec; and the Ontario Volunteer Constabulary.

As shown in its formation of the Canadian Legion War Services and Educational Services, the Legion was also looking beyond the immediate war effort to the rehabilitation of the men and women who would return from the fighting. The lesson of World War I was that it was difficult to remove a million of the fittest people from the country's manpower pool without some measure of dislocation, and it was impossible to make them fit back into society without careful planning. For the first time, the Legion approached the government to ask it to address the problems that would face a new generation of veterans.

"One of the tragedies of this present war," stated the Legion's brief, "is that it should have come at a time when thousands of men are without employment. Now we must frankly admit that when huge forces are mobilized for service, there must inevitably be a number of misfits who, war or no war, would never have made good — who have not the will to work and who would always be drifters. But we are not prepared to admit that among the men we knew in the Canadian Corps of 1914 to '18 there were a number of misfits equivalent to those now unemployed. We can only assume, therefore, that either economic conditions or faulty rehabilitation measures are responsible for existing conditions.

"It is our concern to see to it that in the preoccupation of the new war, the veteran of the last war is not forgotten, and that the men of the new forces may go to meet the enemy with the knowledge that on their return they may expect a fair deal and an opportunity to make a living."

The brief suggested a number of ways in which the government could assist World War I vets who remained in need of assistance. It lauded work that had been done in the field of pensions, medical treatment and the War Veterans Allowance, but warned against complacency and urged steps to safeguard the rights of the old vets while protecting those of the new. It pointed to the chaos in the postwar period that resulted from the rush to install programs that should have been in place in 1915, and suggested ways a similar situation could be avoided.

"It should be possible to evolve schemes for rehabilitation which have a reasonable chance of success, provided always that conditions are favorable. For such favorable conditions, three factors are essential: that economic conditions shall be capable of permitting the absorption of a large number of men in a short space of time; that the men are given a fair chance of orderly absorption; and that the attitude of the men shall be favorable."

Recommendations were made on each of these three factors:

Economic conditions — The Legion foresaw that Canada's foreign markets would be so disrupted by the war that re-employment on a large scale would be difficult. Still, it maintained that young veterans could not be turned loose to wander in search of what work there might be. It advocated conservation of Canada's economic resources and development of employment facilities so that returning vets could find a job. "A place must be found for them, and to that end we recommend that immediate steps be taken to survey the field of employment that it may be developed, even artificially if need be, that a place may be found for every volunteer who enlists."

A fair chance — The brief assumed that every volunteer felt a sense of duty and made certain sacrifices. "If he is young, so young perhaps that he has never been regularly employed, he sacrifices the formative years of his life — the years when he most easily learns the fundamentals of earning a living — and wastes these years in an unnatural environment where he learns little which will be of real use to him afterwards. If he is older and has already started to make his way in life, he loses the opportunity of advancement, the opportunity of mastering the fundamentals of his trade, business or profession. No matter if he returns unscathed, he is definitely handicapped as compared with his friend who has stayed at home. Following the last war, this was one of the most disturbing features of rehabilitation. During the war there had been great expansion and great demand for primary goods for which the producers received exceptionally high prices. There were, therefore, on every side, signs of apparent prosperity, and men who had voluntarily sacrificed good positions to serve found themselves at a great disadvantage with men of their own class who had stayed at home. This created a bitterness which was not conducive to orderly rehabilitation."

The serving man's attitude — "There is no reason why concentration on winning the war cannot be maintained while at the same time a healthy interest in his future is inculcated into the man on service. He should be encouraged to use his leisure time to better fit himself for his return. It is for this reason the Canadian Legion War Services are seeking to develop an educational program."

In addition to these general recommendations, the Legion suggested several specific policies. It advocated equality of pay for fighting men and civilians, and it urged the government to make it law that an employer must reinstate those who left to serve. It also urged preferential treatment for veterans who wanted to enter the public service on their return, and it recommended a program of pre-discharge training for soldiers who wanted to pursue a public service career upon their return to Canada.

Late in 1940, the Legion's concern about the welfare of the new generation of veterans began to bear fruit. The government issued an order-in-council that stated: "immediate action is necessary to bridge the gap between the time at which a member of the forces was retired or discharged and that by which he might reasonably be expected to rehabilitate himself in civil life and obtain gainful employment. This assistance could most readily and effectively be furnished by way of a monetary grant."

The government also announced plans to create a veterans' welfare division within the Department of Pensions and National Health that would interview, advise and assist service personnel at the time of their discharge. Other measures included introduction of a pension for death or disability, pensions for Canadians who had entered the British forces after September 1, 1939, and treatment for men discharged as unfit and requiring hospital care.

Several committees were established to study the problem of rehabilitation. Early in 1941, the Legion appeared before one of these — the Commons committee on pensions and rehabilitation — with a number of specific recommendations.

The principle in any rehabilitation program, the Legion stated, was that "adequate steps should be taken to ensure that those who volunteer for service shall in no way be penalized on their return to civil life and, so far as is possible, shall be assured of that place in civil life which they might reasonably be assumed to have obtained had they not enlisted." This did not mean that the veteran could expect that "the world, and more particularly the nation, owed him a living... It is nothing less than a moral right, however, that a man who has served his country shall, as far as possible, be re-established in society. From the financial standpoint, rehabilitation should be regarded a part of the war and there should be no letting up in the war effort or war expenditure until this problem has been adequately provided for. Rehabilitation must also be considered as an essential part of the postwar reconstruction problem."

The main thing, it stated, was that veterans or their dependants must not be obliged to depend on public welfare between demobilization and re-employment. It noted that the Canadian Trades and Labor Congress supported this view.

On the question of veterans returning to their previous employer, the brief urged the government to appeal to the patriotic leanings of employers and held that it was essential that the transition to civilian life should be accomplished without glutting the labor market and with a minimum of industrial dislocation. To accomplish this, the Legion suggested that a determined effort be made to earmark each veteran for a specific job. Any plan to accomplish this, the Legion felt, should involve both management and organized labor.

The brief reasserted the Legion's stance on public service hiring, and urged the government to amend the Civil Service Act to include the new veterans. For its part, the Legion pledged to help prepare serving men through its Educational Services courses.

It also recommended maintenance of the same facilities for treatment with pay and allowances for war disability as those that existed after World War I, and requested free treatment of all conditions for one year following the cessation of hostilities.

It urged the government to re-establish the Returned Soldiers Insurance Act, and recommended that any land-settlement scheme be carefully studied to avoid the pitfalls associated with the one enacted in 1917.

In conclusion, the Legion brief stated: "(We) believe it will be fatal if the adequacy of rehabilitation measures should be curtailed due to financial alarm or panic. The Legion realizes that this is a natural tendency and wishes to record its opinion that this tendency must be strongly and firmly resisted and the necessary money found to do the job properly. Any other policy will, in our judgment, prove more costly in the long run and the resulting dissatisfaction and unrest will be anything but an asset to our country. The only course is to face the problem and cost involved fairly and squarely in the first instance."

The government's reaction to these and other recommendations came quickly. The committee's report led to important amendments to the Pension Act including extending it to cover the new veterans, and independence for the Canadian Pension Commission, with discretion to award a pension on compassionate grounds. On the question of rehabilitation, the committee recommended that the armed forces retain for six months after the end of the war physically fit men who had no assurance of post-discharge employment. The Legion proposal for free treatment of non-pensionable conditions for a period of up to one year after discharge was provided for by order-in-council, and the committee recommended further provision be made for physical reconditioning of veterans — either for further service or re-establishment.

The committee also urged the government to make plans for retraining special casualties and any new land-settlement program, and it recommended the government carry out constructive policies to include World War II veterans in the Civil Service Act.

The Legion was pleased with what it saw, and Walker offered Pensions Minister Ian Mackenzie the use of branch facilities to assist in rehabilitation programs. The government accepted, making the Legion a partner in the planning and delivery of the rehabilitation program. This was a far cry from the situation that had existed almost 30 years earlier when wounded men began to flow home from the trenches of Europe.

But if the Legion and the King government saw eye to eye on the issue of returning servicemen, the two could not have been much further apart on deciding who might eventually become a veteran.

Throughout 1940 and well into 1941 the Legion kept up its call for full conscription for overseas service. Meanwhile, the prime minister stuck to his 1940 election promise to conscript men solely for the defence of the country under the provisions of the National Resources Mobilization Act.

In October 1941, Walker convened an emergency meeting of the Dominion Executive Council to discuss "profound alarm at Canada's failure, after more than two years of war, to make anything approaching an all-out contribution to the Empire's war effort." In the aftermath of the meeting, on October 21, with the support of some 500 other organizations, the Legion released a manifesto entitled *Call for Total War* that set out five principles:

- immediate, complete and scientific mobilization, organization and utilization of all our resources — spiritual, intellectual, natural, financial, agricultural, industrial, manpower — in such a manner that Canada may be geared to produce essential foods and munitions and to wage war to her maximum capacity;

- the services of all men and women to be employed to the best and most useful effect, according to the age, training, physical capacity and ability of the individual;

- by an intelligent extension of the principles of the National Resources Mobilization Act and by the elimination of the provisions restricting service to Canada only — our armed forces in Canada and overseas, including reserves and reinforcements, to be maintained at the highest possible strength, consistent with our industrial and other requirements;

- an equitable division of the burden of service, sacrifice, contribution and effort amongst all our people to be the basic principle underlying this total war policy;

- the cumulative results of this total effort to be devoted to the single purpose of destroying the enemy.

"We repudiate the statement often heard that Canada is unable to wage total war because of the reluctance or unwillingness of the Province of Quebec," stated the manifesto. "To our certain knowledge there are no greater or more fervent patriots in all Canada than the citizens of that great province. With the assurance of a fair and equitable division of the burden among all Canadians — with favor and privilege to none — the citizens of Quebec, we are convinced, are ready to join in all necessary measures for the annihilation of Nazism. Let us destroy forever this falsehood that Canada cannot wage total war without creating internal disunity. Canada has achieved nationhood and her people can think and act as one; and when the issues are clear, unmistakable and urgent, they will not hesitate to do so.

"It is frequently suggested that members of this government are unable to concur in the total war effort because of certain political pledges given both before and at an early stage in this conflict. The sanctity of the pledged word is to be respected. But these promises were entered into when the extent and further course of the war could at best be seen vaguely. Devastating events have since occurred. Canada now stands in deadly peril. Measures for our individual and national self-preservation, as well as for the victory of our cause must, in the Legion's opinion, take precedence over all else.

"To the Legion the tradition of victory is ingrained and instinctive. Any other outcome is unthinkable. But by hard experience we know something of the cost of victory in blood and effort and suffering and sacrifice. That price must now be paid again, in full. There is no escape from it. We must and can and will prevail, but only if we face facts and meet total war with total war. This the Legion urges, and will continue to urge, with all its strength and all its sincerity."

The manifesto was circulated widely and received endorsements from numerous church groups, labor unions and newspapers, but the biggest boost to its credence came when Japan attacked the U.S. naval force at Pearl Harbor on December 7. King announced his intention to hold a national plebiscite on releasing his government from its anti-conscription promise, but the Legion was not pleased by the prospect. Walker believed that the referendum would lead to a schism within the country and serve only to distract the public from the real issue: the need for a total war effort.

The plebiscite also put the Legion in danger of losing its non-partisan stance. Walker issued a statement expressing dissatisfaction with King's plan and emphasizing that the Legion would not enter into any political controversy surrounding the issue. He reiterated his belief that the government should have enough faith in its right to call for conscription without seeking the public's permission and urged all veterans to "preach the gospel of total war."

The Legionary also attempted to distance the organization from the politics of the vote: "Had the government announced a plebiscite to ascertain whether Canadians are willing to wage total war, then the reference to the Legion's influence might have had some merit. Even so, the Legion would have considered a plebiscite an unnecessary, undesirable, time-wasting, energy-consuming and costly measure at this, the most critical stage of the world's history, when determined, courageous leadership by our government is so desperately needed.

✤

"But the Legion must take a realistic view of the situation. Further opposition to the plebiscite is quite clearly a waste of precious time and energy. It is our duty now to make absolutely certain that the government gets an affirmative vote... If following that the government does not introduce total war, including compulsory national service, then the Canadian Legion may be counted upon to renew its efforts a thousandfold to arouse its fellow Canadians to the full realization of the immediate danger which confronts every man, woman and child in this country."

As Walker predicted, the April 27 plebiscite did little more than magnify the battle lines on the conscription issue. In Quebec, 72.9 per cent voted to refuse King permission to go back on his word; the other provinces voted 80 per cent in favor.

"One wonders," stated *The Legionary*, "whether the plebiscite hasn't resulted in the very opposite of what its authors hoped for; whether instead it hasn't given needless emphasis to a division in our country's makeup which everyone knew existed beforehand. One can only hope that the people of the dissenting province will loyally abide by the verdict of the vast majority of their fellow Canadians.

"In the meantime, it is well to remember that the plebiscite was not a vote against or for compulsory overseas service. Oh no! Nothing as straightforward as that. It was simply a vote to free the government from its pledge not to conscript men for service overseas, to confirm the authority — which it already possessed — of using our manpower in any way it deems necessary for the prosecution of the war."

The delegates who arrived in Winnipeg in late May for the Legion's ninth convention were in no better a mood than delegates had been at the eighth.

"What is the government waiting for?" asked Walker, in a speech broadcast nationally by the CBC. "Hasn't the great majority of the Canadian people told our government that it can go full speed ahead and conscript all of us for service anywhere? Must we wait until our forces in the field clash head-on against the enemy in full battle? Until we have compulsory universal service in this country it is rank hypocrisy for us to talk about making sacrifices... Sacrifice can only be applied to one thing — life itself.

"I give it as my considered opinion that this policy of compromise and procrastination has brought about a state of disunity, doubt and misgiving which would not have existed had the conduct of the war effort been clearcut, vigorous and courageous."

The task of defending the government's policy fell to Defence Minister James Ralston, a respected World War I battalion commander who would eventually resign from cabinet over the conscription question. Ralston attempted to bolster the prime minister's position by talking about the 430,000 Canadians who had volunteered for service wherever they were needed, but neither the delegates nor the media were swayed.

The Globe and Mail stated: "(Ralston) failed to say one thing that the country would like to hear from him, namely that there is no defence for the voluntary system consistent with statesmanship and honor. As has been said many a time it puts a premium on the laggard and a penalty on the patriot. It does not summon the national spirit to a great and righteous crusade, but, as most citizens recognize by this time, it does play into the hands of petty politics, to the shame of the government responsible."

Also high on the convention's agenda was discussion of the government's proposed Veterans Land Act, which had been introduced in the Commons by Pensions Minister Mackenzie earlier in the spring. Designed to settle at least 25,000 returning servicemen on farm land at an estimated cost of $80 million, the plan was endorsed by the Legion with minor recommendations for changes to the proposed interest rate. In general, it was felt that this new plan would avoid the pitfalls that doomed the earlier settlement plan to failure.

Speaking about the Legion's stance on rehabilitation programs, Walker said: "We... believe that the whole problem of rehabilitation and reconstruction, however complex it may be, should be regarded not as a necessary evil to prevent large-scale unemployment when victory is won, but as an opportunity for the greatest human advancement and happiness our civilization has ever seen. If we can afford to win the war, we can afford to win the peace.

"One of the most encouraging signs in connection with rehabilitation is the fact that the common people are beginning to awaken to realities. They want to know why it is now possible to spend billions for armies, navies and air forces when in the years before the war they were told that a few hundred millions to keep starvation from the door meant national bankruptcy. Also, if the present superficially good business conditions can be financed without wrecking the nation, they want to know why large outlays cannot be made in the postwar years on constructive rehabilitation projects and thus benefit the returned men and the nation as a whole."

Not surprisingly, delegates elected Walker for a second term. In fact, the entire executive was returned intact — the only time this has happened in Legion history.

Sadly, though, delegates noted two changes at the Dominion level. Reg Bowler, the Legion's original general secretary since 1929, had committed suicide by drowning in the Ottawa River in March at age 49. A World War I amputee, Bowler was apparently depressed over his declining physical condition. The convention confirmed his assistant, George Herwig, as the new general secretary. Delegates also noted the passing of education officer John MacNeil, a popular teacher at Ottawa's Glebe high school who was killed in the sinking of the *Nerissa* off Ireland.

Among the delegates in Winnipeg was M.G. Ford, president of Young Veterans' Branch in Vancouver, the first of the new generation of legionnaires.

Chapter 9

THE PUSH
TOWARD VICTORY

With a renewed mandate from the Winnipeg convention, Dominion president Alex Walker wasted no time rejoining the fight for universal overseas conscription. He wrote to Prime Minister King demanding immediate action, stating: "Time presses and the preservation of this country and its people, their religions, their rights and their privileges are at stake now. Prompt action is necessary if Canada is to continue to exist. The Legion implores you to act and to act now."

King's answer was viewed as vague and evasive: "...Parliament is now debating a bill introduced by the government to amend the National Resources Mobilization Act to remove the one existing statutory limitation on the powers of the government to dispose of persons, their services and their property for the defence of Canada and the efficient prosecution of the war. It is, as it has been from the outset, the policy of the government to organize the utmost war effort of which our country is capable and to use methods which will most effectively contribute to that end."

The second part of Walker's strategy was to address the people of Quebec directly, excusing them from any malice toward the country and putting the blame squarely on the shoulders of the government.

"I charge our political leaders," he said, "who know that the issues are clear, who know that the need is urgent, with having failed in their patriotic duty to Canada and to Quebec by not coming down here and telling the people of this province the truth — the terrible truth — that confronts us. That truth is that we are *not* winning the war; that we are barely holding our own; that our position may soon become even more precarious.

"The reason Quebec has not been told the truth, the whole naked truth, and the reason we are not fighting a total war by the only fair and decent method of raising men, seems to be a purely political one. It is a sad reflection on the state of politics that, at this crucial stage of our history, the leaders refrain from tackling this vital problem because they are afraid for their political lives. They are putting party strategy first; military strategy second; or in plain English, their own survival first, Canada's survival second."

When, after the amendment King had referred to was passed, the prime minister uttered his famous phrase — "not necessarily conscription, but conscription if necessary" — to describe what would follow, *The Legionary* launched a blistering attack: "In any other democratic country the passing by the national legislature of such an act could only mean one thing — the immediate implementation by the government of Parliament's wishes. But not so in Canada... While in the name of national unity the government of Canada indulges in these time-consuming political gymnastics, the Hunnish hordes are advancing towards the oilfields of the Caucasus and hammering on the gates of Egypt. Considering that the capture of either, or both, may jeopardize the whole outcome of the war, is it too irrelevant to ask a procrastinating government, 'WHEN, in the name of God and our freedom, will you regard compulsory service against the enemy as NECESSARY? WHY, in the name of all that's decent and worthwhile in life, don't we get ACTION? Why, Mr. King?'"

"Those are very strong words," commented the *Globe and Mail*. "No one has any better right to use them than the men who fought for their country in the last war. All the argument and manoeuvering will not change one iota the necessity for unlimited compulsory national selective service now."

Canada's bloody defeat on the beach at Dieppe on August 19, 1942 added fuel to Walker's fury. "Don't let our boys down," he told King. "Heed the lesson of Dieppe by strengthening our army overseas. You, and only you, have the power and authority to do it. Do it now!"

Of course, King continued to dither, refusing to invoke conscription while the war ground on. The Legion kept up its barrage of criticism, but it seemed to have no effect. In fact, the situation had changed very little in the previous two years when the 10th Dominion convention was convened in early June 1944. The war effort and rehabilitation were so dominant that the resolutions committee decided to address only those resolutions that dealt with these two issues.

More than 440 delegates, 194 Ladies Auxiliary members and 112 fraternal members gathered in Vancouver, and only the news that Allied forces had landed in France tempered the bitterness they felt at being ignored by the government on the conscription issue. Once again, delegates voted overwhelmingly in favor of the Legion's policy of total war. Only overseas conscription, they said, would ensure continuous, adequate reinforcements, "particularly at this period of invasion and prospective heavy casualties."

In addition to dealing with this issue, the convention also voted to recommend that the Allies accept nothing less than unconditional surrender from Germany, and it sent a message to King that the Legion would refrain from using political power to pursue its demands.

Walker was acclaimed for an unprecedented third term in office. William Walker of Canora, Saskatchewan, defeated three opponents to become first vice-president, and E.J. Struthers emerged from a field of four candidates to become second vice-president. Allan Piper, 33, of Cornwall, Ontario, became the first World War II veteran on the Dominion Executive Council when he was acclaimed for the newly created position of third vice-president. A captain with the Stormont, Dundas and Glengarry Highlanders, Piper had lost both hands after falling on a live grenade that had been dropped by a trainee. Gordon Rochester and Jack Moore were returned to the positions of honorary treasurer and chairman.

The first cracks in the government's stand against overseas conscription did not appear until the fall of 1944. Following a fact-finding trip to visit Canadian troops in Europe, Defence Minister James Ralston demanded that King reverse his stand. When the prime minister refused, Ralston resigned. In the wake of the resignation, for which no reason was given, the Dominion Executive Council held an emergency meeting and issued another manifesto, this one called *Conscription Now!*:

"...We reiterate our conviction that the time has come when the army of trained soldiers at present inactive in Canada should become immediately available for reinforcements overseas and all further call-ups be for general service," stated the manifesto.

"The Legion as a national organization is profoundly concerned with the problem of national unity. We realize acutely the deep cleavages which have been revealed in our national structure and we have no desire to deepen them. However, our concept of national unity is not that of an amorphous conglomeration of people whose only policy is that of refusing to take a stand on issues where there is divergence of opinion, but rather of a nation with definite characteristics, committed to a definite way of life, the product of our traditions and our common aspirations. If national unity is to be a reality and not a shibboleth, then positive and courageous commitment to that great task is imperative. To abstain from such commitment out of political deference to local prejudice is to deny our nationhood and our destiny."

❀

Shortly after Ralston's resignation, King named Andrew McNaughton as his replacement. The 57-year-old retired commander of Canadian forces overseas had feuded with Ralston throughout the war and was a confidante of the increasingly reclusive King. It was clear to the Legion that the fight for conscription was far from over. On November 6, the new minister appeared at Ottawa Branch to defend King's policy of voluntary overseas service. The 700 legionnaires were in no mood to listen, especially because McNaughton took credit for proposing the concept of voluntary service to King in 1939. Throughout his speech veterans interrupted McNaughton with booing and shouts of "Take the zombies!" — using the derogatory term applied to home-service soldiers. Finally, the meeting chairman called a halt to the proceedings, saving McNaughton from further embarrassment.

Three days later, the Dominion Executive Council confronted King in his office with the Legion's manifesto. "Battle casualties, according to the latest figures, are twice as high as recruitments," the legionnaires told the prime minister. "We are scraping the bottom of the manpower barrel. All this despite the fact that we have some 70,000 fully trained and equipped soldiers in Canada who are performing no useful service. What were these men called up for if not to meet an emergency such as the one that has now arisen? We would urge that the government of Canada now act on the mandate of the plebiscite and invoke the provisions of the National Resources Mobilization Act and send all fully trained personnel called up under that act overseas immediately as essential reinforcements."

Facing open dissension from members of the cabinet in addition to pressure from groups like the Legion, King finally gave in. On November 22, he announced that 16,000 of the home-service draftees would be sent overseas. The Legion viewed the action as barely a partial victory, stating that the number (in fact, less than 13,000 would actually be sent before the end of the war) was far too low. It called on Parliament to stop bickering over the issue and get on with the job of reinforcing the Canadians at the front.

King's decision may have represented too little, too late, but the Legion would reap dividends from its stance on conscription in the form of new members after the war. In his year-end message for 1944, Walker stated: "It is doubtful if in Legion history there has been any more serious challenge than that of the reinforcement issue which was brought — more by Legion efforts than anything else — to a definite conclusion."

Regardless of how rancorous the Legion's relationship with the King government was on the conscription question, the organization continued to make significant strides in the area of rehabilitation policy.

As Walker had noted at the 1942 Dominion convention, Canadians were beginning to realize the importance of legislation and initiatives that would allow military personnel to fit back into society when they returned home. A Gallup poll conducted that year showed 45 per cent of Canadians surveyed believed World War I ex-servicemen had been treated unfairly and 66 per cent wanted the new generation of vets to be treated more generously, especially in job placement.

By early 1943, Parliament had passed three important pieces of rehabilitation legislation: the Civil Employment Reinstatement Act; the Post-Discharge Re-establishment Order; and the Veterans Land Act. The first of these made it compulsory for employers to reinstate former employees, provided the employee had held the job for at least three months prior to enlistment. The Post-Discharge Re-establishment Order provided for unemployment benefits coupled with physical, vocational and educational reconditioning during the period of unemployment. Under these provisions, veterans could pick up their postwar education where the Canadian Legion Educational Services had left off. This included attendance at university for a period equivalent to their service and beyond, depending on academic standing. The Veterans Land Act was much as Pensions Minister Ian Mackenzie had presented it in the spring of 1942, and included provisions for small agricultural holdings and commercial fishing.

Only a few months after these bills became law the government announced further legislative changes, including: increased benefits under the post-discharge order; amendments to treatment regulations to provide complete treatment of non-pensionable disabilities and higher cash allowances, plus allowances for dependants of men undergoing treatment after discharge; and an amendment to the War Veterans Allowance Act to eliminate deductions from allowances because of casual earnings.

In July, the Legion published a wide-ranging blueprint for rehabilitation, which it printed in pamphlet form and distributed to 150,000 Canadians serving overseas. While it agreed that the government's measures "should assist materially in re-establishing ex-servicemen in the immediate postwar period," improvements and modifications would be necessary. Veterans, it stated, should in no way be penalized for having enlisted. Governments at the federal, provincial and municipal levels must coordinate plans to ensure that returning servicemen and women can catch up on the time they have missed. Canadians should be prepared to accept whatever controls are deemed necessary to allow veterans to achieve a decent standard of living and full employment.

The brief expressed the belief that rehabilitation should be treated as part of the war effort and the necessary funds raised by taxation. "The people of Canada generally are not prepared to accept a postponement of social progress because they are told that the country cannot afford it," it stated.

It also recommended an immediate survey of war plants to ascertain which could be converted to peacetime manufacturing and how many veterans could be employed in them.

It advocated the principle of targeted demobilization: "Men should not be discharged from the armed forces except to gainful employment... If the advisory committee on demobilization and rehabilitation has considered retarded demobilization, any recommendations made should be made public as soon as possible... It is to be expected that the troops will wish to return home as soon as possible after hostilities have ceased. Definite steps should be taken to deal with the understandable impatience that undoubtedly will be expressed."

The brief urged preferential treatment for vets in all categories of employment, stating: "The Legion desires to make the point that any plans of reconstruction that do not provide for preferential treatment of the fighting man will be regarded as unjust and will bring bitter reaction. We desire to put forward the proposal that provision shall be made for a general preference to discharged men in all employment, whether under private enterprise or under the federal, provincial or municipal governments throughout the country. The Legion urges the fullest possible use of government employment offices, with no resort to political patronage. Government contractors, both federal and provincial, and government departments for certain types of employment, should be required by law to fill all vacancies through the employment offices and preference should be given to discharged men of this and the last war."

The Legion urged vocational training for returned men to prepare them quickly for civil employment. It also asked the government to embark immediately on a program of purchasing suitable lands for the settlement of veterans. It advocated a public works program of rural road construction, reforestation and soil conservation as a means of creating employment for veterans, and even promoted the idea of increasing Canada's population through immigration, with the proviso that "such a measure should be adopted gradually and after the problems of adequate provision for the return to the Canadian economy of veterans of the present war and those engaged in war work have been established on a sure and satisfactory basis."

As instrumental as this brief was in influencing the course of government policy — Gray Turgeon, chairman of the Commons committee on postwar reconstruction and rehabilitation, called it "the most progressive yet presented to Parliament" — another Legion initiative had wider ranging results. Alex Walker had grown increasingly concerned that administration for veterans' benefits, programs and rehabilitation was too scattered to be of optimum effectiveness. The Department of Pensions and National Health, which had grown out of the Department of Soldiers' Civil Re-establishment and the Department of Health, was responsible for most veterans' affairs. However, administration of the land settlement program was within the purview of the Department of Mines and Resources, and the Department of Labor was responsible for re-training programs and legislation.

During a tour of Ontario branches in the fall of 1943, Walker said: "Regarding the policy and administration of veterans' affairs in general, I fear they may become spread out over too many government departments, opening up possibilities of conflict of opinion and authority. The Legion would like to see all veterans' affairs brought under one ministry. It seems to me that the time is arriving when there should be a department of veterans' affairs responsible for all legislation and administration affecting veterans, including rehabilitation, land settlement, vocational training, university training, war veterans' allowance, veterans' insurance, and any other benefits that may be made available to ex-servicemen and women. Undoubtedly, very close cooperation with other departments of the government will be necessary, but we are satisfied from past experience that veterans' affairs require a separate administration."

Walker wrote to the prime minister, stating: "In setting up such a department (of veterans' affairs) we regard it as essential that that part of the present Department of Pensions and National Health administering veterans' legislation, together with the new welfare division, should be separated from the administration of national health. We also urge that an immediate survey be made of present and future requirements to determine what additional organization and staff is necessary efficiently to provide and maintain the additional services now authorized by new legislation."

✤

Unlike the situation regarding the Legion's ongoing requests for overseas conscription, King's answer was almost immediate. In the Throne Speech to open the new session of Parliament in January 1944 the government listed the creation of the new department as one of its priorities. It also announced its intention to create departments of reconstruction and social welfare. The bill to create the veterans' affairs department was introduced in the spring, and by year's end Ian Mackenzie had been named minister and Walter Woods deputy minister. By V-E Day, the department had 8,000 employees and was looking to hire 4,000 more.

The creation of the Department of Veterans Affairs was not the Legion's only victory on the rehabilitation front in 1944. Parliament also passed the Gratuities Act, which budgeted some $750 million to help ease veterans back into civilian life. Under the act, returning servicemen and women would receive: a rehabilitation grant equal to a month's pay and allowances; a clothing allowance of $100; a gratuity — $7.50 for each month served in the Western Hemisphere, $15 for each month of overseas service, and a week's pay and allowances for every six months' service overseas based on the amount received immediately prior to discharge; and a re-establishment credit to be used for purchase of a home, furniture, etcetera, and to be awarded as an alternative to other re-establishment payments such as vocational or university training or Veterans Land Act benefits.

The Legionary called the Gratuities Act "one of the most encouraging pieces of legislation ever passed by the Canadian Parliament... No other nation is doing better for its fighting men by way of monetary reward. Not that Canada's debt to her sailors, soldiers and airmen can be adequately paid in money, but it is heartening nevertheless that more than five times the amount will be spent on this phase of our servicemen's and servicewomen's rehabilitation than was spent after the last war, in addition to the great sums which will be spent on vocational and university training, land settlement, etcetera. Given adequate employment opportunities at reasonable wages, the present war gratuities and other benefits will give the veterans of this war a much better start in civilian life than the veterans of the Great War had."

The figures bear out this editorial. Almost 250,000 World War II vets took advantage of their re-establishment credits. Roughly 200,000 returned to their pre-enlistment employment, more than 23,000 took up small holdings under the Veterans Land Act, and about 22,000 began farming. Approximately 130,000 vets sought training upon discharge, and more than 50,000 attended university.

Even as the war drew to a close, though, the Legion recognized that work remained to be done. On a three-month overseas tour, Walker encountered men seeking information about rehabilitation and the availability of jobs in the public service. He urged King to address these queries. In April 1945, the Legion participated with the departments of Veterans Affairs, Defence and Labor, along with representatives from private enterprise, in a conference on re-employment of veterans. It also presented a submission to the Royal Commission on Veterans Qualifications, which was set up under Lt.-Col. Wilfrid Bovey, head of the Canadian Legion Educational Services, to study how to adopt military skills to civilian work.

As the troops began to be "de-mobbed" the Legion's attention turned from the empowering legislation to the practical means to make rehabilitation a reality. C.B. Lumsden, chairman of the rehabilitation committee, summed up the problem in his report to the 11th Dominion convention, which met in Quebec City in May 1946: "...the veteran is being frustrated on his return to civil life by a short supply of civilian goods and at the same time by a lack of opportunity for employment. Theoretically, this demand for goods should correct the need for jobs. Actually, we find bottlenecks produced by strikes, low standards of production and general economic inefficiency."

Housing was another serious concern. The shortage of building materials and skilled labor meant that the construction industry could not begin to meet the national demands for an estimated 400,000 new housing units. Calling it "the number one problem of the reconstruction program of the Dominion," the Legion developed a number of recommendations to overcome the shortage, including:

- accelerate the unification of government departments engaged in housing;

- initiate a national housing program to provide homes for low-income families at rents pegged to one-fifth of their annual income;

- establish a veterans' housing act similar in nature to the Small Holding Act to allow urban veterans to acquire homes;

- control the production, distribution and export of all building materials;

- give priority in purchasing materials to builders of low-priced homes.

After up to six years away from Canada the new generation of veterans was impatient to lay claim to the rights and values they had fought to preserve. Many held a grudge against the newly re-elected Liberals over the King government's inability to come to terms with the conscription question, and they knew what it took to get what they wanted. Some 400 of these new veterans answered the call to gather in Quebec City to set the postwar course for the Legion.

In all, 1,137 people registered for the convention, including 744 accredited delegates. Foremost on their agenda was a motion — concurred by the resolutions committee — to extend Legion membership to conscripts who had served in a theatre of war. The debate raged for more than an hour, with some delegates warning angrily that the admittance of conscripts would "split the Legion wide open" while others maintained that the government was to blame for the mess. One young delegate, A.F. MacDonald of Edmonton, admitted his own early prejudice against the conscripts but called for tolerance. Hubert Taylor of Moncton, who lost one of three sons who fought overseas, asked, "How can we decline membership to men who fought on the battlefields?" But the voices of forgiveness were outmatched. The conscripts were refused entry.

The face of the Legion was also shaped by recommendations contained in a report by a special committee Walker had appointed to look at organizational questions. The committee recommended against creating any additional special-interest groups such as the Tuberculous Veterans or Imperials sections, and ruled that no branch should be allowed to use a name that referred to "a racial, religious, political or labor group." It recommended that Dominion Command create a handbook of Legion history and policies, based on a booklet used by Saskatchewan Command. Two other recommendations stand out for the ramifications they would have on the Legion's future: a proposal that the organization become involved at the community level to educate young people about the importance of Canadian citizenship; and the suggestion that a Dominion athletic committee be formed to encourage the growth of sports within and between branches, and in the broader community under Legion sponsorship.

Wilfrid Bovey presented a wrap-up report on the Canadian Legion Educational Services, which had officially ended its wartime work on March 31, 1946. As noted in a previous chapter, Educational Services had provided coursework to more than 200,000 men and touched the lives of many others who availed themselves of its textbooks and other materials. Rather than let the organization die, delegates voted to approve its incorporation to continue to provide services to returned personnel in conjunction with Veterans Affairs Department.

The convention did, however, mark the end for the Legion Educational Services' former parent organization — the Canadian Legion War Services Inc. Its chairman, former Dominion president Alex Ross, recounted the problems the organization encountered by being consistently understaffed and having to deal with the government's complex accounting procedures. In summarizing its goals, Ross said: "We knew that successful rehabilitation depended to a very large degree upon the attitude of mind of the man himself, and we hoped that by the close contact thus established we might be able to do much to create the proper outlook and atmosphere... Also, it was our hope, if we could discharge our duties efficiently and with respect, that we might make the members of the forces conscious of the value of a strong veteran organization and make them organization-conscious on their return and thereby eliminate the possibility of a recurrence of the chaotic conditions following the first Great War. This did not necessarily mean that we expected they would join the Legion... We did, however, desire to show the value of unity and, from experience to date, in this we seem to have been successful."

There was also a feeling of completeness to the election of officers. After six trying years in office, Alex Walker stepped down as Dominion president. Looking back from the vantage point of 1985, another venerable legionnaire, Charles Rhodes Smith, attributed the Legion's political status in Canada to Walker's wartime strategy. "The Legion became a very influential body in World War II under his leadership," said Smith. "He was very sensible in his dealings with King. He never made the Legion's demands a question of partisanship; it was always a question of what was right."

Succeeding Walker, after a four-way race, was Maj.-Gen. Basil Price, who had served as first vice-president from 1938 until his call-up in December 1939. Wounded three times in World War I, which he left with the rank of major, the Montreal dairy executive had been instrumental in securing rights for veterans as a member of the Hyndman Commission in the mid-1930s.

Another business executive, 57-year-old brokerage president Lionel Baxter of Winnipeg, was elected first vice-president. Among those voting for him was his son, a World War II veteran who was an accredited delegate.

Allan Piper moved from third to second vice-president, and 35-year-old Vancouverite Alfred Watts was elected third vice-president. A lawyer who had risen through the ranks quickly in World War II to become director of air training for the Royal Canadian Air Force, Watts had just as quickly established himself in Pacific Command as a man of superior leadership ability. Recommended for the third-vice-presidential post by Basil Price, Watts would be catapulted by fate into a national leadership role faster than anyone in Legion history.

Gordon Rochester and Jack Moore were once again elected as honorary treasurer and chairman, and Lucien Lalonde, a lawyer from Montreal who had commanded the Maisonneuve Regiment in World War II, won the post of vice-chairman, which was reinstated after an 18-year absence.

Chapter 10

THE CHANGING OF
THE GUARD

At Legion branches across Canada rapid expansion had begun. At the urging of Dominion chairman Jack Moore, who headed the membership committee, older veterans began recruiting young returned servicemen and women, and the ranks began to swell. Some branches like Valour Road Memorial Branch in Winnipeg almost doubled its membership in a year. Saskatchewan Command aimed to increase its membership each year, and saw its numbers grow from 13,000 to 20,000. New Brunswick Command concentrated on chartering new branches in rural parts of the province. Some new branches, like Strathcona in Edmonton, were started up by World War II vets. Beginning with just a Quonset hut in 1945, the branch slowly expanded, first adding an auditorium, then buying an adjoining lot to accommodate future buildings.

Communities were anxious to assist the Legion in its growth. Many municipalities sold land to branches for $1, and zoning was seldom a problem. If a branch wanted a licence to serve alcohol, it usually got it, even when other establishments could not.

But this burgeoning growth did not come without a price. While most branches were happy enough to welcome new members and their dues, many were not quick to give any real power to the younger veterans.

"There's no question that the World War I vets ran our branch," said Mervyn Woods, Dominion president from 1960 to '62. "The young vets were eager to work, but we had problems getting into office."

Another future Dominion president, Ed Coley, said: "The World War I vets resented, to some extent, the younger members coming in. I suppose it was a hand-me-down tradition of resentment; the feeling that you had to put in your time before you got their respect."

Yet another latter-day Legion leader, Doug McDonald of Brantford, Ontario, was less sanguine about the situation. "The first branch I belonged to was dominated by World War I vets who badgered the young fellows. They insisted on running things on a paramilitary basis that was left over from their war; that was the last thing the young guys wanted. If they wanted to live in the past — fine. We put up with it for awhile; then we just moved them aside. It was a new age and things had to be changed."

"I'd say that the tension between the two groups was natural," said Donald Thompson, who headed the Dominion Service Bureau in the 1950s and served as Dominion secretary from 1960 to '70. "You're going to get that between any group of 22- and 24-year-olds and people 30 years older. The older vets didn't want to share their power with us at first."

"Oh, yeah, they wanted to have things their way," recalled Winnipegger Bob Smellie, Dominion president from 1972 to '74. "My father and his cronies ran the organization from a room over his store. They let us in, but they made all the decisions. Finally, the younger vets got together, packed a meeting, and voted in one of our own."

Of course, not all branches were obstinate about ceding power to younger members. Many older members recognized the importance of handing over responsibility along with demands for volunteer labor. And, no matter how impatient young members were, or how much older legionnaires dug in their heels, neither side forgot that they had something in common that set them apart.

"We spoke the same language," said Coley. "No one could change that. We had a bond that no other service group had."

"Comradeship was earned," said McDonald. "You couldn't buy it and you couldn't inherit it."

Even at branches where the older vets held stubbornly to the reins, the divisions between the two age groups began to melt away as legionnaires worked together on projects — whether it was fund-raising in the community for branch projects, providing comfort to rehabbing ex-servicemen, or working on the annual poppy campaign. Another leavening factor was that, after their initial foray into branch politics, many young veterans soon found their attention diverted by young families or burgeoning careers. The second-generation recruits would return to the branch in the early 1950s, but in the short term they had other things on their minds.

Housing continued to be a priority, both on the local and the national levels. In 1947, Dominion president Basil Price formed a national housing committee with representatives from all provincial commands to study the problem of shortages and lobby the government for assistance.

However, the King administration rejected the Legion's request for guaranteed mortgages on 90 per cent of the value of land and buildings at an interest rate of 3.5 per cent.

Veterans were more successful in securing government aid on other fronts; those who wanted to start businesses were assisted by the Veterans Business and Professional Loans Act. Under this legislation, the government offered secured loans of up to $25 million at interest rates of five per cent. A year after the act became law, Veterans Affairs deputy minister Walter Woods reported that 60,000 veterans had been helped to set up in business.

In addition to those vets who went into business, 34,000 had been established on the land through the settlement program, 53,000 were attending university and 78,000 had completed some form of vocational training.

Older veterans were faring well, too. Of more than 82,000 who were registered for employment on April 1, 1946, all but 5,166 had been placed in some type of job 18 months later.

Clearly, the planning for rehabilitation that had been spearheaded by the Legion in the early days of World War II was paying dividends.

"I said (in 1945) that the returning veteran would be no problem child, that he would be normal, and a little above average because of his war experience," said Woods. "That view has been completely vindicated. He shows no tendency to lean on the state. He has made full use of the opportunities the country gave him. The problem cases have been few and far between and they very often involve men with no battle record."

As in the days after World War I, the Dominion Service Bureau was extremely active in investigating and processing the claims of veterans. A staff position of deputy chief pension officer was created and the successful candidate was Allan Piper, Dominion second vice-president. With his departure from the Dominion Executive Council, third vice-president Alf Watts was elevated one position. The third vice-presidential position was left vacant in anticipation of the 12th Dominion convention, scheduled for Saskatoon in May, 1948.

Almost 750 delegates, representing 906 of the Legion's 1,896 branches, registered at the convention. Once again, the question of extending membership to conscripts who fought overseas was the main topic of debate, and as in 1946, the motion to admit them was defeated. Although the discussion on the convention floor was as heated as at the previous convention, the margin of defeat was significantly smaller.

✤

Another topic that attracted substantial interest was the problem of the rising cost of living. Taking advantage of the presence of new Veterans Affairs Minister Milton Gregg, former Legion Dominion treasurer, delegates pressed the government for higher disability pensions and war veterans' allowances.

Gregg reported that Canada had 155,699 disability pensioners and dependants, 28,357 recipients of war veterans' allowances, and 13,324 veterans in hospital — of which almost 4,000 were World War I vets.

As at the 1946 convention, the organization and development committee made several recommendations that would influence the future shape of the Legion. It urged Dominion Command to lobby the federal government to remove the restrictions on service clubs and charities that wanted to use bingos and lotteries to raise funds. The committee recommended that the Legion make a greater effort to publish material — including editorial content in *The Legionary* — in French, and set out criteria to sub-divide commands into zones and districts. It recommended that all branches and commands institute the post of immediate past president on their executives, and made provisions for Dominion Command to advise branches on how to conduct membership drives.

Among the other recommendations made by the committee:

- adopt the beret as the official Legion head-dress;

- copies of the Legion's briefs to government committees and other legislative bodies to be sent to branches;

- alter the Legion Ritual to include allegiance to Canada;

- establish Dominion scholarships for the children of veterans from surplus Canadian Legion War Services and Canadian Legion Educational Services funds;

- establish a uniform set of bylaws and regulations to govern Ladies Auxiliaries in various commands;

- convene a service officers' conference for all provincial and Dominion personnel involved in service work;

- establish an annual Legion Week to end on November 11.

Lionel Baxter, the 59-year-old investment executive from Winnipeg who had been involved in the Legion since the 1925 unity conference, moved up the ladder to become Dominion president. A fifth-generation

Canadian originally from Kingston, Ontario, Baxter had first joined the Army in 1908 as a trooper in the 4th Hussars. A lieutenant-colonel in World War I, he served as assistant quartermaster-general at Canadian Military Headquarters in London.

Alf Watts defeated Bill Lumsden, a 55-year-old university professor from Nova Scotia, for first vice-president, Toronto tobacco salesman Ted Evans became second vice-president, and New Brunswick Command president W.A.I. Anglin was elected third vice-president.

Gordon Rochester, Jack Moore and Lucien Lalonde all retained their previous positions.

Delegates were saddened to learn that, after 23 years of Legion involvement, Sir Richard Turner was resigning as grand president. He was replaced by Gen. Harry Crerar, commander of the Canadian Army Overseas in World War II.

In the weeks following the convention, the Legion formally presented its case for increased war pensions to the government, which responded by raising them 25 per cent. It was to be one of the last achievements made by the Legion during the 22 years of the Mackenzie King government. King used a November 10 letter to the Legion to announce his imminent resignation, and conducted his last official act on November 13 at a 90-minute meeting with the Dominion Executive Council.

A change in leadership within the Legion itself did not receive as much publicity, although it was almost as significant an event. Shortly after assuming the office of Dominion president, Baxter suffered a heart attack. Although no official announcement was made, Watts assumed Baxter's duties, shifting the leadership of the Legion to a World War II vet for the first time.

Another change in Legion leadership came with the death of George Herwig, Dominion Command's general secretary since 1942. He died at age 59 after a lengthy illness, having served the cause of Canadian veterans since his tenure on the staff of the Great War Veterans Association in the early 1920s. He was succeeded as general secretary by his assistant, T.D. Anderson.

The last vestiges of the Great War Veterans Association — the branches that had existed in Newfoundland since 1922 — were also about to change. With Newfoundland's decision to join Confederation on March 31, 1949, a plan was required to provide for representation of the new province's estimated 10,000 veterans. Early in 1949, Legion officials visited

St. John's to discuss a possible amalgamation. Once the Legion agreed to assume responsibility for the smaller organization and recognize the honors and awards it had bestowed upon members, amalgamation was strictly a matter of attending to the necessary legalities. At Bell Island on October 12, the Great War Veterans Association of Newfoundland voted to surrender its charter to the Legion. For veterans on the island, joining Confederation meant that their Imperial pension rates automatically came within the Canadian scope of payments, which were larger. They also received additional re-establishment credits and were able to benefit from the provisions of the Veterans Land Act.

It did not take long for Newfoundland Command to demonstrate that its members shared the same concerns as their comrades in other parts of Canada. At its first convention in Corner Brook, the command voted to donate $6,000 to the Legion's latest national project — a program to assist the estimated 12,000 Canadian children whose fathers had been killed or fatally wounded overseas. The brainchild of Dominion chairman Moore, the Foster Fathers Program began in his native Winnipeg, where the Legion sponsored some 60 boys who had lost their fathers. Moore's concept was that the project would go far beyond providing for a child's physical welfare — although the project did help with such necessities as clothing and food — to assist with education and provide the guidance of dedicated adults. Speaking in support of making Moore's project a nationwide initiative, Watts said: "This problem cannot be solved by a modest allocation of branch funds. It will take your individual and personal time and application."

The foster fathers concept — renamed the Legion Children's Program — became one of the main items for discussion at the silver anniversary convention, which found the Legion back in Winnipeg for the third time. Moore relinquished the chair to address the 684 accredited delegates and 85 fraternals in a passionate plea to support the program. Supporting him in the Manitoba delegation were several men who had benefited from Moore's personal assistance after their fathers had been lost in World War I. A pamphlet addressing the goals of the project was distributed to every delegate. The convention voted overwhelmingly to "take such steps as may be necessary to properly implement the plan."

With the Korean War almost three months old and Canadian troops committed to join the United Nations' military force, delegates were unanimous and extremely vocal in calling for "total preparedness," a concept that had also been endorsed at the previous two conventions. Addressing the opening ceremony, grand president Crerar said: "Potential military strength, which the democratic powers undoubtedly possess, but which they have not developed, can be completely futile. War can spread so fast and far under the conditions today, that such potential power may never get the chance to be converted into real dynamic force... To a nation, a temporary high cost of living is nothing compared with the permanent high cost of dying..."

Defence Minister Brooke Claxton assured the legionnaires that Canada would be enlarging the regular and reserve forces of all three branches of the service, as well as training air crew from Britain under what amounted to a revival of the British Commonwealth Air Training Plan.

For the third consecutive convention, the question of admitting overseas conscripts to the Legion was raised. The 90-minute debate was only slightly less acrimonious this time, but the tide had turned. The conscripts were finally in.

Once again, the organization and development committee — now expanded to include the issues of immigration, settlement and membership — introduced several resolutions that had lasting impact. Primary among these was a recommendation that the Legion adopt a standard uniform: blue beret, blue blazer, and grey pants or skirt.

Outgoing Dominion president Baxter reported on flood relief in his native Manitoba — a project that had occupied many branches through the spring and early summer. Following the record-setting flooding of the Red River, which drove 100,000 people from their homes and inundated 15,000 farm buildings and businesses, Legion branches and commands had raised more than $60,000. Delegates voted to have the flood relief committee continue to disburse funds until all cases had been dealt with and use any surplus for the future relief of ex-service personnel affected by natural disasters.

The Dominion Service Bureau reported on its hectic schedule: since the previous convention, it had adjusted 1,522 claims, winning almost $500,000 in additional benefits for its clients; it had received 4,065 claims, conducted 11,775 interviews, written 24,167 letters, and searched 36,595 files.

Almost overlooked in the furor over preparedness for the Korean War and the acceptance of conscripts was a motion requesting the government to increase pensions by 33.3 per cent, in order to catch up to the soaring cost of living. Given that the gap between pensions and the average unskilled laborer's wage – the benchmark that had been set by J.L. Todd back in 1915 — had widened significantly since 1945, the resolution seemed innocuous enough. No one guessed at the time that it had set the stage for one of the Legion's toughest battles.

As expected, the convention voted unanimously for 39-year-old British Columbia native Alf Watts to become the first World War II vet to officially fill the post of Dominion president. Bill Lumsden was elected first vice-president. Joseph Kennedy of Saint John became second vice-president and Very Rev. John Anderson of Winnipeg won for third vice-president. Prince Edward Island native Ronnie Stewart, a 54-year-old Veterans Affairs employee, became the Legion's fifth honorary treasurer, taking over from Gordon Rochester, the fellow Ottawa civil servant who had filled the post for a decade. Jack Moore was elected chairman once again, and 53-year-old railroad auditor Erle Burgess of St. Thomas, Ontario, became vice-chairman.

Watts' ascension to the post of Dominion president was not the only sign that the day of the World War I vet was waning. Within the space of five months, the Legion lost two men who had helped steer the organization's course through its first quarter-century.

The first to go was Moore, Dominion chairman from Day One. A casualty at Vimy Ridge, Moore was living proof that, in the Legion, you checked your rank at the clubhouse door. As chairman, the jovial, burly former sergeant commanded the respect of everyone — from fellow non-coms like Alex Walker to senior officers like Alex Ross. A retired shop foreman for the Canadian National Railway, he died suddenly in his native Winnipeg at age 68, just three weeks after winning his 14th consecutive election.

The following March, Dominion Service Bureau director Dick Hale died of kidney failure at age 63. A former TB patient in Ontario's Muskoka Sanitorium, where he organized the Invalided Tubercular Soldiers' Welfare League, he is credited with personally handling 20,000 pension claims.

As obvious as it was that the torch was being passed at the Dominion level, it was even clearer at the branch level. All across the country, eager young veterans were establishing themselves at meetings, working on committees and speaking out with new ideas. The future of the Legion could be found in small communities like Estevan, Saskatchewan, where a brilliant young lawyer named Bob Kohaly was working his way up in his branch's executive. Severely wounded leaving the beach at Dieppe, Kohaly had been introduced to the Legion through its wartime educational services and joined as a matter of course as a law student in Saskatoon in 1947. After moving to rural Estevan to establish his own practice and transferring his membership, he recognized that veterans shared a common bond. In his fellow vets he saw the same qualities that opened up the West.

"Veterans learned self-reliance and they learned responsibility for the other fellow," he said in an interview for the Legion's diamond jubilee aural history project. "They brought these unusual qualities back with them, and it made them better truck drivers and mayors and store-owners."

If only you could harness all this energy, he thought, you could influence enormous change in Canadian society. The Legion, he realized, was just the catalyst to make it happen. In 1950, two years before he became president of his remote branch, Kohaly was formulating a plan that would revitalize the Legion and make its second 25 years even more impressive than its first 25.

Section 3

1951 - 1965

THE BOOM YEARS

Chapter 11

OLD BATTLES/ NEW WAYS

On November 10, 1950, the Dominion Executive Council presented a brief to Prime Minister Louis St. Laurent's cabinet outlining the request for pension increases and other changes that had been passed at the Dominion convention two months earlier. The Legion made five specific requests:

- increase all pensions by 33.3 per cent to offset increases in the cost of living;

- increase the basic rate of War Veterans Allowance to $50 per month for a single recipient and $100 per month for a married recipient, and increase the allowance for income from other sources to $250 for a single person and $500 for a married recipient;

- increase War Veterans Allowance rates to $60 per month, single, and $120 per month, married, when the recipient was permanently and completely unemployable and had no other sources of income;

- give consideration to the plight of the children of War Veterans Allowance recipients;

- extend benefits to Canadian veterans living outside Canada.

The Executive Council urged the government to consider these amendments a top priority, despite the mounting increases in defence spending, which were reported to be straining the budget to the limit. Dominion president Watts pointed to rising costs as calamitous to the pensioner, who was portrayed as "living on relief with sub-marginal standards."

With Parliament in recess, the new year brought no answer from St. Laurent's government, and the Legion decided to take the offensive, using *The Legionary* as the vehicle. In the April issue, which was scheduled to be delivered to all newspapers and MPs just as the House reconvened, first vice-president Bill Lumsden wrote a scalding article entitled "Pensioners' Plight" that said the government's failure to act was "tantamount to cutting rightful awards by 30 per cent." He noted that the cost of living had increased an additional five percentage points since the Legion had presented its brief. Quoting statistics from the Toronto Welfare Council and the government's own cost-of-living index, Lumsden made a case that, after paying for basic housing, clothing and food, a person with a 100-per-cent disability would have nothing left for heat, light or anything else. He contrasted this to the Depression years, when the same pensioner would have had almost $39 a month left over to pay for such basics as fuel, hydro and personal amenities.

Citing the government's failure to respond to the Legion's brief, he charged that St. Laurent intended to hold the line on any pensioners except those who could qualify for supplementary allowances by passing a means test – anathema to all the Legion stood for. "...(If) this is actually under consideration by responsible officials," he wrote, "we should oppose it as inadequate and as constituting a fundamental and undesirable departure from basic principles as they have become established over the years.

"One does not have to argue the obligation of the country to compensate men disabled in battle. That is accepted without dispute as a moral obligation...

"As an organization of ex-servicemen we must insist, and back that insistence with all our massed strength, that the country recognize and meet its obligation to these casualties... To try and limit the country's obligation to those in desperate need is to introduce into the Pension Act a means test, a humiliating and unjustifiable insult to men who have earned their compensation. It is to scuttle the historic norms of wages and costs by which pensions are determined and to put in their place the whims of officials...

"We must press then unremittingly for a full and ungrudging assumption of our country's obligations to these disabled veterans and their dependants, and recognize that adequate pensions for the disabled are as much the price of defence as the cost of steel or aluminum and that there is no greater moral obligation resting on the government of Canada."

John Hundevad's editorial in the same issue contained a lightly veiled threat of what an all-out Legion attack might mean to a government intent on pulling its weight in the United Nations: "With casualties coming back from Korea and a new group of war pensioners being created, what would they and their friends have to say if their disability compensations were not at least on a par with World War II pension values at the time they were awarded? It is not unreasonable to assume that their reaction might well affect the new recruiting campaign and make it doubly difficult for the government to obtain, by voluntary means, the 50,000 men needed for the expansion of our regular forces."

In the next issue, the Legion resumed its attack in an editorial bearing the headline, "The Cost of Living vs. The Cost of Keeping Alive": "The difference between the cost of living and the cost of keeping alive must be clear to all who have eyes to see, ears to hear, and hearts and minds to understand. Whereas rising living costs to the majority of Canadians have meant skimping a bit and doing without certain luxuries, to many disability pensioners and all War Veterans Allowance recipients, the result has been a deplorable lowering in their already low living standards. They have already earned a better deal than that which the government is proposing to give them."

The information Lumsden had acted on proved accurate. When Parliament reopened, Veterans Affairs Minister Lapointe introduced legislation that would alter the way pensions were assigned. In response to the uproar that followed, the government struck a special committee on veterans' affairs to study the matter.

On May 17, Alf Watts — the sharp, 40-year-old lawyer who had vaulted a generation of veterans to take charge of the Legion — and Lumsden — the biblical literature professor who had lost an arm at the Somme — appeared before the committee to launch one of the organization's toughest battles. They were a formidable team, and they were not about to be swayed from the belief that they were fighting for a moral obligation.

The government's proposed legislation, Watts claimed, indicated an "attempt to ignore a debt of honor. It is retrograde, alarming, dangerous and pernicious... The Canadian Legion cannot be satisfied with the legislation before this committee. There are no recommendations for improvement in the basic rate of pensions, nor is there any mention at all of War Veterans Allowances — the two principal problems affecting our veterans today. Worse still, the supplementary estimate of $2 million now before you would alter the tried and proven pension policy in a manner not desirable to the veteran nor, we suggest, to the Canadian public.

"The supplementary estimates and the administrative proposals are in effect a means test on a pension. It will be so understood and administered. It involves no increase in the basic rate of pension in spite of the outrageous rise in the cost of living. If the value of the dollar continues to fall, the suggested policy would involve a steady march toward a means test on *all* pensions."

Watts told the committee that the government's proposal would mean that only 6,000 totally incapacitated veterans would qualify for an increase, while 160,000 others with disabilities would go without anything.

Picking up Watts' lead, Lumsden took over in his scholarly way, citing numerous statistics and projections to show how the legislation would harm disabled veterans. He countered the government's argument that rising defence costs precluded introduction of the cost-of-living increases the Legion had requested by suggesting that if Canada could afford the 4-per-cent rise in the cost of living since February, it could certainly afford the cost of increasing pensions. If the cost-of-living index roughly indicated the increased defence costs, he said, that 4-per-cent increase represented more than $35 million added to the $1.6-billion defence budget. The Legion's recommendations were estimated to cost a total of $60 million. "It is not a case of being *unable*," said Lumsden, "but it *may* be a case of being *unwilling*."

Concluding the Legion's case, Watts suggested that the committee's terms of reference were not broad enough to handle the urgent problems of the veterans. He asked that it return to the Commons to request a broader mandate to study the issue and recommend solutions.

A week after the Legion's presentation the committee defeated a motion to seek new terms of reference. A subsequent appearance by Lumsden before the committee led to an angry clash with MP Leslie Mutch, Lapointe's parliamentary assistant, over the Legion's contention that passage of the $2-million supplement would mean that pensions would eventually be awarded on a need basis rather than a basis of right. "It is an outrageous presumption," Mutch thundered, "to say that by accepting a palliative you are closing the door to any basic increase in the pension in the future... What basis have you for that assumption other than pure conjecture?"

Lumsden replied that the difficulty the Legion faced in getting the basic increase it had requested indicated how much harder it would be once the supplement — and, more importantly, the principle underlying it — had been accepted.

It was becoming clear that the committee was going to recommend the supplement to Parliament, but MP W.J. Henderson moved an amendment recommending that the government give further consideration to the request for a basic increase, as well, when the fall session convened. The motion on the supplement passed by an 18 to 10 vote, and the amendment received unanimous support. The amendment had left the door open for the Legion, but it had its work cut out if it was going to swing opinion to its side. There was not even a guarantee that Parliament would revisit the question before the end of 1951.

The Legion fired its first salvo in the new attack with a blistering editorial in *The Legionary*: "...(The) result of the committee's work was a very great disappointment to the Canadian Legion, as indeed it must have been to many members of the committee. To the great majority of war disability pensioners and their families, who in spite of the dreadful rise in living costs will receive no increase whatsoever in their pensions at this time, the result is nothing less than a calamity.

"If it is true, as reported, that the fall session will be brief and will be called solely to secure parliamentary approval of the old age pension legislation (and to make legally possible an additional $4,000 indemnity to members of Parliament), then it could well be that no action will be taken at that session either.

"In fact, judging by the shocking lack of sympathy displayed by certain government members and officials, this is almost sure to happen — unless the cabinet is made to realize in the interval that the whole veteran body and the public and press of the Dominion are really aroused over this glaring injustice. It would be well, therefore, if Legion branches everywhere made their views known in no uncertain terms to their local members while they are home for the parliamentary recess, and requested their local newspapers to continue with the magnificent support which so many of them have given the Legion in this crucial debate...

"We are quite sure neither Parliament nor the people of this country ever dreamed when the principles of Canada's pension legislation for her fighting men were established more than 25 years ago that any government would be so devoid of feeling, understanding and gratitude as to treat the war-disabled pensioners in such a parsimonious fashion at a time such as this."

For his part, Watts took off across the country to speak at every provincial convention — no easy feat in the years before jet travel. "Knowledge of the situation and the issues at stake must serve as the springboard for individual action on the part of every member of the Legion," said Watts. "The facts must be impressed upon your federal member of

Parliament by as many members of your branch as possible and as often as it is necessary to ensure that he will not return to Ottawa without a full understanding of the Legion's position on this vital question. If you can contact him personally, so much the better. If you live a long distance from him, write him a letter. What is essential is an urgent reminder of the need, together with a strong appeal to support the Legion's request for an over-all increase in war disability pensions and War Veterans Allowances at the next session. Let every member of Parliament realize the need for immediate action. The success of our appeal depends entirely upon the efforts of our combined membership across Canada."

Throughout the summer and early fall Watts worked the phones, as well, constantly encouraging the command presidents to push the issue with local MPs and the media.

The campaign quickly gained the support of newspapers across the country, several of which weighed in with editorials:

The Toronto Globe and Mail: "Government pensions are given for the purpose of providing the recipient with a certain standard of living; if prices go up, pensions must go up... It is surprising that a government which just last fall intervened in a strike to fix a minimum wage increase by statute on the grounds that higher prices made such an increase necessary, should have to be bullied on this point. The workers of the nation are not its direct responsibility. The veterans are."

The Vancouver Province: "The government's plan is both ungenerous and unjust. When Canada gets into a jam, as she did in 1914 and 1939, she is very ready to call on the services of her young men and make them promises. How is she fulfilling these promises? Certainly not in that spirit when she offers a bit of cold charity to her needy veterans. The government's parsimony is singularly unsuited to the times. Once more the country is in a jam. Once more it is appealing for volunteers for the armed services. What encouragement does it offer in its pensions, which are far below the wage of common labor, and in its objectionable 'unemployability' sop?"

The Windsor Star: "The ($20 per month) amount is paltry; limiting benefit to only 6,000 even more paltry. But the cheapest policy of all is the means test which accompanies it."

The Fort William (Ontario) Times-Journal: "No matter how one squirms at the very thought of upping further the money which the government spends on services, only the most unfeeling among us can quarrel with the claims of the veterans."

The first indication that the government might be shifting its stance came in a letter to Watts from Veterans Affairs Minister Lapointe. He announced his intention to introduce legislation to revise basic rates under the Pension Act, but gave no indication as to how much those increases might be. In addition, he told Watts that any change to the War Veterans Allowance would have to be referred to a parliamentary committee.

While the Legion was disappointed about the government's refusal to make immediate changes to the War Veterans Allowance, it was encouraged by Lapointe's letter and reiterated its support for across-the-board increases.

On November 16, Lapointe announced that he was introducing legislation to institute pension increases averaging the Legion's requested 33.3 per cent, and withdrawing the legislation for the controversial means test.

"The government's action indicates they are fully aware of the seriousness of the effect on war pensioners of the increased cost of living," said Watts after he received the news. "The Legion feels that the interest and concern shown by members of all parties in this problem is heartening to those who served since it shows that, in the midst of all other problems of major importance, the welfare of those who made sacrifices in the service of our country has not been forgotten by the elected representatives of the country."

Looking back over 35 years, Watts reflected in 1986: "This was our biggest victory. It was tremendously important for the beneficiaries and for the Legion."

The increase applied to 161,000 veterans, 125,000 children and 20,000 widows. The 100-per-cent disability rate for a single veteran went to $125 per month from $94. The cost to the government was $28 million. More important was the reinforcement of the principle that a war disability pension is a right independent of all other income. Unfortunately, the legislation provided no permanent solution to the question of determining pension rates. It would be more than 20 years before the federal government adopted a means to guarantee regular pension increases. Even so, the November 1951 decision represented a landmark, and effectively erased any lingering doubts World War I vets might have had that younger men like Watts would be as committed to ex-servicemen's rights as the earlier leaders had been.

As a backdrop to the Legion's fight to entrench the principle of veterans' pension rights, sweeping changes were taking place at the Dominion Command Service Bureau. Its new director was 29-year-old Don Thompson, a native of Saint John who had served as New Brunswick Command's secretary. Like Watts, Thompson brought new ideas on how responsibilities should be split between the Legion at the community level and Dominion Command. To support Watts' view that it was crucial to strengthen the lines of communication between Ottawa and the branches, Thompson began to travel across the country to meet as many provincial service officers and local legionnaires as possible.

As part of the decentralization process, the Legion initiated a program to recruit and train branch service officers who could act as a first point of contact — a face-to-face one — with veterans who wanted information on pension claims. Under him, the department developed an information kit that local service officers — or the branch secretary if the branch was not large enough to warrant its own service officer — could use to familiarize themselves with the federal legislation and what the Legion could do to help veterans. Branches were encouraged to open their doors to the Veterans Affairs Department's travelling welfare officers, so that their clients were encouraged to come forward with claims, and came to associate the Legion branch with the concept of service. The Service Bureau emphasized that the Legion took on service work free of charge for any veteran, dependant or survivor, regardless of where they lived. During Thompson's tenure, approximately 75 per cent of the Service Bureau's work was undertaken for non-Legion veterans.

"The important thing," said Thompson, "was that the vets or their dependants didn't feel like they were handing their case over to a stranger. They came to know the service officer at the branch, and knew where to go, either for help from us or to meet the Veterans Affairs officials. It strengthened our bond with the community."

Opening Legion doors to the department's welfare officers also helped smooth over any hard feelings that might have developed during the Legion's fight with the Veterans Affairs minister. "There was a good working relationship between the Legion and the DVA in the 1940s," said Thompson. "We certainly had sharp disagreements on occasion, but, in general, the relationship was good."

Although the processes were formalized and some of the work shifted to the local level, the goal of the Service Bureau remained consistent with what the Great War Veterans Association had established in the early 1920s. A year after Thompson was hired, a special committee of the Dominion Executive Council set down the bureau's goals: "The importance of service work to the Canadian Legion cannot be too strongly emphasized. Its recognized facilities and will to prosecute claims for Veterans Charter benefits for individual veterans and their dependants distinguishes the Legion from all other Canadian veterans' organizations. Without this distinguishing ability to serve, the Legion could not have built up the high esteem which it enjoys with the Canadian public and which makes it so influential in veterans' affairs. What is equally important is that, without its facilities for service work, the Legion would have no sound basis of information and experience for the development of its policies or for the preparation of sound and therefore effective representations to governments, parliamentary committees and governmental departments and commissions. The service principle is the very heart of the Canadian Legion."

The report outlined four goals for the Dominion Command Service Bureau:

- To assist veterans and their dependants with their claims for various benefits provided by legislation.

- To study carefully the pattern of the administration of legislation as indicated in individual decisions on claims submitted through the Bureau and to try to have rectified any trends or policies that are felt to be detrimental to the interests of the veterans.

- To keep the officers and members of the Dominion Executive Council and the Dominion secretary advised on developments in legislation, and to bring to their attention certain legislation or aspects of the administration of that legislation which do not appear to be in the best interests of veterans and their dependants.

- To pass on to the Legion membership, through Service Bureau bulletins, individual correspondence and personal contact, as much information as possible on veterans' legislation so that the Legion will be fully equipped to advise and assist the veterans and their dependants at all times.

With Thompson heading up the Service Bureau and 55-year-old Erle Burgess of St. Thomas, Ontario, as Dominion chairman, it was a different looking — and substantially younger — Legion that opened its 14th convention in Montreal on May 18, 1952.

Once again, defence issues were foremost on the minds of the 768 accredited delegates and 119 fraternals. The convention heard reports on the progress of the Korean War from both Defence Minister Brooke Claxton and Brigadier John Rockingham, recently returned from his duty as commander of the 25th Canadian Infantry Brigade in Korea. Both speakers disputed the need for the total call-up of available men that the Legion had been lobbying for, and Claxton's speech led to the wording in the resolution on the matter being changed from "conscription" to "selective service." In the end, the motion passed by the convention asked the government to speed up defence measures and introduce "some form of selective service" for the defence of Canada. The delegates also called on the government to establish a royal commission to study the formation of Canada's reserve forces.

Immigration was another pressing issue. Since the end of the war, legionnaires had expressed concern about Canada harboring possible subversives. Previous conventions had voted on resolutions calling for the expulsion of Canadians of Japanese origin, and warned the government about nascent communists. This time, delegates voted to strongly urge the government to tighten up its screening of German immigrants to keep out "swashbuckling bullies" with fascist or communist tendencies. Some delegates voiced their concern that Germans were taking Canadians' jobs in Northern Ontario. Another resolution demanded that the federal government introduce legislation that would force immigrants to apply for Canadian citizenship within six months of their arrival or face deportation.

Fifty-seven-year-old Bill Lumsden was acclaimed president, making him the first army private to hold the office. A stretcher-bearer in the 25th Battalion, Lumsden had joined the Great War Veterans Association in 1917 and the Legion in 1936. A Yale University graduate, he had taught at Acadia University in Wolfville, Nova Scotia, since 1937.

Very Rev. John Anderson — the personal choice of Watts — was elected first vice-president, putting the 39-year-old World War II veteran in a key position that would have significant ramifications for the Legion. Ted Evans of Toronto returned to the Executive Council as second vice-president, the same position he held from 1948 to '50. George Gleave of Edmonton was elected third vice-president. Burgess was acclaimed for his first full term as chairman, and A.G. Munich of Montreal was elected vice-chairman. Ronnie Stewart was acclaimed for his second term as honorary treasurer.

As part of his committee's report on organization and development, Anderson introduced a section entitled "The Legion's Future" that prescribed several steps to determine the future course of the organization. As a preamble, the document stated: "The quarter century that has elapsed (since the Legion's founding) has seen great growth and development in this country. There has been a radical change in outlook and an increased understanding of social services and governmental responsibility in this field (of veterans' benefits). The situation which confronts us now is substantially different from that which prompted the effective cooperation of our comrades of an earlier day. If the Canadian Legion is to continue as an effective instrument for the good and welfare of those who have served their country in time of war, it is becoming increasingly obvious that the time has come to give serious consideration to a revaluation and reconsideration of its aims, objects and methods of operation.

"There is a growing concern amongst many members as to the appeal and purposes of the organization. It is clear that the pressure of original needs has largely been met through governmental legislation and monetary support. It is also obvious that the veterans of the Second World War do not have the same strong unit associations as the veterans of World War I. Something more is needed now if we are to maintain the sense of service and comradeship which all ex-service personnel seek to express in one way or another."

The committee made three recommendations:

- that the Dominion Executive Council be instructed to set up a commission to study, evaluate and re-examine the aims and objects of the Canadian Legion, its methods and purposes;

- that this commission report precisely upon the needs and opportunities which changed conditions have brought about;

- that in particular they give serious consideration to the needs of older aged veterans, and study and present such fresh approaches to the organization and enlistment of younger veterans in the Canadian Legion in such ways as may meet the needs of the present day.

Unlike the questions of defence preparedness and immigration, Anderson's proposals did not elicit significant debate, but whether delegates realized it or not, he had laid the groundwork for massive changes that would alter the public's perception of the Legion forever.

Chapter 12
SPRINTING PAST THE CROSSROADS

"John Anderson was largely responsible for changing the face of the Legion."

Looking back on the Legion's evolution from being strictly a veterans' champion to Canada's largest community-service organization — the story of the Legion in the 1950s — former Dominion president Mervyn Woods had no doubt about who drove that change.

If one thing symbolizes Anderson's place as the architect of the "new Legion" it is an article he wrote for *The Legionary* in 1955, during his term as Dominion president. In it, he picked up the themes he had introduced in his organization and development committee report at the 1952 convention: "The society in which the Legion operates is changing, and the Legion must adjust with the times... The Legion has a brilliant record of achievement. But where do we go from here?

"Today, the task of obtaining adequate legislation is about complete... The Legion has fulfilled, and will continue to fulfil, obligations to the nation's war dead and wounded... There is a definite need for increased Legion activity in community affairs, particularly in matters pertaining to youth. Many branches have already undertaken vigorous community programs. We have organized sports, recreational activities, housing projects, educational programs, and participation in drives such as the blood bank and polio campaign. These activities should be intensified. The Legion might also place emphasis on sponsoring lectures and discussion groups in citizenship (for new Canadians)...

"The Canadian Legion is at the crossroads. We have a noble record behind us and two paths ahead. The Legion can continue to be a vital, active force in Canada's future. Or it can go into gradual decline where members sit in the lengthening shadows, contemplating the lost days of their youth."

His phrase, *at the crossroads,* became one of the most memorable in Legion history. Independent of each other, as part of the aural history project conducted for the Legion's 60th anniversary, former presidents Bob Kohaly and Doug McDonald, and former Dominion secretary Don Thompson all remembered it as a vital rallying cry.

"Anderson was something of a philosopher," said Kohaly. "He realized earlier than most that the Legion had to either move into the community or move out."

"The members, at the branch level, could see what the community needed," said McDonald. "The service aspect wasn't enough to keep a large organization going and all the members motivated. Anderson realized that the Legion was a sleeping giant."

"Right across the country, the Legion had a whole new crop of members," recalled Thompson. "They saw other organizations — the Lions Club, Kiwanis, Rotary and so on — getting involved at the community level, and they knew there was still lots of good work to be done. It was a chance to help the country, and to use the size and strength of the Legion for the common good."

Very Rev. John Ogle Anderson was in a unique position to judge the needs of the community. A native of Rathwell, Manitoba, where he was born in 1912, Anderson was the Anglican Church's dean of Ottawa and rector of the city's Christ Church Cathedral. An Army reservist from 1929 to '42, he saw active duty as a chaplain until being seriously wounded in Holland when his jeep detonated a land mine. He joined Crescentwood-River Heights Branch in Winnipeg in 1945 and served on Manitoba Command's council as third vice-president from 1947 to '51. He was chairman of the Dominion convention committee in Winnipeg in 1950, where he was elected Dominion third vice-president.

As a cleric, Anderson was well aware of the importance of community work — both in terms of what it meant to the beneficiaries and how it could give a large organization purpose — and he had the dynamism necessary to rally enthusiasm for the idea across the Legion. Of course, as he said himself, the concept of community involvement for the Legion was not new; many branches were already deeply involved in the affairs of their municipalities.

Woods said that it was a natural evolution in Saskatchewan Command, where he was president in the mid-'50s. "We found that we didn't have a lot to do after we came back from the war," he said. "One man at the branch could pretty well look after the local vets who needed help, so you had thousands of people on your hands. The question was, what to do with them? That's where community service work really began. We urged branches throughout the command to take on local projects, and they found things that suited them. It was usually a case of answering a need; for instance, a mayor would go to a branch president with a request for funding for a new rink and the request would be discussed at the next meeting."

In Ontario Command's District D, for example, local MPP Bill Beech — who was also the Legion's national housing director — got the branches involved in building low-rent apartment units for elderly vets, dependants and widows.

In Alberta, the command adopted the fight against polio as a principal cause, and branches raised more than $200,000 in the first five months of 1954.

"At the local level, it wasn't really a conscious decision to turn to community work," said former Dominion president Bob Smellie. "It was really just a matter of seeing a need and filling it. In Russell (Manitoba), it was supplying ambulance service to the community, but the interests differed, depending on need — and on what the leaders perceived as need."

"It was a natural thing for us after the war," said Woods. "We had been trained to get a job done, and we had collected a wide variety of skills. The man who had been to war had a post-graduate degree in a number of things."

Anderson's call-to-arms was a reaction to seeing this potential go wasted in areas where there was little or no coordination. After his article appeared, there was a significant increase in the number of branches that began to reach out to their communities, and substantially more communication between legionnaires about what their individual branches were doing.

Housing remained a primary concern — one that served both the needs of the veteran community in addition to the larger community. The project that started in Toronto with Ontario District D spread quickly, and Legion branches adopted similar projects in Ottawa, Kitchener, North Bay, Winnipeg and Charlottetown. By the end of the decade, Legion housing projects were valued at more than $3 million, with developments in Vancouver, New Westminster, Abbotsford, Chilliwack, Prince Rupert, Cranbrook, Fort William, Montreal and Moncton. Most were designed to house vets or their dependants, but some, like the project in Fort William (now amalgamated into Thunder Bay), were open to all.

The Foster Fathers Program — the pet project of former Dominion chairman Jack Moore — continued throughout the '50s with varying degrees of commitment across the country, and the Scouting and cadet movements became other leading beneficiaries of Legion support. By 1960, the Legion had grown to be the largest single sponsor of Scouts and Cubs in Canada, supporting 134 units and some 7,000 boys. About 6.5 per cent of all Legion branches sponsored Scout or Cub units, and many others gave funds to the movement. Many branches also sponsored sea, army or air cadets, often by providing training facilities.

The rising concern about juvenile delinquency spurred many branches to adopt citizenship programs for local young people, including public-speaking and essay contests, and scholarships.

However, far and away the largest single area of sponsorship for branches from coast to coast was sports.

The connection between the Legion and sports was a natural one. Most ex-servicemen had grown up with an affinity for sports, which was only reinforced by the recreational activities they pursued during their leisure time in the forces. Throughout North America, the major professional sports saw a tremendous upsurge in interest as players returned from military service and veterans came home with a new thirst for spectator events. Other competitive sports like curling, darts and billiards also underwent revivals as young veterans sought ways to maintain the camaraderie they had discovered in wartime. The obvious next step in this evolution was to transfer this love of sports to their children and their children's peers — the massive population bulge of baby boomers who would quickly come to dominate society's focus.

In 1946, the Legion initiated Operation Fitness, designed to bring the fitness level of Canadian children up to world standards. In that year, the Dominion organization and development committee recommended the formation of a national sports committee, which it hoped would eventually lead to the establishment of a Canadian Legion athletic association. A "Legion sports" page became a regular feature in *The Legionary* as a means of spotlighting branches that were sponsoring local sports programs, and the young athletes who were participating. In the late '40s, Winnipeg and Montreal had Legion hockey leagues, and Montreal branches also sponsored six basketball teams.

At the 1950 Dominion convention, the national sports committee implored delegates from other areas to get involved: "Canada is growing rapidly. This means more children... need guidance into channels that will carry them to physical and mental stability. Existing agencies that are set up for this purpose — voluntary and otherwise — are not going to be able to provide all the training necessary to ensure that every youngster in Canada gets a proper opportunity to grow to manhood in fullness of stature and prepared to enter into the struggle ahead with the stamina that living today requires. So the Canadian Legion should accept this call to its fullest capacity and capabilities."

In 1951, the Legion created a sports medal bearing its crest, which it hoped would be purchased by provincial commands for use in awards ceremonies. The following year, committee chairman George Machum again implored delegates to the Dominion convention to urge their comrades to make support for local sports a priority. He urged the chairs of provincial sports committees to exchange ideas and develop new approaches. But Machum was faced with a mammoth task. With more than 2,000 branches across the continent, it was difficult to keep track of all the activities that were going on. As with the branches' other community projects, there was no real national coordination; no vision of how to bring it all together.

His report to the 1954 convention, held in Toronto in early August, expressed some frustration, and introduced some themes that would continue to ring through Canadian society for decades to follow: "The primary objective of our Legion sports program is not to develop champions in any line of sport, but rather to improve the general physical fitness of the mass of our youth and by so doing to raise a physical standard of the nation as a whole. There is a great need to steer our younger people into the paths that lead to fitness, especially in these days with so many counter attractions forcing themselves on the attention of our youngsters and sabotaging their desire to excel in sports.

"It is a deplorable fact that in this country we are far too much over-entertained for our own good. There is too much temptation to sit down, push a button, and let some mechanical contraption do the rest. Youngsters, as soon as their studies and their chores are finished, should be seeking the nearest playground, there to mix with others of their own age in the pursuit of athletic development, of adventure on the road to physical and mental fitness, but far too often these future pillars of our national institutions are found ruining their health and their chance of happiness in the disgusting pursuit of some so-called entertainment coming out of a raucous box in the foul, smoke-filled atmosphere of a darkened room... Can we build future citizens of strength and physical and moral stamina on the hero worship of some dim-witted crooner of nauseating songs or some greasy-haired strummer on a mandolin?

"There was some shocking news in the press a few weeks ago. It reported the findings of a survey committee under the auspices of the New York University-Bellevue Medical Center on the muscular development of school children across the larger part of the world. This two-year study disclosed that North American children were nowhere nearly as well developed muscularly as the children of countries like Italy and Austria, for instance, which we have been in the habit of considering underprivileged areas after the ravages and depredations of war. The answer is that youngsters in those countries across the sea still have to work for their fun. It isn't handed to them on a silver platter. They walk or run wherever they need to go. They are not transported in luxury. We are killing our youngsters with kindness, and it is time we woke up and worked out their salvation."

As it turned out, the solution — from the Legion's standpoint at least — lay in one of those many branch programs that escaped the view of the national chairman. Ontario Hydro Branch, so named because of the many hydro workers who were members, was an active sponsor of something called the Canadian Olympic Training Plan. Since 1953, Robert Saunders, chairman of Ontario Hydro, and George Duthie of the Canadian National Exhibition had been operating the program, which brought athletes and coaches together at the Canadian National Exhibition's facilities in Toronto to train for international track and field meets.

The program came to the attention of the Legion's national leaders when Norman Shannon was hired as the organization's public relations director in 1955. His previous employer had been Ontario Hydro, so when he learned that Anderson and the Legion were looking for a national sports program to support he knew just where to point them.

At the 1956 Dominion convention, delegates voted to publicize the existence of the Canadian Olympic Training Plan throughout the Legion, and approach each command for authority to finance the project. Support for the project began in earnest in 1957, with $20,000 given to the program — renamed the Canadian Legion Sports Training Plan — to bring Austrian track coach Franz Stampfl and others to Toronto to conduct a clinic prior to the trials for the 1960 Summer Olympic Games. Stampfl returned to run the clinic again in 1958, and was replaced in 1959 by Don Canham from the University of Michigan and Dave Rankin from Perdue University. That summer, Canada sent 30 track and field athletes to the Pan-American Games; 26 were graduates of the Legion's program.

Machum's successor as national sports chairman, Fred O'Brecht, was, if anything, even more passionate about the Legion's responsibility for the fitness of Canada's youth. Born in Mount Forest, Ontario, in 1910, O'Brecht became a flight lieutenant in the RCAF in World War II before returning to rural Ontario to run a dairy. Elected president of Ontario Command in 1957, he became Dominion third vice-president in 1958 and assumed the stewardship of the track program.

As promising as it was, the program was beset by funding problems that stemmed from the 1956 decision to solicit contributions from each command rather than introduce an additional per capita levy. None of the commands met the targets set for them by Dominion Command in 1957, and several contributed little or nothing in subsequent years. Nevertheless, by 1959, O'Brecht was reporting that the program was reaping tremendous benefits, both in athletic achievement and in publicity for the Legion. In addition to the meet at the Canadian National Exhibition grounds, Waterloo Branch also staged a meet in conjunction with the coaching clinic. Together, they were the only two track meets in Canada at which athletes from all 10 provinces were represented. O'Brecht also held up New Brunswick Command as an example since it was the only command that took the program all the way down to the zone and district levels.

At the 1962 Dominion convention, O'Brecht reported significant progress in expanding the program from the top down. Pacific Command had introduced the Junior Olympic Training Plan, which providing coaching to 12,000 boys and girls, Manitoba-Northwestern Ontario Command had build its own $16,000 indoor track and was sending coaches out to rural communities each summer, and New Brunswick Command's Youth Leadership course was drawing more than 300 competitors. At the branch level, many track events were being held, the most significant of which were in St. Lambert, Quebec, Waterloo, Ontario, and Saskatoon.

He also reported on a significant funding development. After deciding the previous November to excuse the commands from funding the national clinic, the Legion had approached the federal government for assistance to hire a full-time coach and conduct a national meet. It received $50,000 from the Department of National Health and Welfare. Immediately, O'Brecht had the plans for the 1962 program altered. Instead of bringing in three coaches and 75 student-coaches, the 10-day clinic at Guelph, Ontario, expanded to a dozen coaches and 160 student-coaches.

One of the coaches who had been on O'Brecht's original list was a 47-year-old former British army major named Geoffrey Dyson. The chief national coach of the British Amateur Athletic Association since 1947, Dyson had coached three Olympic teams and written a book, *The Mechanics of Athletics*. He also had a refreshing attitude about sport, summed up in a remark he made in 1966: "If a sport is worth playing, it is worth playing badly."

Dyson was a perfect fit for the full-time spot the government assistance had opened, and the Legion hired him in early 1963 for a five-year term as national sports director. In addition to conducting coaching clinics across the country, Dyson was also a popular speaker at sports dinners and awards banquets. In the wake of Canadian sprinter Harry Jerome's record-tying 100-yard-dash performance in 1962, track and field was suddenly a high profile sport in Canada, and the Legion was front and centre.

At the 1964 Dominion convention, O'Brecht and Dyson reported on "a period of intense activity and phenomenal growth." The Legion's coaching camp, said Dyson, had been hailed by a U.S. track and field magazine as "the largest and most comprehensive clinic of its kind in the English-speaking world." The American State Department had adopted some of the Legion's ideas for its own national clinic. The Legion's 1963 clinic had attracted 210 student-coaches to Guelph, and plans for 1964 included space for 235 students, a staff of 22, and demonstrations from several world-class athletes, including Jerome. The federal government supported both with grants of $50,000 each.

O'Brecht noted that track programs had spread to Nova Scotia, Prince Edward Island and Newfoundland commands, and he recommended that branches add indoor sports programs to keep the interest of young people during the winter months: "The formation of athletic clubs by branches and the continuation of a national and provincial track and field program can be the combination which would change the face, not only of track and field, but of physical fitness in Canada."

Chapter 13

MEMBERSHIP AND "THE MAFIA"

As beneficent as John Anderson's goal of moving the Legion into the community was, there was an ulterior motive as well. Charitable works would improve life in municipalities across Canada, yes, but they would also serve as an advertising and recruiting tool for the Legion. There was no denying that the organization needed a boost; when Anderson became president in 1954 only 15.8 per cent of Canada's 1.2 million veterans were Legion members. Almost two-thirds of that total were World War I vets well into their 50s.

The reasons for the Legion's inability to attract the interest of eligible young men and women were varied and not always valid: the concentration of many people on raising families and building careers; the perception of the Legion as being unfriendly to younger veterans; the view that the organization was dominated by former enlisted personnel; and the Legion's image as a place to drink beer and reminisce about wartime experiences. The unspoken part of Anderson's crossroads message was that it was up to legionnaires to change those perceptions — right or wrong — or they *would* find themselves sitting "in the lengthening shadows, contemplating the lost days of their youth."

Anderson may be best remembered inside the Legion for his crossroads article, but his decision to appoint the organization's first national membership committee in 1955 was of equal importance.

Anderson's vision and strong personality could have made him a natural long-term leader in the mould of three-term president Alex Walker, but the cause of veterans was obviously not his only calling. Forty-three years old when the Legion's 16th Dominion convention was held in June 1956 at the Hotel Vancouver, Anderson was still a young man by clerical standards. As rector of a large church and dean of Ottawa, he had an active career outside of the Legion and the Anglican Church also recognized his leadership abilities (he would eventually be named Bishop of Winnipeg).

✳

The Legion's well-established pattern of succession would normally ensure a simple transfer of power, but Anderson's decision to resign as president created an unusual vacuum at the top. None of the serving vice-presidents was interested in putting aside his career to replace him. So, for the first time since 1928, when Sir Arthur Currie was parachuted into the presidency, the role would be filled by someone without experience on the Dominion Executive Council.

After a three-way fight between David Burgess of Ontario, Ted Brown of Alberta and Robert Macnicol of British Columbia, the 846 delegates elected the 65-year-old Burgess, the second consecutive Ottawan to hold the post. Born near Orangeville, Ontario, Burgess had served with the RAF in World War I, winning the Military Cross as a lieutenant and finishing the war as a captain. After the war, he was one of the 31,000 to become a farmer under the Soldiers Settlement program, and one of the 10,000 to give up the farm during the program's first decade. He moved to Ottawa in 1930 to become the private secretary to Robert Weir, the federal minister of agriculture. At the time of his election he was about to retire as the department's chief of supply. A legionnaire since the organization's inception, he had been president of Ottawa Branch and a member of the Dominion constitution and laws committee.

H.W. Sutherland, a 43-year-old lawyer from Campbellton, New Brunswick, moved from second to first vice-president, Don McTavish, a 45-year-old lawyer from Salmon Arm, British Columbia, stepped from third to second vice-president, and a third jurist — 56-year-old judge Clare Sparling of Flin Flon, Manitoba — became third vice-president. Ronnie Stewart was acclaimed honorary treasurer for the fourth time, Erle Burgess was elected for his third term as chairman, and Alan Macdonald was uncontested for his second term as vice-chairman.

In his report, membership chairman John Henderson pointed out that only one in six veterans was a legionnaire, while more than 70 per cent of the organization's welfare work was to benefit non-members. "For over 30 years," he said, "the Legion has been accepted as the voice of the veteran. We have indeed been fortunate that the government has listened to this voice with respect. But now, more than a decade after the war, the question arises as to whether this voice will continue to... elicit government support."

Henderson recommended initiating a two-year recruiting drive with the goal of doubling membership by the following Dominion convention. "It is granted that we have shown a gradual increase in the past four years, but we have not yet begun to tap our membership potential. A full-scale campaign, properly promoted, with participation by all branches, could not only make our target attainable, but the interest and activity created by such a campaign would, we think, carry on beyond the next convention, in a continuing membership campaign."

The primary target, he suggested, should be the 891,000 World War II veterans who did not belong to the Legion, and he told the delegates that reaching them must involve everyone: "The most important factor in the whole campaign will be the local branch. Regardless of what momentum or support is provided by the provincial and Dominion commands it is up to the branches to realize and accept the responsibility for the success of the campaign."

He outlined five points that the membership drive should stress:

- remembrance and service work;
- legislation for veterans and dependants;
- the Legion's work in the community;
- Legion scholarships and education;
- housing.

To sweeten the lure for non-members and renewals, the committee recommended holding two draws for new cars, to be held in 1957 and 1958.

One of the committee's aims — to determine the characteristics of existing Legion members — was carried out through a survey in *The Legionary*, which now went out to every member as part of their per capita dues. Based on the 3,500 questionnaires that were mailed back to the magazine, the organization gleaned some interesting details about the average member. Almost certainly male, the average legionnaire was married and owned a mid-priced car, as well as most modern electric appliances. One-third were between 35 and 45 years of age; 61 per cent were older than 55. Annual income was $4,502, compared to the national average of $3,700. Educational background was 10 per cent higher than the average Canadian. Almost one-third owned their own business. Three-quarters owned their house, and another 10 per cent were planning on building soon. Fewer than 20 per cent lived in cities with more than 100,000 residents; 67 per cent lived in communities with fewer than 10,000 inhabitants. Preferred hobbies included gardening, hunting and fishing.

❦

The indication at the recruiting campaign's halfway mark was that, while membership was climbing — reaching almost 227,000 — the goal of at least 500,000 was unrealistic. Indeed, when 868 delegates and 410 fraternals met in Edmonton for the 17th Dominion convention in May 1958, the membership stood at 237,000.

Henderson did not live to report on the campaign, dying at his Truro, Nova Scotia, home just days before the convention.

Once again, one of the main influences on sluggish membership growth — non-Legion interests — was reflected in the organization's top ranks. H.W. Sutherland dropped out to pursue his burgeoning law practice and fellow lawyer Don McTavish chose to contest the opening at vice-chairman created by Alan Macdonald's decision to challenge for the post of chairman.

Burgess was acclaimed president, and yet another jurist, 49-year-old Saskatoon law professor Mervyn Woods, vaulted into the post of first vice-president, defeating G.H.A. Trudeau of Quebec Command. Trudeau dropped down to challenge Clare Sparling for second vice-president and lost again. Riding the early success of the Legion's sports program, 47-year-old Ontario dairy owner Fred O'Brecht defeated Bert Hidson and John Murray, both of Alberta, for third vice-president. Incumbent Erle Burgess defeated Macdonald for a fourth term as chairman, and Ronnie Stewart was acclaimed for his fifth term as honorary treasurer.

The Edmonton convention was widely remembered in Legion circles for three reasons: the western hospitality; the record-setting attendance; and the presence of Prime Minister John Diefenbaker — the first time a sitting Canadian leader had opened a Legion convention. In retrospect, however, the 1958 Legion parliament was remarkable for the slate of vice-presidents it elected. Unlike previous vice-presidential groupings, which were broken up by resignations or war, the Woods-Sparling-O'Brecht triumvirate would have tremendous influence on the Legion's direction. All would eventually become Dominion president, and each would leave his mark through the men he recruited to follow him onto the Executive Council.

One area where these men's influence was not felt immediately was membership; it continued to increase slowly across the entire Legion — reaching 242,000 in 1959 — but four commands actually registered a decline during the 1955 to '59 period. In his 12-man committee's report to the 1960 Dominion convention, Jim Insley of British Columbia set out to explore the reality of the membership situation. "While the (membership) figures themselves may not be conclusive," he reported, "when studied together with the provincial convention reports available to us it became apparent that some provincial commands have been kidding themselves, to put it bluntly. For the most part these reports were laudatory, noting the enrolment of new members and speaking of the ever-increasing membership, disregarding a fact that should have been apparent — that some of them were losing members at a greater rate than they were gathering in new members."

To illustrate his point, Insley used his own command as an example. Between 1951 and 1959, British Columbia enrolled 50,972 new members, but 41,580 allowed their dues to lapse. The command's net gain over the nine-year period was 9,392. "The membership campaign commencing in 1956 could not succeed as long as we were losing four members out the back door as fast as we brought five new members in the front door," he said. "In order to show a net gain of one member we have had to enrol five."

In fact, he reported, Henderson's recruiting drive had resulted in 150,000 new members — more than halfway to its goal — but 129,000 members had been allowed to slip away. "Was there a wrong basic concept to the membership campaign? We think not. The problem apparently is that we have unwittingly applied ourselves to the task of obtaining *new* members without applying even greater efforts in retaining our *present* ones."

Insley's committee concluded that the solution was to set an attainable goal and concentrate on the people who were already members. "There will always be a natural influx of members," their report stated. Recording its belief that the Legion's prestige could be harmed by a "hard sell" campaign for new members, the committee recommended that the Legion celebrate its 35th anniversary by attempting to increase its membership by 35,000 by the 1962 convention. "If all branches retain every member they had as of December 31, 1959, and with the natural influx of new members this can be done. Your committee suggests no magic, no catch phrases and no gimmicks. We believe that if you have a good product or worthwhile service to offer, you do not need these things and reputable organizations don't use them."

As good a product as the Legion was, Insley's strategy was not the ticket to success. When Erle Burgess brought the gavel down to open the 1962 convention in Halifax figures showed that membership had increased by just over 8,000.

❦

The new membership chairman, Art Adams of Ontario, admitted that mistakes had been made: "At the last Dominion convention the membership committee recommended that the main efforts... should be directed primarily to the retention or renewal of the present membership. With this your (present) committee agrees, but we feel that somewhere along the line the main source of our membership has been overlooked. We agree that we lose a goodly percentage of our membership each year through lack of renewals, but we are losing sight of the basic requirement to a good membership drive — the personal contact.

"Your committee is of the opinion that a campaign aimed solely at (new members or renewals) is unbalanced... both objectives are equally important."

Adams expressed surprise that, despite the fact that membership had been identified as a Legion priority seven years earlier, some commands still did not have a membership chairman.

Seldom, if ever, had a committee report openly criticized previous decisions that had been approved by convention. It was clear that the membership issue was out of control and in dire need of leadership. No one in a position of power was better suited to step into that void than 41-year-old Bob Kohaly, the Estevan, Saskatchewan, lawyer and former member of the legislative assembly, who had taken his vision of the Legion's future from his small-town branch to the presidency of Saskatchewan Command. In 1961, Mervyn Woods had hand-picked him to chair a special committee to study the question of extending full membership privileges to ex-service personnel who had served in peacetime. Already eligible for non-voting, "associate" membership, they represented a large pool of potential legionnaires who shared many of the concerns of veterans.

Kohaly had organized and led several successful membership drives in Saskatchewan, and was enthusiastic in his conviction that the secret to increasing membership was to "give people a reason to join and fulfill the reason" once they were on board.

"The thing you had to admire about Kohaly was that he was always moving toward a goal," said Bob Smellie after both had served as Dominion president. "He could always recognize the pitfalls and potential of a situation. He maps his course of action and then he persuades people to follow him. He was, perhaps, the best Legion leader of his time."

"Nobody can touch Kohaly," agreed former president Doug McDonald. "He had an uncanny way of getting things done. You had to read what he wanted to do, though, because it wasn't always evident from what he said or did."

"He was quite bright, and a very skilled courtroom lawyer" said Jean Lamy, Dominion secretary from 1971 to '82. "He was a persuasive speaker, and he almost always got what he wanted."

What Kohaly wanted in 1962 was a free hand to run a membership campaign the way he envisioned it. Looking back, 24 years later, he outlined his four elements for running a successful recruitment drive: "I had to have long-term support from the Legion. I wanted the freedom to choose the members for the committee. The committee members had to be committed to the cause and ready to be there for the long term. And, I had to have an adequate budget."

The newly elected third vice-president, Kohaly left the Halifax convention with the delegates' approval to conduct a 10-year membership campaign, a commitment from Woods, the immediate past president, and Sparling, the new Dominion president, that they would back him in his choice of committee members, and a budget of $9,500 — an unprecedented amount for a Legion committee.

The only thing he needed was committee members who shared his vision.

Of course, he had "official" committee members — the regular provincial representatives who sat on national Legion committees — but Kohaly's goal was a small standing committee of like-minded workaholics who were ready to give whatever it took to get the job done. His idea was to look at the district level and below, where he felt he could find hard workers who were in touch with the bulk of the membership. In the meantime, he worked with what he had.

"I was lucky to start out with some strong people," he said. "I had John St. Germain from Quebec and Mac Heckbert from New Brunswick who was really highly organized."

In the first two years of the new campaign, Kohaly organized his attack, meeting with his standing committee members — St. Germain, Heckbert, Jack Oldham and Gordon Wakefield — four times to plan strategy and holding meetings in Fredericton, Montreal and Toronto to exhort commands to get involved. His idea was to eventually visit as many parts of the country as possible and personally preach the gospel of membership recruitment and renewal at seminars. "Our philosophy was to catch people's attention by using actuary figures. We had to impress upon them the urgency of building the membership, to say, 'Look! Here are how many members are going to die over the next few years.'"

When he reported to the 1964 Dominion convention at Winnipeg, Kohaly laid out a 12-step plan that he assured delegates would net 85,000 new members by 1971. That would be enough to offset his projected loss through death of 100,000 World War I vets and 15,000 from World War II minus a projected 30,000 new members who would join without any encouragement. He established a diminishing quota system, whereby the target for 1962 to '63 was 30,000, for 1964 to '65, 20,000, for 1966 to '67, 15,000, and for the final two periods, 10,000 each. His 12 steps included:

- establishing quotas — "The quotas set can and will be obtained and the problem solved with the cooperation of all commands. These quotas will be fulfilled *if* Dominion and provincial commands provide the necessary leadership..."

- use of *The Legionary* — "Our objective (is) to have and keep a more informed general membership by increasing the number of campaign articles and contributions..."

- writing and rewriting pamphlets — "Remember, there is not a member in a carload of paper. It can only be done by YOU at the branch level. The national standing committee prepares the material, but it must be ordered from your provincial command."

- aids and crutches to membership — "These have been adopted for the most part from ideas received from all across the country."

- proper use of membership statistics — "Some inaccuracies in statistics previously listed have been corrected..."

- fall-out problems — "To bring members in the front door is fine, provided that the lack of programming does not let them out the back door soon after."

- dual chairmen (new and renewal) — "Can your branch afford the luxury of ignoring either the renewal of the old or the addition of the new?"

- regional meetings — "(Essential) due to the size of our country and the varying problems facing each different command..."

- reaching the French-speaking veteran — "It is not sufficient to merely translate English material into French. It just won't work."

- determining the unexplored areas of membership — "...there are 50,000 ex-servicewomen in Canada who... have been referred to the auxiliaries... Greater emphasis must be placed on (veterans in) the metropolitan areas... In Canada's armed forces there are literally thousands of veterans who have never been invited (to join)..."

- committee organization — "The entire executive at every level should be absolutely membership-conscious and should form part of the membership committee. Budgets should also be provided at all levels where possible and feasible."

- possible benefits of panel discussions — "...proved highly effective in that it combines membership information and audience participation..."

Stressing the importance of taking initiative, Kohaly held up the example of two men named Garrett — Vernon Garrett of Charlottetown Branch who personally recruited more than 125 members, and Bert Garrett of Renfrew, Ontario, who signed up more than 250 members. "Men like these have made all of us look good," he concluded.

In his overview of his plan, Kohaly said: "(The 1962 convention) indicated that the comrades were not fooling in the field of membership and that whoever was charged with the responsibility of leadership had better carry out a unique and strong campaign... The first two years of the 10-year program have elapsed. This convention must now approve, reject, amend, add to or scrap the campaign. The future of the Legion depends on this program being complete and sufficient. If we are wrong, we are sitting in on the terminal illness of the Legion.

"The program material and manpower are at work in 2,000 branches. The future of the Legion, built as it must be upon membership, is assured. We are moving up well over schedule. If we are to extend our active life based on present qualifications for membership we must increase our membership markedly to withstand the natural loss by death, both within our ranks and from our potential field of recruits.

"No program of the Legion can survive without membership. No program will suffer if we build and maintain our numbers and their interests. The strength of our legislative voice, so badly needed now, will be in direct relationship to our numbers. Membership has been, is now, and will forever be the lifeblood of the Legion."

Leaving the Winnipeg convention with the backing from the delegates to carry on, Kohaly set about recruiting a team of men to help him in his quest, looking, as he would put it, "where there's water." Following his theory of recruiting from below the command level, he found some talented people. His network of contacts started to pay off right from the start.

"I had an entrée into Ontario Command's district commanders from a presentation I made to their caucus at the Halifax convention," he said, "and that's where I found McChesney."

Bob McChesney was a fast-rising insurance executive from Kirkland Lake, Ontario, and, as a salesman, the polar opposite to Kohaly's frenzied intensity, though no less effective. The two clicked immediately, and McChesney became Kohaly's lieutenant. Kohaly also recruited Paul Burden from New Brunswick, Paul Richard from Quebec, and another hard-driving businessman from Ontario, Doug McDonald of Brantford.

Although several others were involved in the membership drive — either as members of Kohaly's national committee or as regional counterparts — a core group began to form: McChesney, McDonald, Heckbert, Burden and Dave Hunter from British Columbia. "There was a great spirit among us," said Kohaly. "We travelled together, holding seminars all over, and we talked on the phone constantly. We became good, close friends with a common goal and a common view of how things should be."

With their high profile at the Dominion level, their single-mindedness and their ability to get things done Kohaly's way, it was natural that other Legion members started to view them as something of an elite group, and natural enough that someone should hang a name on them.

"It was (Saskatchewan Command secretary) Linton MacDonald who coined the name 'Legion mafia' to describe us," said Kohaly. Outsiders may have seen some negative connotations to the term, and some would use it against them in a derogatory fashion, but in 1986 Kohaly and Doug McDonald still relished the name that set them apart. "Understand," said Kohaly, "we never looked for glory for ourselves, but we got involved in issues on principle if we were asked. Sometimes people would wonder what they had gotten themselves into by asking us, because we got things done — our way."

"I suppose some of what we did was devious," said McDonald, "but we did it because it had to be done."

During the quarter-century — from Kohaly's first membership drive to its re-emergence during the organization's 60th anniversary year — that the "mafia" (with a few personnel changes) would be on the Dominion scene, it would exert enormous influence on policy, leaving its mark on almost every aspect of the Legion.

Chapter 14

TURNING OVER
A NEW LEAF

"**T**he assumption must be," wrote Stephen Bayley, a British design critic, "that those who can see value only in tradition, or versions of it, deny man's ability to adapt to changing circumstances."

The winds of change were blowing hard as the 1950s came to a close. Tradition — so respected in the nine years of relative stasis under Prime Minister Louis St. Laurent — was suddenly being challenged from all sides. Television was changing the way information was transmitted, the children of the wartime baby boom were listening to music their parents did not understand, African nations like Ghana were breaking away from their colonial masters, and the Soviet Union was rising to challenge the established powers of the West — gaining the upper hand in space with the launch of two Sputnik satellites in 1957. The average World War I veteran was over 65 — not an age when change is accepted easily. In a world gone crazy with change, the Legion still offered a refuge; a place where the old ways were still respected as the best ways. It is not surprising, then, that when rapid change challenged legionnaires on their own ground, they bucked against it.

The first change was precipitated by events on the other side of the world. Meeting in Canberra in early 1958, the British Empire Service League voted to change its name to the British Commonwealth Ex-Services League. In reaction, delegates to the Legion's 17th convention in Edmonton voted to change the official name of the Canadian Legion of the British Empire Service League to simply the Canadian Legion. An official request was made to Queen Elizabeth for permission to affix the term "royal" to the name, which would receive her consent in 1960.

Some felt that other name changes were needed, as well. Delegates in Edmonton debated a motion to drop the term "Dominion" in favor of "national," but the idea was not a popular one and the resolution fell by a large majority.

Those were the easy decisions. More difficult was the choice of what to do about the Legion's badge, designed by George Inglis in 1926. Following the Edmonton convention, the incoming Dominion Executive Council requested a new design incorporating the Legion's main elements from Alan Beddoe, the retired lieutenant-commander who had directed work on the World War II Book of Remembrance. His final design — combining a red maple leaf, the word "Legion," a crown, three poppies and the Latin motto "*Memoriam Eorum Retinebimus*" ("We Will Remember Them") — was approved by Council and printed on the cover of *The Legionary* in November 1960, but the decision did not please many in the Legion's rank and file.

What followed was one of the most acrimonious debates since the conscript question had arisen at three consecutive postwar conventions. In fact, the debate raged for more than a year. Letters — pro and con — flowed into *The Legionary*, spurring Mervyn Woods, who had been acclaimed president at the 1960 Dominion convention, to hit the road in defence of the new badge at many of the provincial conventions in the summer of 1961. Using words that would come back to haunt him, Woods told legionnaires that the maple leaf was an appropriate symbol because Canadians had worn it on their uniforms in both world wars. But there was little consensus across the country. At the Pacific Command convention Woods received a standing ovation; in Nova Scotia delegates demanded that the badge be re-designed to include the Union Jack and the words "Royal Canadian Legion." Others wanted a bilingual French and English badge. Overall, Ontario, Saskatchewan, Quebec and New Brunswick stood in favor, while Alberta joined Nova Scotia on the negative side of the argument.

Looking back, Woods took an ironic view at the situation. "Feelings ran very high," he said, "but the reasons were mixed. For example, Ontario Command wanted a change because it had a big business in supply and stood to gain a lot if the new badge was issued."

He believed that the issue was mishandled. "More leadership should have come from us in the executive," he said, "because the question had to do with our national image. The discussion got out of hand."

The issue was finally settled at the Dominion convention at Halifax in 1962, when delegates voted in favor of Beddoe's proposal.

Don Thompson, Dominion secretary at the time, was more sanguine than Woods in his reminiscence of the affair. "The controversy was inevitable," he said. "It would have been surprising to me if there had been no reaction. Once it became clear that this was the new design the differences were quickly forgotten."

If the differences over the badge were forgotten, it is likely because legionnaires had an even more bitter fight on their hands.

The debate over the design of a Canadian flag can be traced back to Confederation. When Canada officially became a sovereign nation in 1867 the Union Jack was adopted as its flag, although the Red Ensign with a distinct Canadian badge was flown occasionally. In 1925, during the wave of Canadian nationalism that swept the country after World War I, Prime Minister King appointed a committee to study possible designs for a distinctive Canadian flag, but nothing came of it. For years after, the question of a new flag was introduced in Parliament on a regular basis, but no action was taken until 1946, when another committee recommended a new version of the Red Ensign with a maple leaf in the fly in place of the coat of arms.

Ten years after that report the issue of the re-designed Red Ensign reached the floor of the Dominion convention in Vancouver. After extensive debate, the issue was deferred to the next convention in Edmonton. There, delegates approved a design that combined the Union Jack and an autumnal maple leaf "proportioned so that the size and position of the maple leaf in relation to the Union Jack will identify it as a symbol distinctive of Canada."

Two years later, at the 18th Dominion convention in Windsor, the Legion reversed itself, voting in favor of the traditional Canadian version of the Red Ensign. Delegates to the 1962 convention endorsed that decision and requested that the government move to adopt the design as Canada's official flag. By that time, however, Prime Minister John Diefenbaker's government — which also favored the Red Ensign — was embroiled in the debate over nuclear weapons that would eventually lead to its defeat at the polls on April 22, 1963. When Lester Pearson assumed power after his Liberals squeezed past Diefenbaker's Conservatives, creating a unique Canadian symbol was one of his priorities.

Working with MP John Matheson, Pearson began to promote the idea of a flag that would graphically represent the country. The design they favored — a cluster of three red maple leaves bordered by wide blue vertical stripes to symbolize the oceans — pleased few Canadians. In opposition, Diefenbaker continued to pull for retention of the Ensign, while Tommy Douglas' New Democrats supported a design similar to Matheson's, but with only one leaf.

The Legion plunged into the fray, launching a series of strident editorials in *The Legionary,* which began to carry a traditional Red Ensign on its cover, with the admonition, "This is Canada's flag. Keep it flying!" In the pursuit of fairness, though, the Dominion Executive Council voted to recommend that Pearson call a national referendum on the flag issue. *The Legionary* wrote: "In a free, democratic country, where public opinion is neither regimented nor suppressed, instances occur when the people are stirred to the innermost depths of heart and soul. Then it is that government by the people, for the people, is given true effect by a national vote on the issue at stake, and on that only... We sincerely believe that (a plebiscite) is the only means of avoiding, as far as it is possible to do so, making it a partisan issue."

It was tradition for the Legion to invite the Prime Minister to address a Dominion convention, and the 20th convention was certainly no exception — especially when the Legion was marking the occasion by returning to Winnipeg for the fifth time and delegates were concerned about the government's intention of transferring veterans' hospitals to local authorities. With almost 1,000 delegates registered to attend, the convention would be the biggest to date. The invitation to open the convention went out to Pearson's office, and was accepted enthusiastically.

"We should've known we were going to get diddled, because Pearson was the consummate politician," said Bob Kohaly, third vice-president at the time and himself a former politician. "We damn well knew we were in trouble with the flag issue so hot. We tried to cancel his appearance, but it was too late. We should have been wise enough not to invite him."

Having failed at heading off Pearson's opening speech, the Legion's officers decided to deflect any comments he might make about the flag issue by meeting his plane at the Winnipeg airport and speaking to him before the speech. The Prime Minister's plane taxied into the debarkation area — flying the Red Ensign outside the pilot's window — and he was whisked away before the Legion delegation had a chance to meet him.

The second indication Kohaly had that the fat was in the fire was the amount of media present at the Capitol Theatre for the Sunday night opening. "When the CBC crew arrived we knew that Pearson was going to use the speech as a national platform. He was going to talk right over our heads to the Canadian people, and no matter what happened he would be able to say that he had faced the toughest opposition on the issue, and done it on their turf."

More than 2,000 people were assembled for Pearson's speech, which began with his reassurance that the Legion would be consulted in any decisions regarding veterans' hospitals. But it did not take long to get to his main topic.

"When it became known that I was going to have (this) honor," he said, "I got a good deal of advice as to what I should discuss — or not discuss... (One) subject which I was advised, for obvious reasons, not to mention at all — the flag. That advice, of course, was well meant. It was also impossible to accept."

Wearing horn-rimmed glasses and miniatures of his service medals from the First War on a dark business suit, an unruly cowlick on the back of his head shaking as he emphasized his main points, Pearson lit into a lengthy defence of his policy on the new flag: "This mutual awareness of our attitudes, I believe, precludes any possibility that I should appear before you tonight and attempt to dodge the flag issue. After all, you are men who know what it means to go into battle. So I intend to talk briefly, but frankly, about this issue; to put my own feelings, my beliefs, my judgment squarely and honestly before you. You would expect me to do this and I believe it is my duty also. I expect dissent. I also respect it.

"When I went overseas in 1915 I had as comrades in my section men whose names were: Cameron, Kimura, English, Bleidenstein, DeChapin, O'Shaughenessy. We didn't fall in, or fall out, as Irish Canadians, French Canadians, Dutch Canadians or Japanese Canadians. We wore the same uniform, with the same maple leaf badge, and we were proud to be known as Canadians, to serve as Canadians and to die, if that had to be, as Canadians.

"I wish our country had more of that spirit today, of unity, togetherness and resolve; the spirit that was shown by Canadians in time of war when the survival of our country was at stake. Well, the survival of our country as a united and strong federal state is also at stake today.

"What we need is that soldierly pride in Canada — that confident, passionate pride in Canada that men had who wore the uniform with the maple leaf badge on it; a pride, I remember, which used to lead to a scrap or two in the canteens with others who didn't always show sufficient respect for our Canadian status or our Canadian uniform.

"What we also need is a patriotism that will put Canada ahead of its parts; that will think more of our future destiny than our past mistakes; that rejects emphatically the idea that, politically, we are, or should become, a federation of two associated states — some kind of pre-war Austria-

Hungary. We should have none of such separatism or of petty, narrow nationalism of any kind.

"I believe that today a flag designed around the maple leaf will symbolize, will be a true reflection of, the new Canada.

"Today there are five million or more Canadians whose tradition is not inherited from the British Isles, but who are descendants of the original French founders of our country. There are another five million, or more, who have come to Canada from other far-away lands, with a heritage neither British nor French.

"I believe that a Canadian flag, as distinctive as the maple leaf in the Legion badge, will bring them all closer to those of us of British stock and make us all better, more united Canadians."

By this point, Pearson's voice was rising over a chorus of boos and shouts of "no, no." Dominion president Clare Sparling stood up to admonish the nay-sayers, and Pearson plunged ahead.

"Would such a change mean any disrespect for the Union Jack or its rejection from our history? No.

"I would not agree to that. I have served under the Union Jack in war and I have lived under it in peace. I have seen it flying above the smoke and fire and crashing bombs in London's blitz. I have seen it flying proudly in some desperate moments in 1915. I know it stands for freedom under law, justice and the dignity of man; for the glorious history of a brave breed of men. The Union Jack should still be flown in Canada — not as our national flag but as a symbol of our membership in a Commonwealth of Nations and of our loyalty to the crown.

"You will recall the great Legion debate just a few years ago, in 1960, when you were choosing a new Legion badge; you will remember the arguments put forward in defence of your executive's decision on that new badge.

"As described by your then-president, Mr. Justice Woods, it was correct according to heraldry; it was distinctive; it embodied the right symbolism to represent those things the Legion stood for. It was strictly your own and could not be confused with the badge of any other organization. Its central, dominant feature was the maple leaf.

"You will recall also that the suggestion made at the time, that the question of your new badge should be determined by referendum throughout your membership, was rejected by your executive as impractical.

"As in the case of your new badge, so it is in any question of changing symbols. It asks a lot of human nature to expect ready acceptance of something that is going to alter that which is venerated and has been for long honored by many.

"So any suggestion for change is bound to provoke strong criticism as well as support. This is all part of the democratic process.

"We who are elected to serve Canada in Parliament owe those who elect us more than the advocacy of non-controversial ideas. We owe Canada our best judgment, and we fail Canada if we fail to exercise that judgment, or if we pass our responsibility for judgment back to the electors who sent us to Parliament.

"I believe most sincerely that it is time for Canadians to unfurl a flag that is truly distinctive and truly national in character — as Canadian as the maple leaf which should be its dominant design; a flag easily identifiable as Canada's; a flag which cannot be mistaken for the emblem of any other country; a flag of the future which honors also the past; Canada's own, and only Canada's."

Pearson was only about halfway through his prepared remarks, but he had effectively skewered the Legion's opposition by using the organization's own words and actions against it. He was going to move ahead with his plan to introduce a new flag, and there would be no referendum.

Embarrassed by the disrespect shown to the prime minister by the booing, jeering audience members, yet seething over the content of the speech, Sparling nevertheless followed the Legion's script and concluded Pearson's remarks by presenting him with an honorary life membership. After the convention, *The Legionary* would attempt to put the best face on the booing incident, stating that it was mild compared to what went on daily in Parliament, and that "reaction was grossly exaggerated by sensation-hungry press, TV and radio commentators." Regardless, Kohaly claimed that Sparling, an intense, earnest man, was scarred by the incident.

The controversy did not end with Pearson's speech. The following day, delegates were buzzing with the news that the prime minister had held a press conference in Winnipeg to announce the design he proposed to submit to Parliament. He gave more media interviews after his return to Ottawa, and on Wednesday the press reported that cabinet had already approved the new flag. Delegates began to reach the same conclusion as Kohaly — that Pearson had used the convention as part of his strategy and was forcing the Legion into breaking from its tradition of non-partisanship.

🍁

Before adjourning, the convention passed a resolution adopting the Red Ensign as the Legion's official flag and the only flag that could be flown by branches and commands.

On June 15, debate on the flag issue began in Parliament, and the July issue of *The Legionary* weighed in with what it called "a final appeal" to take the question to the Canadian public. "*The Legionary*... strongly urges the Prime Minister to let the Canadian people decide it, one way or another, through a national plebiscite," wrote editor John Hundevad. "It is the most democratic way of solving this problem. It is the *only* way to ascertain what the *people* really want. And the request for a plebiscite is sure to be warmly supported by all Canadians of goodwill and moderation because, no matter what the result, if the issue were settled by a parliamentary vote only, grave doubts would arise in the minds of a great many citizens that it represented the will of the people. These doubts would linger on for many years and would remain a serious obstacle to the attainment of national unity.

"So please, Mr. Prime Minister, let the people decide. It would be a statesman-like solution and might well be a nation-saving move."

As the debate raged on in Parliament, *The Legionary* continued to hammer away, running a small Red Ensign in the upper corner of the front cover with the modified motto: "This is the Legion's flag. Keep it flying!"

"It was an anxious time," remembered Mervyn Woods. "I thought opposition was a big mistake, that we were letting sentiment overrule reason, but I faced a lot of opposition from the executive. It wasn't easy to remain to be seen as non-partisan when the debate came down to one between Pearson and Diefenbaker."

Throughout the late fall of 1964 interest over the new flag continued, with magazines and newspapers polling readers on their views and the Legion's opposition to any change constantly in the news. Finally, on December 15, Pearson invoked closure on the debate in Parliament, forcing a vote on the single maple leaf design. The new flag was accepted by a 163 to 78 vote, and a Senate vote followed suit on December 17. Queen Elizabeth proclaimed the new flag on January 28, 1965, effective February 15.

With the red maple leaf Canada's official symbol, the Legion faced a dilemma that teetered on the edge of becoming a constitutional crisis.

"We were torn in two directions," recalled Charles Rhodes Smith, the Legion's longtime constitutional expert. "Loyalty to the flag is paramount in our original aims and objectives, and we were getting requests from some branches for permission to fly the new flag. Yet, we had a decision from our convention that we would oppose it. In the end, we had to face the fact that we couldn't continue as an organization with a flag that was not the flag of Canada."

Fred O'Brecht, the new Dominion president, wrote a guest editorial in the February issue of *The Legionary*, stating: "Every law-abiding Canadian citizen must recognize (the new flag). In particular, it must be recognized by every member of the Royal Canadian Legion who, on joining our organization, swore loyalty to our sovereign and country, and obedience to the law of the land.

"Now, when a good citizen obeys the law, it is not as a rule because he has any particular liking for it, let alone love. It is because, as a citizen of a democratic country, he recognizes the supremacy of Parliament, which makes the law. Sometimes he may question the wisdom or desirability of a proposed piece of legislation. If he has strong views about it he will oppose it and fight against its adoption by Parliament with every legitimate means at his disposal. That is his inalienable right as a citizen of a democracy...

"(The Legion) rallied around the flag under which so many of its members had served and which in death had covered the bodies of many of their fallen comrades. Through every legitimate means the Legion endeavored to persuade the government, Parliament, provincial legislatures, municipalities and individual fellow citizens that Canada already had a national flag, full of heraldic meaning and historical significance. It was a gallant and a fair fight, one of which the Legion can always be proud. That it did not succeed was in large measure due to the unfortunate fact that the flag issue became a political party matter — a field into which the Legion as a non-partisan organization could not and would not enter.

"What of the Canadian Red Ensign as the Legion's flag? Our members are aware that their accredited delegates to the last Dominion convention... decided to adopt (it) as the official color of our organization. (This) resolution remains in effect... until such time as another Dominion convention may decide otherwise. Our commands, branches and members may be assured that it is perfectly lawful to continue flying the Ensign over Legion halls and headquarters...

"At this crucial juncture in the history of our beloved country I commend to members of the Legion, and to all Canadians of tolerance and goodwill, the following words... 'Let bitterness and wrath and anger... be put away from you.'"

In a move filled with more than a little irony, the Dominion Executive Council directed *The Legionary* to replace the Red Ensign on its cover with the Legion's badge — the symbol that Pearson had used as ammunition. The magazine said that "in the best interests of Canadian and Legion unity" it would refuse to publish any further letters or branch resolutions on the flag issue.

There were certainly some legionnaires prepared to admit defeat gracefully and accept the new flag, and Pearson likely harbored no ill will against his comrades who had fought to retain the Red Ensign, but the fight rubbed feelings raw within both the Legion and the government. One thing that fell victim to the Legion's stance was the government's plan to build a monument to honor Canadian casualties in World War II and Korea on Ottawa's Nepean Point. Controversial because of its $1.5-million price-tag, the project — a variation of which was suggested by the Legion in 1956 — was scrapped in the heat of the debate. At least one future Dominion president, Redmond Roche, believed that relations with the government suffered because of the battle. "You can't fight politicians," he said, "you have to be a diplomat. My predecessors meant well, but they didn't always understand politicians. Before Bob Kohaly took over (in 1968) there was a basic distrust of their motives that didn't serve us well. Relations were not very good."

Chapter 15

COMING OF AGE IN
THE SIXTIES

The changing of decades creates a convenient place for people to reflect on achievements and plan for improvements, and 1960 seemed a particularly good time for the Legion to look back at its past and ahead to its future. The year marked the 35th anniversary of the organization, and to celebrate it the Dominion Executive Council had commissioned Clifford Bowering, a government information officer and frequent contributor to *The Legionary*, to write an official history.

At the Dominion convention that year, which attracted 796 accredited delegates and 423 fraternals to Windsor's Cleary Memorial Auditorium, the Legion gave all the signs of an organization that was operating smoothly and efficiently. Even the election of officers was relatively uneventful.

After two terms as Dominion president, David Burgess stepped down to make way for the acclamation of 51-year-old Mervyn Woods of Saskatoon. A member of the Legion since his discharge in 1945 from the Royal Canadian Navy with the rank of lieutenant-commander, Woods had practised law for several years before joining the staff of the University of Saskatchewan's school of law.

Clare Sparling and Fred O'Brecht also faced no opposition in moving up the ladder to first and second vice-president respectively.

There was a four-way race for third vice-president among Tom Young from Nova Scotia, Ron MacBeath from New Brunswick, Bill Rorke from Alberta and Robert Hall from British Columbia. New Brunswick Command president MacBeath, a 48-year-old building contractor and former Army captain from Moncton, was the eventual winner.

Ronnie Stewart defeated E.K. Brunton of Sudbury, Ontario, to retain the post of honorary treasurer for a sixth term.

Chairman Erle Burgess was challenged by vice-chairman Don McTavish but emerged victorious to serve a fifth term. Jean Miquelon, a 50-year-old Montreal lawyer and World War II Army major, defeated Dai Morgan of Alberta and J.J. McIsaac of Prince Edward Island to become vice-chairman.

In his report, outgoing president David Burgess reviewed some of the Legion's achievements, concluding that the organization was healthy and growing, albeit not at the rate the membership committee had hoped for. "Comrades," he said, "the Canadian Legion was founded on the principle of service to others. For 35 years it has gained strength through the performance of such service. This increased strength has enabled us to do a better job for veterans and to expand our concept of service to include the community at large.

"Service through strength: Strength through service! This, comrades, should be the theme which carries us into the next 35 years."

Burgess detailed the numerous briefs the Legion had made to government officials for improvements to various aspects of veterans' legislation, noting that these had resulted in few changes. "The failure of the federal government to act on our recommendations regarding the Pension Act — especially pension rates — has been a matter of grave disappointment to me. Our requests were based on careful study, and I believe pensioners were justly entitled to the increases which were urged. We must continue to make strong and unified representations on this most important matter.

"As veterans of both wars grow older, problems relating to pensions and allowances will increase. As the rate of veteran deaths increases we can also expect an increase in claims on behalf of widows and dependants. The processing of such claims is becoming more complex and time-consuming each year and will continue to fully engage our Dominion Command Service Bureau staff for years to come."

In fact, the Service Bureau's workload had grown by 25 per cent since the previous convention. That, and a key resignation, had prompted a number of changes at Dominion Command. Three months prior to the convention, Dominion secretary T.D. Anderson had left to become chairman of the Canadian Pension Commission after 10 years on the job. He was succeeded by Don Thompson, the director of the Service Bureau since 1951. Thompson's move made way for the promotion of Murray MacFarlane, a lawyer who had worked at the bureau for four years. Two new men, Bill Conyers and Ed Slater, had joined the staff, bringing the number of service officers to six. Thompson reported that the service officers were now spending more time than ever before studying cases and referring men to medical specialists. Over the two years since the 1958 convention, the bureau had won awards totalling about $300,000 for 1,000 veterans or their dependants. In November 1958, the Service Bureau had held a conference for provincial service officers to coordinate efforts; another was scheduled for later in 1960.

The annual poppy campaign continued to be a major source of funding for veterans' welfare. Between 1954 and 1959, the number of poppies distributed had increased from 4.8 million to 6.5 million. The number of wreaths had grown from 50,000 to 64,000. In 1958, more than $500,000 was used from the Poppy Fund for welfare work. The national poppy committee chairman, former Dominion president John Anderson, urged greater participation from branches: "If we could say that we could count on the personal efforts of every member of the Legion and the Ladies Auxiliaries for even one day each year, what a tremendous difference this would make.

"This is the challenge: to set your sights on achieving the greatest possible participation by individual Legion members and auxiliaries in carrying the poppy emblems to every citizen that can be reached by personal contact. In this way we may come closer to realizing our obligations to the dead and those they left behind."

The committee's goal was to distribute a poppy to every Canadian.

Some concern was expressed at the 1960 convention about continuing efforts by other charitable organizations to subsume the poppy campaign as part of their fund-raising campaigns. Delegates voted unanimously for a resolution "to maintain its own identity insofar as the poppy campaign is concerned and... not go in with the Community Chest, United Appeal or Red Feather Campaign."

Although the Legion was largely preoccupied by the controversy over the new badge during 1961, the organization kept up the pressure on the government to adjust pensions and War Veterans Allowance payments. In his report to the 1962 Dominion convention in Halifax Woods stated: "...While we cannot take full credit for government legislation, we do not feel immodest in believing that our well-documented and carefully prepared submissions had much to do with the government's decision to increase pensions and War Veterans Allowance by 20 per cent, as well as the other items of legislative improvement which were submitted to Parliament."

Woods did not seek a second term in office, leaving Clare Sparling alone on the ballot. A legionnaire since 1938, the 62-year-old Sparling had served as an officer with the 5th Mounted Cavalry Brigade for 12 years before transferring to the RCAF as a flying officer in 1940. In addition to his military service between the wars, Sparling had practised law since graduating from the Manitoba Law School in 1922, and after his discharge from the Air Force he had served in a number of judicial positions in Manitoba. In 1958, he was made a judge of the province's juvenile and family courts.

As in 1960, there were no additional nominations for the posts of first or second vice-president, so both Fred O'Brecht and Ron MacBeath moved up one rung. As noted previously, Bob Kohaly was elected third vice-president, defeating Bill Rorke of Alberta, Jack Pothecary of British Columbia and Jean St. Germain of Quebec.

Ronnie Stewart was acclaimed for a seventh term as honorary treasurer.

Three men, including five-term incumbent Erle Burgess, competed for the post of chairman. Burgess and O.F. Howe of Ottawa were defeated by Chester Merriam of Tara, Ontario. A 52-year-old hardware retailer, Merriam was a flight sergeant in the RCAF in World War II. He had served as chairman of Ontario Command since 1957.

Acclaimed as vice-chairman was Myles Murray, the first sitting member of a provincial legislature to hold Legion office at the national level. A native of St. John's, Murray was Newfoundland's minister of provincial affairs, in addition to being a former president of his command.

It was reported that the Service Bureau had handled 2,732 new cases since the previous convention and reopened 215 old files. It had successfully adjusted 1,054 cases for a value of $297,000. Service officer Bill Conyers had left the bureau since the last convention, and two others, George Cracknell and Robbie Robinson, had retired. Robinson, 65, was a charter member of the Tuberculous Veterans Association, and had been a Dominion service officer since 1941. Two new service officers, Kerry Dunphy and Leo Trottier, had joined the staff.

The planning committee reported that former Dominion secretary T.D. Anderson was representing the Legion on a government committee that was investigating ways of marking Canada's centennial in 1967. Delegates voted to form a national committee under Anderson's chairmanship to coordinate the Legion's centennial projects at the local, provincial and national levels.

The convention was informed about arrangements for an upcoming pilgrimage to Canadian war cemeteries in Holland, the first of its kind since World War II. The idea of bringing the next of kin of Allied casualties had originated shortly after the war with Herman Goetzen, a banker who had served in the Dutch Resistance. He organized a group called the Netherlands War Graves Committee and began sponsoring charter flights from Britain to Holland. In 1956 Goetzen approached the Department of Veterans Affairs to send Canadians over, but the government demurred, citing the lack of money for administration costs. The Legion had agreed to take on the project and supplemented its Dominion Command staff to handle arrangements. The cost of the trip — including return air fare from Montreal, accommodations, meals and ground transportation during 10 days in Holland — was $200, of which Goetzen's committee would pay $50.

Delegates were told that 750 Canadians had applied for the trip, which could handle only 79. It was decided that this initial pilgrimage would be restricted to parents of war dead over the age of 70.

In September, the 79 pilgrims flew from Montreal's Dorval Airport to Amsterdam, where they were met by committee members and transported to Dutch homes where they would be billeted. Few of the Canadians on the trip were prepared for the personal attention provided by their Dutch hosts to the 6,331 graves in their care. Many Dutch families had "adopted" specific Canadians, tending their gravesites as if they were members of their own family. The Canadians were also impressed by the warmth of the Dutch government; Queen Juliana received the pilgrims at Soesdijk Palace during their stay.

The 1962 pilgrimage turned out to be the first of 17 made over the following 10 years. Eventually, more than 2,000 Canadians made the trip.

The Legion was also involved in another pilgrimage, this one to mark the 20th anniversary of D-Day in 1964. Restricted to 125 veterans of the Normandy campaign as a pilot project for possible other pilgrimages, the trip was planned to take in sites in France, Belgium and Holland along the "Maple Leaf Up" route as well as Normandy.

As noted elsewhere, the controversy surrounding Prime Minister Lester Pearson's proposal to adopt a new Canadian flag dominated Legion affairs in early 1964 and led to the largest convention turnout in history — 995 accredited delegates and 514 fraternals — at Winnipeg's Marlborough Hotel. It was a far cry from the 60 veterans who had gathered at the hotel to hammer out the shape of the Legion in 1925.

❦

Clare Sparling declined to stand for a second term, and Fred O'Brecht, the 53-year-old dairy owner from Mount Forest, Ontario, was acclaimed president.

Ron MacBeath was acclaimed first vice-president, and Bob Kohaly was the only legionnaire nominated for second vice-president. Five men faced off for the post of third vice-president: Jack Oldham, Medicine Hat, Alberta; Clarence Wood, Paris, Ontario; Don McTavish, Salmon Arm, British Columbia; J.J. MacIntosh, Dartmouth, Nova Scotia; and Redmond Roche, Montreal, Quebec. Roche, a 57-year-old law professor and court of sessions judge, had the backing of former Dominion president Basil Price and won on the first ballot.

Ronnie Stewart was unopposed for an eighth term as honorary treasurer.

Chairman Chester Merriam was also acclaimed, and Vice-Chairman Myles Murray staved off challenges from John MacIsaac of Prince Edward Island and Manitoba's Fred Orchard.

The other contentious issue at the 20th convention was the future of the veterans' hospitals that the government had administered since 1916. Based on the findings of the Glassco Report, which had been produced for the Diefenbaker government, Veterans Affairs had expressed its desire to transfer some of the hospitals to local agencies, which would make them available for wider community use. This, the department felt, would prevent deterioration of care standards. After receiving assurances from the Pearson government that the matter would be studied and the Legion consulted, it was announced that plans were underway to transfer Calgary's Colonel Belcher Hospital to civil authorities.

Veterans Affairs Minister Roger Teillet and 18 members of the Commons committee on veterans affairs arrived in Winnipeg to address the issue. Teillet outlined the reasons for the decision, citing the difficulty in attracting top-quality medical staff to work in chronic care units. Delegates listened politely to his presentation and a lively question-and-answer session followed. The prime minister also had a few things to say on the matter. He told delegates: "...in anything we seek to do about veterans' medical and hospital care the government's primary consideration will be to protect the interests and promote the welfare of the veterans themselves. They are not problems but people. Veterans, especially older veterans, deserve and must receive special and humane and generous consideration. There will be no change which will remove control of veterans' admissions and their treatment and their domiciliary care from the Department of Veterans Affairs. That department is not going out of business."

After a lengthy and heated debate, delegates passed a resolution drafted by a sub-committee headed by former Dominion president Bill Lumsden. The resolution stated that no hospital be transferred "to civilian administration... without full consultation at the outset of negotiations and mutual agreement with both Dominion and provincial commands..." In addition, the convention said that adequate domiciliary care must be in place before any transfer, and that Veterans Affairs must control the admission, care and discharge of veterans.

Thanks to Kohaly's effective presentation of the membership picture there was somewhat less debate about extending ordinary membership to postwar service personnel. The motion passed, opening up a huge pool of potential legionnaires.

Organization and development committee chairman Mervyn Woods reported on the progress of the special centennial committee that had been formed after the 1962 convention. Made up of Woods and several other former Dominion presidents, the committee had originally decided to recommend funding a national youth hostel and conference centre in Ottawa. Changes in the policies of the Canadian Youth Hostels Association had overtaken their plans, however, and the committee had reached a decision that the best course would be to establish a fund that could be used to seed future projects. "The committee, in considering these proposals," said Woods, "attempted to visualize the future of the Legion as an organization which has a naturally dwindling potential of eligible membership over the next 30 or 40 years, and could see the possibility that this was a means by which the aims and objects of the Legion might be furthered, even if it no longer exists as a war veterans' organization. The committee feels that the objective should be $1 million."

The committee proposed that the money should be raised on a voluntary basis and that interest from the fund could be used to finance such projects as bursaries or student exchanges with other Commonwealth countries. Its formal mandate stated that the fund would "provide a perpetual memorial to those who have fallen in the service of Canada, by continuing the activities of the Royal Canadian Legion — including the promotion of education, sports, Commonwealth unity, and all other forms of national and community service which, in the light of changing conditions, the trustees may deem consistent with the aims and objects of the Royal Canadian Legion."

❦

Although Woods had some reservations about the plan, he was asked to chair the fund-raising campaign, which kicked off on April 9, 1965 — the 48th anniversary of Vimy Ridge. Woods had barely started on the mammoth project when Veterans Affairs Minister Teillet approached him to head a special committee to examine the work of the Canadian Pension Commission. The Legion had benefited significantly over the years from Woods' hard work and good judgment, but the result of his study of the state of veterans' legislation over the following three years would be far-reaching changes in the treatment of ex-servicemen and women.

Section 4

1966 - 1980

RENEWAL

Chapter 16

WIN ONE, LOSE ONE

Fifty years after the first casualties of World War I began to return home to Canada the basic shape of the country's veterans' legislation remained relatively unchanged from the design of J.L. Todd and Ernest Scammell. Despite major victories like the introduction of the War Veterans Allowance Act in 1930 and the pension increases of 1951, benefits continued to be based on a system that was growing progressively outmoded. Since the 1920s the Legion had sought to convince the government to adopt a satisfactory way of automatically escalating pensions in tune with cost-of-living increases. Other elements of the legislation had also failed to stay in step with the evolving system of social assistance in Canada.

"Case after case had shown how the legislation had failed veterans," said Colin Graham, a longtime Dominion Command service officer who served as Dominion secretary from 1982 to '85. "There was a presumption of medical fitness. The benefit of doubt had not been extended in many cases."

Veterans Affairs Minister Roger Teillet's appointment of former Dominion president Mervyn Woods to chair a committee of inquiry into the Pension Act promised to help rectify the stagnant situation.

In 1966, the Legion appeared before the four-man Woods Commission in Ottawa to present its views on how the system needed to be changed. It took three days to present the organization's 136-page brief. In all, the Woods Commission held 41 hearings in Ottawa, Toronto and Quebec City to gather input from various interested parties before retiring to prepare its report.

Meanwhile, the Legion continued to press for immediate changes, including an increase in war disability pension rates and a cyclical review of pension and War Veterans Allowance rates. It recommended that the basic rate structure be adjusted to reflect the wage paid to a cleaner in the civil service. In April 1966, addressing the 21st Dominion convention in

Montreal, Teillet said that the government could not introduce a cyclical review until a new basic rate yardstick was established, and he was not prepared to accept the Legion's recommendation. Undaunted, the record-setting 1,063 delegates voted to demand that the government set the basic rate at a level comparable to what a fully disabled man could earn if he had not suffered his injury — an amount equivalent to just under $4,000 a year.

In November 1966, the government introduced a 15-per-cent increase, but for the first time the raise was only applicable to pensioners or their widows. The Legion disputed the exclusion of wives and children from future increases as a dangerous precedent and lodged a protest with cabinet. The government relented and altered the plan, and later introduced another increase. By 1968, the basic rate had risen to $3,180 — still a substantial amount less than what the convention delegates had requested.

Woods and his commission members labored on. It would be March 1968 before their report — a massive three-volume, 1,300-page document with 149 recommendations — was presented to cabinet. By then, Prime Minister Pearson had resigned. Pierre Trudeau would soon become the new leader and the government would prepare to go to the polls. Nevertheless, Teillet, who had failed to win the Liberal nomination in his St. Boniface, Manitoba, riding, told the delegates to the Dominion convention in Penticton, British Columbia, that he was sure massive changes would follow a thorough review of the Woods Report by the new government. He called the report "the most comprehensive and complete study that has ever been done in Canada on the subject of pensions for service-related disability and death."

The Legion had begun to respond to the report as soon as it became public. As soon as the staff of the Dominion Command Service Bureau read the report it was clear that Woods was proposing the types of sweeping changes the Legion had long desired. But it was also clear that changes of this magnitude would be difficult for the government to implement — particularly a new government. Bob Kohaly, who as first vice-president was in line to become Dominion president at the Penticton convention, knew that it would take a combined effort on the part of the Legion and the non-aligned veterans' organizations to push Woods' recommendations through. "The government had always played the National Council of Veterans' Associations of Canada off against the Legion to deflect action we believed was needed," said Kohaly. "This time we had to ensure that we had a united front."

First, Kohaly approached Cliff Chadderton, the influential national secretary of the War Amputations of Canada who had served as secretary to the Woods Commission. Through Chadderton, Kohaly convinced groups like the Army, Navy and Air Force Veterans and the Hong Kong Veterans Association that a joint effort was needed. The groups met in May 1968, and agreed to establish a common policy to support all but two of Woods' proposals.

After his election to Dominion president, Kohaly became chairman of a special Legion committee to push for the implementation of the Woods Report, in addition to being chairman of the united veterans' group. Working closely with Chadderton, Service Bureau director Murray MacFarlane, service officer Ed Slater and Dominion secretary Don Thompson, Kohaly formulated a response that called on the new Trudeau government to implement four main points of Woods' study: establishment of the Pension Appeal Board; acceptance of the basic rate of pension principle; adequate compensation for those suffering from multiple disabilities; and special legislation relating to Hong Kong veterans. The brief was ready by October 1968, but it could not be presented to the Commons standing committee on veterans affairs until the government had published a white paper on the Woods Report.

In February 1969, while waiting for the white paper, the joint veterans' group sent its brief to all MPs. When the white paper was finally published on September 9, 1969, it proposed substantial modifications to many of the report's recommendations and sent the joint committee back to work. On September 18, Kohaly presented a new joint brief to the Commons committee, but it was clear that the government was becoming increasingly concerned about the cost of implementing Woods' proposals. In December, Kohaly and his committee released a third brief, this time allotting priorities to Woods' recommendations in an attempt to alleviate the government's monetary concerns.

The government still was not convinced, and appointed a special study group of Veterans Affairs and veterans' representatives to come up with some solutions that would satisfy everyone. This group met 16 times throughout the winter of 1969-70, and created a report that stated that the veterans' proposals would cost more than $8.2 million, contrasted with $5.5 million for the white paper's recommendations.

In March 1970, the veterans' committee filed a fourth brief with the House committee, outlining a new compromise position that attempted to meet the government's requirements for restraint. A month later, Veterans

Affairs' deputy minister appeared before the Commons committee to buttress the white paper's findings, and on April 9 Kohaly filed yet another brief to rebut the bureaucrat's argument. As Kohaly reported to the 1970 Dominion convention in Ottawa: "We have adopted a flexible and reasonable approach to many of the (Woods) recommendations in view of the monetary implications. Thus we have reason to hope that the committee's report to Parliament will give considerable support to our cause.

"We will have more to say then, and when legislation is introduced to improve the Pensions Act, we will continue to fight to obtain the improvements that we feel are necessary to correct the flaws and inadequacies in the present system."

As it turned out, Kohaly's hopes were realized. The committee endorsed most of Woods' recommendations, and the legislation that the Trudeau government finally introduced included some significant changes, including:

- strengthening and clarification of the guidelines in the benefit-of-doubt section of the Pension Act;

- the introduction of an exceptional incapacity allowance for 100-per-cent pensioners with an outstanding burden of disablement;

- the establishment of an independent Pensions Review Board;

- the establishment of the Veterans Bureau as an independent body and re-definition of its functions;

- special recognition for Hong Kong veterans.

Foremost among the gains that veterans made in this new legislation was a paragraph that stated: "The provisions of this act shall be liberally construed and interpreted to the end that the recognized obligation of the people and government of Canada to provide compensation to those members of the forces who have been disabled or have died as a result of military service, and to their dependants, may be fulfilled." Finally, the promise made to the men of the Canadian Expeditionary Force by Sir Robert Borden in 1917 was coming true.

"There's no question that the Woods Report was one of the most important factors in the history of veterans' legislation in Canada," said Thompson, who left the Legion in 1970 to become chairman of the War Veterans Allowance Board.

The new Pension Act became law on March 30, 1971. "Practically everything we proposed was enacted," said Woods. "The new act straightened out a lot of inequities."

Missing from the new law was the establishment of a satisfactory basic rate of pension, and the Legion quickly turned its sights on settling that issue. This time, however, many of the players were new — including Dominion president Redmond Roche, Dominion secretary Jean Lamy, Service Bureau director Bert Hanmer, and Veterans Affairs Minister Arthur Laing — and the Legion was determined to take a different approach.

Roche, a 63-year-old court of sessions judge and former colonel, was determined to establish cordial relations with Trudeau, avoiding what he felt had been an overly adversarial approach by some of his predecessors. His attitude was augmented by Lamy's, which was to build bridges between the Legion's elected officers and the Veterans Affairs bureaucrats. A seasoned administrator who had come to Dominion Command in 1968, Lamy believed in using his staff's expertise to become a valuable resource to a government that was seeking direction in the area of veterans' benefits. "I felt that any briefs we made should be couched in positive terms," said Lamy. "It was important that we got to know the people who actually made the decisions. In the past, it had been the custom for the entire Dominion Executive Council to troop up to Parliament Hill to meet with the prime minister; that was a waste of time, and something prime ministers used for their own promotional purposes."

In May 1972, Veterans Affairs Minister Laing introduced an amendment to the Pension Act that would provide for annual adjustments in pensions and allowances, based on changes in the Consumer Price Index. The first increase of 3.6 per cent was made retroactive to January 1. This was a partial success, but did not meet the Legion's long-held belief that a 100-per-cent pensioner should be compensated to the level of government clerks. In the summer of 1972, after Bob Smellie had been elected president at the 24th Dominion convention in Regina, Lamy suggested a luncheon to introduce Smellie and Laing. Out of their conversation and subsequent letters between them, Laing developed the idea for a joint study group composed of Chadderton, Lamy, Hanmer, Slater, and representatives of Veterans Affairs and the Canadian Pension Commission. Lamy was to be vice-chairman.

The group returned with the recommendation that the basic rate for a single 100-per-cent pensioner be based on the average composite after-tax salary of five categories of unskilled laborers in the federal public service.

It also recommended a continuation of the principle of the pension not being taxable, and the establishment of a relationship between the basic rate and the pension paid to dependants so that the rates for all of them would change automatically with a change in the basic rate. The report also recommended that adjustments be made annually on a fixed date in accordance with changes in the average wage rates in the five categories selected.

The new basic rate principle was not enshrined in legislation, however, and eventually the suggestions were altered so that the automatic increases to the basic rate would be the higher of increases to the five civil service categories or the Consumer Price Index, ensuring that pensioners kept up with any future inflation. Subsequent changes tied the War Veterans Allowance to Consumer Price Index increases, as well, and introduced quarterly adjustments to the allowance.

One immediate effect of the new legislation was a deluge of work for the Legion's service bureaus at every level. Colin Graham, who was one of four service officers at Dominion Command, said: "The new avenues for claim reviews brought in a huge volume of work. We were almost overwhelmed by paperwork."

In addition to preparing cases for the Canadian Pension Commission, the Entitlement Board and the Pension Review Board, the Dominion Service Bureau also found its hands full bringing the service officers at the provincial and branch level up to speed on the new legislation. By 1976, 71 per cent of the Legion's 1,862 branches had a service officer, with the percentage being much higher — 97 per cent — at branches with more than 500 members.

One of the initiatives introduced by the Dominion Service Bureau was a biennial conference for service officers. Held over three days, these conferences allowed provincial service officers — and occasionally command secretaries — to attend briefings on legislative changes, exchange information with representatives from other commands, and meet government officials. At the 1975 conference, for example, guest speakers at the conference included three members of the Canadian Pension Commission, War Veterans Allowance Board chairman Thompson, officials from the army, navy and air force benevolent funds, and the director of the Veterans Welfare Service.

Out of these meetings developed an idea to contact every veteran, widow or dependant of a veteran in Canada to find out if they were aware of all the benefits available to them under the Pension Act. The germ of the idea had come from a speech Veterans Affairs Minister Dan MacDonald had

GRAND
*P*RESIDENTS

■

Field Marshal Earl Haig of Bermersyde
KT, GCB, OM, GCVO, KICE
1925-1928

General Sir Arthur Currie
GCMG, KCB
1929-1933

Lieutenant-General Sir Percy Lake
KCB, KCMG
1934-1940

Lieutenant-General Sir Richard Turner
VC, KCB, KCMG, DSO, VD
1942-1948

General H.D.G. Crerar
CH, CB, DSO, ADC
1948-1965

Major-General The Honourable George R. Pearkes
VC, CB, DSO, MC, CD
1966-1976

Brigadier-General J.A. de Lalanne
CBE, MC, OSt.J, ED, BA, CA
1977-1984

His Honour Judge Alfred Watts
AFC, ED, QC
1984-1991

The Honourable J. Gilles Lamontagne
CP, OC, CD, BA
1991-1994

The Honourable D. Gordon Blair
BA, LLB, BCL
1994-present

DOMINION PRESIDENTS

Lieutenant-General Sir Percy Lake
British Columbia, **1925-1927**

Lieutenant-General Sir Arthur Currie
Quebec, **1928**

Lieutenant-Colonel Leo R. LaFleche
Ontario, **1929-1930**

Major John S. Roper
British Columbia, **1931-1933**

Brigadier-General Alex Ross
Saskatchewan, **1934-1937**

Lieutenant-Colonel W.W. Foster
British Columbia, **1938-1939**

Alex Walker
Alberta, **1940-1945**

Major-General C.B. Price
Quebec, **1946-1947**

Lieutenant-Colonel L.D.M. Baxter
Manitoba, **1948-1949**

Group Captain Alfred Watts
British Columbia, **1950-1951**

Dr. C.B. Lumsden
Nova Scotia, **1952-1953**

Very Reverand John O. Anderson
Manitoba, **1954-1955**

D.L. Burgess
Ontario, **1956-1959**

Justice Mervyn Woods
Saskatchewan, **1960-1961**

Judge C.C. Sparling
Manitoba, **1962-1963**

F.T. O'Brecht
Ontario, 1964-1965

R.E. MacBeath
New Brunswick, 1966-1967

Robert Kohaly
Saskatchewan, 1968-1969

Justice J. Redmond Roche
Quebec, 1970-1971

Robert G. Smellie
Manitoba, 1972-1973

Robert D. McChesney
Ontario, 1974-1975

Douglas McDonald
Ontario, 1976-1977

Edward C. Coley
Alberta, 1978-1979

Al Harvey
Newfoundland, 1980-1981

Dave Capperauld
Ontario, 1982-1983

Steve Dunsdon
British Columbia, 1984-1985

Anthony Stacey
Ontario, 1986-1987

Gaston Garceau
Quebec, 1988-1989

Fred Williams
Newfoundland, 1990-1991

Jack Jolleys
British Columbia, 1992-1993

Hugh Greene
Alberta, 1994 - present

The history of The Royal Canadian Legion would not be complete without capturing some of the images that have been suspended in time through the art of photography. The collection displayed on these next few pages is designed to show some of the highlights of that history as well as a representation of Legion programs as they existed in the past and as they are today.

FIRST DOMINION CONVENTION, CANADIAN LEGION OF THE B·E·S·L.
WINNIPEG, JANUARY 24TH-29TH.1927

The first Canadian Legion Convention was held in Winnipeg, Manitoba between January 24 and 29, 1927.

The 1994 Convention, attended by more than 3,000 delegates and observers, was held in Calgary, Alberta.

The Vimy Pilgrimage and the unveiling of the Vimy Monument was a major event in the Legion's history, and one that was extremely emotional for those who made the voyage.

*R*oyal visits have always been memorable for veterans. In May 1939 His Majesty, King George the VI, and Queen Elizabeth attended the ceremony of the unveiling of the National War Memorial where they paused to shake hands with many of the World War One veterans who had gathered.

In November 1957, Her Majesty, Queen Elizabeth II met veterans from World War Two as she toured Canada.

Veterans and royalty continue to meet. His Royal Highness Prince Charles chats with legionnaires while on a visit to Prince George, British Columbia in 1986.

At the other end of the country, His Royal Highness, Prince Edward meets Fred King on a visit to Newfoundland.

■

During its 50th Anniversary year, The Royal Canadian Legion produced a song book of wartime favourites which is still in demand today although it is long out of print.

For the 50th Anniversary the torch became a major symbol of the Legion and its work.

In 1975 The Royal Canadian Legion was appointed as the godfather for Prince Floris of the Netherlands. In 1990 Dominion President Gaston Garceau chatted with the 15 year-old prince during a Veterans Affairs Canada pilgrimage to mark the 45th Anniversary of the Liberation of Holland by Canadian troops.

Thousands of military men and women upgraded their educations while serving during World War Two thanks to the Legion's educational programs. As can be seen, some of the "classrooms" were less than ideal.

At the beginning of World War Two the Canadian Legion of the British Empire Service League mobilized its resources to provide welfare, recreational and educational services to troops at home and abroad. The Canadian Legion War Services and the Canadian Legion Education Services were major efforts.

■

The Legion's mobile canteens were a source of news and a method for troops overseas to keep in touch with events at home.

CLWS clubs followed then troops wherever they went, even to Hamburg.

■

*C*LWS *huts, staffed by volunteers, like this one at the Prince of Wales Armouries in Edmonton, Alberta served hundreds of thousands of meals during the war. In this case it was it was just a tea break for soldiers following a route march.*

Troops overseas were provided with writing rooms by the CLWS, like this one in Brighton, England, 1943.

Reading rooms stocked with material provided by the Legion were common where military forces gathered. This typical reading room was at Yorkton, Saskatchewan.

The Legion was also in the theatre business. The Strand Theatre at the Canadian General Hospital in Italy had a line up to see Bob Hope's "Caught in the Draft".

■

The Legion provided numerous travelling entertainment troupes during the World War Two like the Canadian Legion All Stars.

■

Troops returning after the war were also cared for by the CLWS. The troops here are in a "Welcome Home Coach" in the Canadian National Railways coach yards at Pointe St. Charles, Quebec.

The Veterans Guard also provided security services at home.

A CLWS sports storage area in England during World War Two. The Legion supplied equipment and instructors to units.

On the home front Legions took care of those in hospitals...

...and provided entertainment and relaxation services for those who weren't.

There are numerous Legion programs for veterans, seniors, youth and the communties in which branches exist. Millions of dollars are used annually along with hundreds of thousands of volunteer hours.

∎

Remembrance and the poppy campaign are the major programs run by the Legion. The National Remembrance Ceremony is held annually in Ottawa on November 11. This ceremony was held on Parliament Hill with a temporary cenotaph prior to the unveiling of the National War Memorial in 1939.

On November 11 Canadians gather at cenotaphs and memorials across the nation to remember those who served and died for Canada. This group waiting to lay wreaths in Prince Rupert, British Columbia is representative of all those who attend these ceremonies.

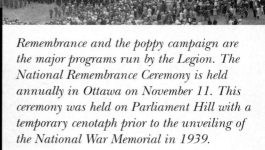

The Vice-Regal Group at the National War Memorial November 11, 1990.

A common occurrence around Remembrance Day is the appearance of veterans in schools to talk about their war time experiences and why remembrance is so important.

Remembrance is a year-round activity for legionnaires. New cenotaphs and memorials are always appearing like this one at the Honourable John Diefenbaker Branch in Laval, Quebec.

The poppy blooms every fall in Canada as a constant reminder to Canadians of those who went to war. Donations received are used to help veterans but thousands of poppies are distributed to school children free of charge to help promote remembrance.

Poppies were made by Vetcraft employing veterans until it ceased operations in 1995.

Veterans housing has been a priority since the formation of the Legion. This example of housing provided during the depression of the 1930's...

...stands in stark contrast to the housing ventures for veterans and seniors in which the Legion is involved today.

Seniors programs are many and varied in branches. It may be something as simple as a barbecue donated to a nursing home as was done in Fredericton Junction, New Brunswick by the Gladstone Branch Ladies Auxiliary...

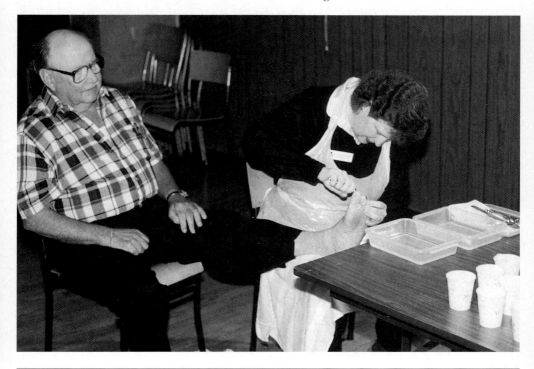

...or it could be the provision of seniors clinics such as this foot-care clinic run by the Victorian Order of Nurses provided by Northern Memorial Branch in Port Loring, Ontario.

Legion sports programs are popular and national championships are the end result. Curling is just one of the many played by members. Note the contrast in clothing from this competition in Summerside in the 1950's...

...to the clothing worn at this seniors meet in 1994.

Cribbage is a hotly contested game at most Legion branches and the national championship is a prize to be proud of. Prince Edward Island versus Ontario in this game from the 1994 championships.

Community support is the mainstay of the branches and medical equipment donations have always been a way for Legions to be involved in the community. In 1965 these wheelchairs were presented to the Department of Veterans Affairs Shaughnessy Hospital in Vancouver.

Today the demand continues for newer and better equipment like the fire and rescue equipment donated to the Milton, Ontario Fire Department by the Private Joe Waters Branch....

...and this trauma bed donated to the Lacombe, Alberta Community Health Centre by the Ladies Auxiliaries in Alberta Northwest Territories Command.

The Legion Book Depot closed in 1994 but in its heyday it provided hundreds of thousands of used books for troops in isolated areas and on missions around the world.

Youth programs are many and varied but the track and field program dates back to before this 1962 photo showing a travelling clinic reviewing the places it has conducted training.

■

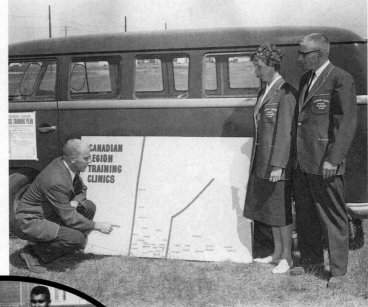

The quality of the athletes partaking in the training and the coaching is shown in this photo of Harry Jerome conducting training at a clinic. The program grew to become the national meet and clinic which celebrates its twentieth year in operation in 1995.

Cadets are sponsored by numerous branches across the country and appear at many Legion sponsored events such as the dedication of the Brock Fahrni veterans extended-care pavilion in Vancouver...

...or as cook's helpers at the Legion Convention in Calgary.

delivered in 1974, in which he estimated that there were about 500,000 former servicemen who might not be aware of the benefits for which they were eligible. Dubbed Operation Service, the project was launched on Vimy Day, April 9, 1976, as part of the Legion's 50th anniversary celebrations. It began with five pilot projects spread across Alberta, Saskatchewan, Manitoba-Northwestern Ontario and Ontario commands.

Reporting to the 1976 Dominion convention in Winnipeg, chairman Bert Harris told delegates: "There is, all our efforts notwithstanding, an abysmal ignorance of veterans' benefits even within our own ranks. What then of the veteran or dependant who has no affiliation with any veteran or veteran organization? We are aware that we cannot entirely cure the problem, but we are resolved to be a part of the solution."

Realizing that the success of Operation Service would depend entirely on the involvement of every branch, a two-hour seminar on the project was integrated into the golden anniversary convention. Billed by incoming Dominion president Doug McDonald as the Legion's "last great effort to ensure the veteran is aware of what the veterans' legislation provides," Operation Service was granted a budget of $250,000 by the delegates.

Looking back on the project 10 years later, Jean Lamy recalled that Operation Service "worked as well as we could have expected. It began with a lot of enthusiasm, but it's always hard to sustain that kind of enthusiasm for a long period. Some branches certainly got behind it fully." So much so that, in some communities, legionnaires literally went door to door asking about the status of the inhabitants. As the project wrapped up in 1978 the government reported that pension claims had increased by 49 per cent, largely as a result of the Legion's efforts.

Flush with the success of the changes to veterans' legislation and the early enthusiasm of Operation Service, the Legion received a cold splash of water in the fall of 1976 when news leaked out that the Trudeau government was planning on relocating the Department of Veterans Affairs from Ottawa to Charlottetown.

"Fortunately we found out about the plan from (NDP MP) Stanley Knowles before the official announcement was made, so we had time to prepare a response," recalled Lamy. On October 29, the day after the government stated its plans, the Legion formally announced its opposition to the move on the grounds that it would lead to a deterioration of services for veterans. The findings of a government task force on the move seemed to bear out the Legion's fears; only 20.5 per cent of Veterans Affairs' headquarters staff said they were prepared to make the move to Prince Edward Island. Still, Minister MacDonald insisted that this would be sufficient to ensure continuity of service after the move.

MacDonald's heart attack slowed development of the plan, but on January 27, 1978, the minister announced that a site on Charlottetown's waterfront had been selected for the new Veterans Affairs headquarters. Later in the year it seemed that the government's restraint policy, which called for the department to cut $30 million from its budget, might scuttle the move. There were problems with MacDonald's favored site, too. The waterfront site proved too costly, and negotiations began to purchase another downtown piece of property.

Without warning, on November 28, MacDonald announced plans to begin moving Veterans Affairs' employees in 1979, two years ahead of the previously announced timetable. Quickly, the Legion stepped up its campaign to have the move quashed. Legion Magazine (the name adopted by The Legionary in 1969) had been hammering away at the plan in its editorials. Then, in February 1979, Dominion president Ed Coley wrote to all MPs and senators to elicit their support against the move: "We are in sympathy with the plan to create jobs in Prince Edward Island but not at the expense of disabled war veterans. We, therefore, wish to enlist your support in our endeavors to keep the pension commission and its 250-300 staff members in Ottawa. Alternate plans could be devised to move another agency to Prince Edward Island in order to cater to the economic needs there, without adversely affecting the status of war veterans.

"We wrote to the president of the treasury board twice — in October and November 1978. His response did not offer any encouragement that the government was prepared to examine a possible change of plan.

"We now wish to make all honorable senators and members of Parliament aware of the urgent need for action to keep the pension commission in Ottawa."

A new ray of hope appeared in June 1979, when Trudeau's Liberals were defeated by the Progressive Conservatives led by Joe Clark. Clark's appointment as Veterans Affairs minister, Allan McKinnon, promised a full review of the proposed move. Unfortunately, McKinnon did not pull a lot of weight in Clark's cabinet. As secretary of state, Prince Edward Island MP David MacDonald was far more powerful in the prime minister's so-called inner cabinet — a fact that became clear when MacDonald publicly embarrassed McKinnon over a story in the Charlottetown Guardian. No sooner had the paper published a story stating McKinnon would cancel the move of the pension commission if he discovered that two provisos had not been met — 1) that plans had not advanced past the point of no return, and 2) that the overall move would not cost more than $35 million — than MacDonald announced that Clark supported the move. McKinnon immediately issued a news release, stating: "In accordance with the prime minister's recent announcement, that the ministers of the new government would undertake a full review of departmental plans and projects, the minister has examined the proposed relocation plans and decided that the advantages of relocation to the province of Prince Edward Island, warranted the decision to proceed."

"A full review?" scoffed a *Legion Magazine* editorial.

Mirroring early campaigns against the proposed pension means test and the new flag, the Legion stepped up its pressure on the Clark government to recant. *Legion Magazine* published anti-relocation editorials from the *Globe and Mail* and quoted statistics indicating that service would surely suffer if the move went ahead. Coley and Lamy had an acrimonious meeting with Secretary of State MacDonald, but their threats to use the force of the Legion's 560,000 votes against the Conservatives went nowhere. In an attempt to show legionnaires just where their local MP stood, *Legion Magazine* devised a plan to poll all 282 members of the House and 103 senators and publish the results. Conducted two weeks before the sudden fall of the Clark government, the survey indicated 80 MPs in favor of the move, 59 opposed, 11 undecided and 132 failed to answer. Twelve senators voted in favor, 20 were opposed, four undecided, and 67 failed to answer. The results were published in full in the January 1980 edition.

Clark's unexpected defeat on a motion of non-confidence put the relocation question up for grabs, and while the Legion did not succeed in making it a national election issue, Lamy believed that it was responsible for the defeat of David MacDonald in his riding, despite the long-standing policy of non-partisanship. "The P.E.I. Legion worked against him," said Lamy, "and whether or not legionnaires succeeded in rallying support against him, MacDonald paid for his stand."

"Back to the trenches" was the title of the lead editorial in *Legion Magazine* in March 1980, which called for legionnaires to make newly elected MPs aware of the issue. But the writing was on the wall. With Dan MacDonald back in the Veterans Affairs portfolio in the new Trudeau government it was obvious that the move was not going to be stopped. Opposition to the plan quietly disappeared from the magazine's pages, and Legion officials got on with the business of pushing for a smooth transition from Ottawa to the East Coast. In November 1980, just over a month after the minister's sudden death at age 62, the Dominion Executive Council went on record as accepting the move to Charlottetown and embraced the idea of naming the new headquarters after him. "No one can win them all and grace in defeat is worth cultivating," stated a *Legion Magazine* editorial.

Chapter 17

CHANGING WAYS...
AND MEANS

By the mid-1960s the Legion had established itself as one of Canada's most active community-service organizations. Aside from its tradi- tional role in assisting veterans, their families and survivors, it had become ingrained in the social life of every community where a branch was located. And while charity began at home, it did not necessarily end there. In response to a personal plea from Lord Louis Mountbatten, grand president of the British Commonwealth Ex-Services League, Dominion president Fred O'Brecht committed the Legion to provide aid to overseas veterans.

Mountbatten was the Legion's special guest in Montreal for the 21st Dominion convention in April 1966. He regaled the 1,474 delegates and their guests with anecdotes and impersonations of the late Winston Churchill, and left with O'Brecht's promise that the Legion would assist veterans in the developing countries of the Commonwealth. Noting that Canada was about to celebrate its 100th birthday, Mountbatten asked dele- gates to look ahead to the second hundred years. "What can you contribute to the second century?" he asked. "This, I trust, will be the underlying theme of this convention. The Legion today is stronger than at any time in its history. It has made bold changes in the past and it needs boldness for the future..."

He said that if the Legion wanted to find new challenges, it should look no further than the plight of millions of destitute veterans around the world in emerging Commonwealth countries.

Assistance to the Commonwealth was not the only pressing financial concern, either. For many years the Legion's central staff had worked as much out of devotion to the veterans' cause as any financial reward, but times were changing. Bob Kohaly, chairman of both the ways and means committee and the newly formed Dominion Command financial advisory committee, recognized that the staff's salaries and benefits needed to be upgraded if the Legion was going to continue to attract talented people.

The national sports program was another leading expense, and, while it was achieving its goals, the ongoing membership drive also demanded a considerable investment.

"Going to the convention every two years with your hand out for small per capita increases was useless," recalled Kohaly. "We needed to build up a reserve of funds, but we knew we'd have a fight on our hands if we put it that way." Faced with Mountbatten's request for additional funding, Kohaly devised a way to raise capital that became a part of Legion lore.

"Fred called me to his hotel room where he was having breakfast with Lord Louis," he remembered, "and he told me that he had just made this promise to assist the BCEL (British Commonwealth Ex-Services League). 'I want you to come up with a way to raise the money,' he told me. Now, I only had about an hour to think of something, so I decided to tell the boys a story."

His story involved a midnight walk he told delegates he had taken the previous night. He said he had wandered over to Montreal's cenotaph, where he had encountered an impoverished veteran searching through a trashcan for food. With that image planted in the delegates' minds, Kohaly made his pitch for an unprecedented per capita increase of 50 cents.

"Then, I sat down and ate an apple while I waited to get a seconder to the motion. That speech is still legendary across the Legion. No matter where I go, someone will come up to me and ask me if I want another 50 cents from them.

"But that made the Legion fiscally responsible. It gave us the capital we needed to work with, to build the organization into what we knew it could be."

Delegates also acclaimed Kohaly first vice-president, in an election that saw Ron MacBeath acclaimed president. Fifty-four years old, MacBeath was a Moncton native who had served with the New Brunswick Rangers and the North Shore Regiment in World War II. Discharged as a captain in 1945, he had returned to New Brunswick and built a successful contracting business. While not part of the so-called mafia that was quickly rising to power, others in the upper ranks of the Legion considered him a well-organized, thoughtful man who recognized the talents of those around him.

Redmond Roche, the Montreal judge, was acclaimed second vice-president. Art Adams, 64, a retired Bell Telephone executive from Toronto, defeated Jack Oldham of Medicine Hat, Alberta, and Donald McTavish of Salmon Arm, British Columbia, for third vice-president.

Ronnie Stewart defeated former vice-chairman Jean Miquelon of Ottawa to begin his ninth term as honorary treasurer. Incumbent Chester Merriam was unopposed in his bid to return as chairman. Vice-chairman Myles Murray defeated Henry Harvey of Ottawa and John MacIsaac of Borden, Prince Edward Island, to retain his position.

Kohaly's per capita increase was not the only financial matter before the delegates in Montreal. Significant interest was also focused on the first report of the Centennial Fund committee, now chaired by Bob Jones. He reminded the convention of the principles that Mervyn Woods had established for the fund before resigning in the fall of 1965, which included:

- projects to be funded could include bursaries, the Legion Sports Training Plan, student exchanges with other Commonwealth countries, promotion of Commonwealth unity, and memorial projects;

- funds were to be invested by a trust company with administration by a board of trustees under guidance of the Dominion Executive Council;

- funds were not to be used for operating expenses, but could be used to continue welfare services to veterans and their dependants;

- each command would appoint a Centennial Fund chairman;

- command quotas were to be based on approximately $4 per member, as of December 31, 1964.

Jones said that returns had been slower than anticipated because of the amount of organization required within each command. To date, the fund had reached about 30 per cent of its goal of $1 million. A questionnaire was circulated among delegates, seeking suggestions of how the fund might be used.

In the months following the convention, an Executive Council subcommittee on the Centennial Fund met and appointed five trustees to administer the fund: Dominion president MacBeath; past president O'Brecht; Brig. James deLalanne, a retired chartered accountant and a veteran of both world wars; H.D. Graham, former president of the Toronto Stock Exchange and a retired lieutenant-general; and L.T. Price, a businessman from British Columbia. The trustees met for the first time on October 21, 1966, and officially signed the indenture to create the fund. At subsequent meetings in 1967 and 1968, the trustees determined to invest the money from the different commands in various securities on the advice of five different investment houses, rather than relying on a trust company. The average annual yield on the investments was seven per cent.

Unfortunately, the money was not flowing into the Centennial Fund as quickly as planned. In the spring of 1967 it became clear that the fund would not reach its goal by July 1. In fact, by the end of 1967, only Prince Edward Island, New Brunswick and Saskatchewan commands had reached their targets. When the 1968 Dominion convention was convened in Penticton, British Columbia, the fund was still $70,000 short of its goal. Faced with this shortfall, Ontario, Alberta and the host Pacific commands stepped forward to make up the difference. Quebec Command, which had only reached 57 per cent of its quota, presented Bob Jones with cheques totalling $17,500 — boosting its tally to 86 per cent of its goal. By the end of the convention, the fund stood at $1,014,030.

Voting on the report of the fund's trustees, the record-setting 2,121 delegates determined not to touch the principal or interest of the fund until after the 1970 convention. In the intervening two years Dominion Command would canvas all branches to obtain suggestions for use of the fund.

As expected, Kohaly completed his steady climb to the top of the Legion's ladder with his acclamation as Dominion president. Both Redmond Roche and Art Adams also moved up one rung by acclamation.

The fight for third vice-president was more interesting. Most Legion insiders had assumed that "mafia" member Dave Hunter was a shoo-in, but early in the proceedings he became embroiled in a shouting match on the convention floor over a minor issue. His outburst cost him the election, allowing Bob Smellie, a 44-year-old Manitoba lawyer, to defeat him, Jack Oldham of Medicine Hat, and Jack Tattrie of Truro, Nova Scotia.

Ronnie Stewart, the honorary treasurer since 1950, had resigned the previous December, and the convention confirmed the Executive Council's appointment of the 71-year-old Montrealer James deLalanne as his successor.

Chairman Merriam was acclaimed, and vice-chairman Myles Murray defeated Jaimer Hall of Trail, British Columbia.

As ordered by the convention, Dominion Command conducted an all-branch survey in early 1969 to gather suggestions about possible uses for the Centennial Fund. At their meeting in October that year, the Executive Council approved a recommendation from the fund's trustees that neither the principal nor the interest be touched until at least 1974 and that utilization of the fund be reviewed at two-year intervals. That recommendation was the subject of protracted debate at the 1970 Dominion convention in Ottawa — a meeting dominated by financial concerns.

Many among the 1,379 delegates objected to the decision to leave the Centennial Fund's accrued interest untouched, and the Executive Council's recommendation was amended to reflect their desire. With that decision in hand, a motion was introduced to use some of the interest to support the Legion Sports Training Plan, which had lost its government funding. After vigorous debate, the motion was defeated.

The other main financial issue resulted from a dramatic increase in postal rates for magazines in Canada. The cost of mailing *Legion Magazine* had increased by 1,400 per cent in 1969 — from half-a-penny to seven cents a copy — forcing the Legion to switch to a smaller format, reduce the number of pages per issue and drop two monthly issues. Faced with this crisis, the provincial commands had voted for a one-time per capita allocation, but if the magazine was to continue, said Kohaly, delegates would have to agree to a $1 annual per capita increase — bringing the total fee to $3.40. This additional money would double the cost of a subscription to *Legion Magazine* to $2 per year. The members agreed to the increase.

The 1970 convention was also notable because of changes to the elected officer structure introduced by the national standing committee on organization and planning, which had been formed in July 1968. In its report to the convention, the committee stated: "Under the present system, it has become almost axiomatic that the person elected to the office of third Dominion vice-president will succeed to the presidency six years later. This method practically commits the candidate for third vice-president to be willing to serve on the sub-executive committee for the next 10 years. Such a commitment must surely limit the candidates for financial, business and domestic reasons.

"As a broader and more effective system, we propose that a group of four executive officers would be elected without specific reference to precedence within the group and, further, that each Dominion convention would elect one vice-president only.

"Your committee also considers that the position of Dominion vice-chairman is redundant and that the Dominion president should be empowered to appoint an acting Dominion chairman as the need arises."

The recommendations were accepted by the convention, and voting proceeded under the new guidelines.

Redmond Roche was unchallenged for president. A lawyer since the early 1930s, he had enlisted in the Army in 1939 and ended the war with the rank of colonel. A member of Montreal's elite Jean Brilliant VC Branch, he had first become involved in the veterans' movement as Quebec president of the Army Benevolent Fund. He was elected Quebec Command president in 1963, a year before being recruited by former Dominion president Basil Price to stand for election to the Dominion executive.

As might have been anticipated, the new voting procedure produced a race for the position formerly known as first vice-president — the first since 1958. Nominated were second vice-president Art Adams and third vice-president Bob Smellie. While Smellie, when he first entered the national scene, had not gained the immediate support of Kohaly and his influential devotees because they felt he had not put in the requisite years at the branch, zone and provincial command levels, he had won their respect. At age 46, he was seen by them as being considerably more progressive than the 66-year-old Adams. Smellie got their support, and the post of vice-president.

Five men contested the four executive officer posts: Dave Hunter of Vancouver; Bob McChesney, Kohaly's protégé from Kirkland Lake, Ontario; Jim Fagan of St. John's; Ed Coley of Edmonton; and Rupert McCabe of Edmundston, New Brunswick. Hunter, McChesney, Fagan and Coley were elected.

Incumbents Chester Merriam and James deLalanne were acclaimed as chairman and honorary treasurer respectively.

The sweeping changes instituted by the organization and planning committee indicated how much power it had accumulated in less than two years. Led by Doug McDonald, the 44-year-old Brantford, Ontario, businessman — a hard-driving and outspoken confidante of Kohaly — the committee had a broad mandate to "recommend the improvement of or the addition to (the) organization and programs in the face of changing conditions."

In his initial report to the convention, McDonald stated: "We are aware that many practices and procedures that exist in the Legion today have been a part of the Legion since its inception, and this has been part of the Legion's strength. However, we must recognize that the Legion has grown immensely in numbers and accomplishments. This remarkable growth has also produced a situation whereby more immediate executive decisions and administrative action are required so that these heavier demands can be more effectively managed.

"(The) committee considers that there is a continuing need for the Legion to examine itself with a view to being better prepared to face the future..."

McDonald was always careful to acknowledge the input of all commands, but his message was clear: the Legion is too prosperous and active to operate by consensus — leadership by muddling about, as it became known in the business jargon of the 1990s. It was time to run the Legion like the big business it was — to get lean and, when necessary, mean. "We set our priorities," said McDonald, "and we had a scheme to change the whole organization to make it more effective." The committee's motto, introduced at the Ottawa convention, was "Soar into the '70s."

One area that both McDonald and Kohaly recognized needed changing was the relationship between the provincial commands and Dominion Command headquarters. In his farewell speech as president, Kohaly made a point of explaining the role that headquarters staff played as secretaries on national committees and in preparing background on projects. McDonald's report made it clear that there was a lack of communication and trust between the staff members in Ottawa and the membership in the provinces.

"The staff were considered deadweight by the membership," recalled Kohaly in 1985. "People on the other side of the country couldn't necessarily see how dedicated these people were to veterans and the organization."

In Jean Lamy, who took over as Dominion secretary on April 1, 1971, the Legion found an administrator determined to make the most of his staff. "There was a very bad atmosphere," said Lamy. "People were constantly sniping at headquarters and some bad feelings had been allowed to build up... Most of the problems could be solved by talking."

Lamy found a staff that had been polarized by their dealings with various elected officers. "Some officers had allied themselves with particular staff members, and they would use those relationships to get things done their way. That had to stop. One thing I insisted on was that the staff had to report directly to me; that was the only way to overcome petty jealousies and favoritism. Things had to be run like a business."

One project that Lamy instituted immediately was to computerize the Legion's membership list and manage renewals with pre-punched computer cards.

Another initiative was to encourage staff members to generate ideas, which could then be moved up to the various committees for discussion.

"Branches will do the job, but they need leadership," said Kohaly. "Dominion Command planted many of the seeds that subsequently grew from the bottom." One of Kohaly's other pet theories was that competition bred the best ideas, which had led him to create McDonald's organization and planning committee, as well as a leadership and development committee, which was chaired by Dave Hunter.

"The membership committee had too many strong members," said Kohaly, "so we spun off these new committees and sent them out to start recruiting all over again."

Formed on July 28, 1968, the leadership and development committee had a two-pronged mandate: to plan and promote the best possible officer training, branch activity and programming at all levels of the Legion; and to establish and maintain close liaison with the national organization and planning committee, as well as with the standing membership committee. In concert with McDonald and membership chairman Bob McChesney, Hunter's committee set out eight goals for itself:

- prepare and promote leadership seminars and workshops;
- assist each command to organize a provincial leadership committee to conduct seminars or workshops at the zone and district levels;
- give other assistance to provincial commands or committees;
- prepare materials for command seminars and workshops;
- explore modern techniques in seminar and workshop presentation, especially in the field of motivation;
- develop programs and activities recommended by the organization and planning committee;
- assist the membership committee;
- encourage an administrative chain of command in all commands that will benefit all levels of the Legion.

Viewed in isolation, the formation of the organization and planning and leadership and development committees, and their cross-ties with the membership committee, makes crystal clear the strategy of Kohaly's "mafia." The lifeblood of the Legion, as had been said so many times, was membership. As the clout behind the organization's lobbying efforts, as the source of operating income, and as a workforce for the benefit of the community, new legionnaires were essential. Kohaly may have left behind the role of membership chairman, but he had never lost sight of the goal he set himself at the 1962 convention. One way or another, the Legion's membership was going to grow.

"My philosophy has always been, if you're not moving ahead you're moving backwards," he said. "The Legion was on a terminal course, but it didn't need to be."

Chapter 18

NEW AVENUES FOR GROWTH

I n 1966, four years after Bob Kohaly accepted the challenge to reorganize the Legion's membership campaign, there were just over 280,000 legionnaires. That represented a growth of 30,000, but Kohaly was far from satisfied.

In his report to the 1966 Dominion convention, he delivered a blistering assessment of the Legion's health, and laid the groundwork for the changes he would institute two years later:

"The Royal Canadian Legion is unknown. Nobody from the Dominion president to the newest member knows the Legion. Each of us may think he does. We know a segment of it, perhaps, like the blind man exploring an elephant, but each of us depicts it as something different and something very incomplete.

"For instance, how many delegates can accurately tell this convention what the total Legion expenditure on low-rental housing for our senior citizens now stands at? Or how many children participate in our overall sports programs? Even the most ardent welfare officer cannot accurately tell us what our annual welfare disbursements are, or how much money we spend annually on education. This is what we mean by the 'unknown Legion.'

"Most of us are aware that the above activities are taking place. We know that the Legion is creating an impact on the nation. But we are ignorant when it comes to knowing the full extent of the Legion's role on the Canadian scene.

"Why do we have such ignorance of our organization?

"Because:

1) We are suffering from poor communications and liaison at all levels.

2) There is a lack of training and education in Legion matters.

3) There is a lack of continuity.

4) There is a lack of enthusiasm.

"How can we justify these statements? These views, comrades, are not merely the thoughts of your membership committee; they are also the statements which your committee has heard over the past two years in conducting membership clinics across Canada.

"These remarks kept recurring at places such as Fredericton, Winnipeg, Vancouver and Toronto, as member after member in workshop discussions indicated that these four points were among the major problems facing branch officers. For instance, in Winnipeg we heard that much of the membership material which has been in use for at least three years had never been seen before by many branch representatives. This, we suggest, is the result of poor liaison between the personnel who received the mail and those on the membership committee to whom the mail was directed.

"The workshops at both Winnipeg and Vancouver expressed a desperate desire for some form of formal training in Legion matters. Other branch officers report that the lack of continuity in branch chairmen and officers tends to inhibit the progress of programs.

"There was a consensus that while branch members might be willing to serve on a given committee, they were getting no guidance and not enough leadership.

"In order to effectively tell the Legion story to the public and to members we must have planning, knowledge of what is going on, and personnel who are capable of interpreting these programs to others...

"It is the firm belief of all committee members that it is imperative to continue to maintain a vigorous membership campaign. While this does involve money, time and considerable planning, we feel that without a continuing program membership will falter and drop. Furthermore, the money spent on membership is offset by the increase in revenue..."

In the months following the 1966 convention the membership committee set out across the country again, holding clinics in nine cities. Each clinic began with a session that included everyone, then the participants broke off into smaller workshop groups with assigned topics. In addition to membership, the topics also covered the importance of public relations and good leadership.

In his committee's presentation to the 1968 convention in Penticton, Kohaly reported that membership had climbed to 295,000, and was expected to reach the 300,000 mark by year's end. Although he was more upbeat than in 1966, calling the increase since 1962 "not only gratifying but amazing," he outlined the need for continued efforts to reach out into the community and attract eligible members.

"I would ask you to become objective — to put yourself in the place of the non-member — before answering my next question," he said. "Why should a veteran join the Legion today?

"Consider this. Your World War II veteran has been out of service for 23 years — almost a quarter of a century. He has made a life for himself, has various interests such as church, sports, professional and other community undertakings. He is re-established — that word itself is almost obsolete — has few pension problems and little sentimental attachment to the old days.

"Why should such a man consider joining the Legion?

"Would he join because of the Legion's role in the establishment of veterans' legislation, or would he be impressed by the work of the veterans' poppy fund in his community? Perhaps he would join because he suddenly felt an admiration for the Legion's community service program, or because his son or daughter had become involved in the Legion's sports training plan.

"The member we want would join because of all these factors.

"But he will not remain in the Legion unless he is given some challenge, some opportunity to participate in a constructive program.

"The branch needs an image. Furthermore, it must live up to that image by holding a member's interest. Each member must feel that he is needed and is making a contribution to something worthwhile. This can only be done if every member is systematically given an opportunity to serve.

"We fail our branch and we fail the new member when we make him a vague offer of comradeship and service in exchange for his dues, and an equally vague appeal for his assistance on some undefined project at some undetermined time.

"Perhaps this man at some time in the past had the appalling experience of sitting through a poorly conducted branch meeting; perhaps he was once a member who was completely ignored by the branch during a lengthy illness. Or he might be a stranger who is most unimpressed by what he sees at the local branch."

He praised several commands for conducting their own membership and leadership courses, and told delegates to insist that their commands accept their share of the responsibility to get the job done. "We must proceed with the training of officers at all levels at the fastest possible rate. We must use all means available to make the Legion more attractive to others. This applies to management, public relations and programming."

He stressed pragmatism, and told members that a "hard sell" was needed to combat the growing use of the media for other community causes.

"Let us not be so emotional about the Legion that we fail to realize that over 50 per cent of our population today has no recollection of the war. Also, let us not be deluded into thinking that the public is going to remain pro-veteran when they cannot even remember what the war was all about. The public is changing. It is preoccupied. It is cynical and is bombarded daily by good causes.

"There are many worthy organizations today in any community. You cannot turn on the TV without being deluged with messages from a multitude of worthy causes. Most of these are very current. They apply to what is going on in India or Asia today. The public feels a tremendous sense of urgency when they look at a photograph of a starving child with a distended stomach, holding out its hands for a bowl of rice. The same applies to the heart fund, the blind, the arthritic and the handicapped. All of these things evoke a great deal of sympathy because they are things which are here, today, in front of us.

"As I said, over 50 per cent of today's population does not even remember World War II. They are more concerned about the war in Vietnam or the possibility of a third world war than they are about the Second World War or the historical First World War. Whereas after World War I the public was quite veteran-conscious, today this no longer applies."

One factor that went unmentioned in Kohaly's report but that continued to rankle the membership committee and other Legion officials — particularly with the financial woes besetting the organization in the late '60s — was the presence at branches of so-called fraternals. Since the earliest days of the Legion, branches had reserved the right to open their doors to people who wanted to take advantage of the social atmosphere offered there. Most were not eligible for membership, but many were.

To the "mafia" these social members presented two problems. First, they represented hundreds of thousands of dollars in potential per capita tax, and second, they bolstered the Legion's image as a drinking establishment. The Legion's association with alcohol — beer in particular — has offered a challenge to public relations efforts throughout its history.

"A lot of the three-B image (booze, beer and bingo) is our own fault," said Al Harvey, Dominion president from 1980 to '82. "We haven't always been good about publicizing the other facets of the organization, so that's what people at the community level see of us."

"The veteran originally encouraged the beer-drinking image when he returned from war," agreed Kohaly. "You can't blame them, because they drank a hell of a lot of muddy water out of a helmet to pay for it, but still it's something we have to live with."

The use of the Legion's influence in some areas to obtain liquor licences, or favorable treatment, did not help either. In Manitoba, for many years, the Legion hall was the only licensed establishment where a man and woman could drink together. In Prince Edward Island, the Legions were the only licensed establishments, so the provincial authorities forced them to provide public areas on their premises. Still, in 1976, only 56 per cent of Legion branches were licensed, although every large branch with more than 1,000 members had a licence.

To the branches who welcomed fraternals, though, image was less important than the revenue realized from beer sales. What was the harm, they argued, of taking the money of these outsiders since it was being used for all of the branch's good works at the community level. But social members could drink at the branch — or participate in intermural sports — without any type of formal affiliation to the Legion. As long as this was so, Kohaly and his cronies in the leadership and planning and organization and development committees felt that the organization would be tainted in the eyes of some potential members. It fell to Doug McDonald, chairman of the organization and development committee, to introduce the unpopular motion to force fraternals to pay Legion dues.

"The showdown came at the 1970 convention," he recalled. "The resolution was in my report along with the changes to the officer structure and voting procedures. We wanted every advantage possible, so we scheduled the vote on it right after lunch to try and limit debate on it. We also forced a secret vote on the motion to ensure that it would be a free vote. But, even with these manoeuvers, we knew it was going to be close."

Debate on the motion — which would leave the acceptance of fraternals to each command, limit the number of fraternal affiliates to less than 30 per cent of a branch or command's total ordinary, life and associate membership, and restrict the granting of fraternal status to those not eligible for other types of membership — was long and heated. Many members spoke out against Dominion Command imposing its will on the branches, in contravention, some said, of the principle of branch autonomy. The vote, which included ballots by proxy, was 1,357 in favor and 1,320 against.

"There was a lot of bitterness over it," said McDonald. "After the vote people came up to my hotel room and ripped up their membership cards."

At its regular post-convention meeting, the Dominion Executive Council decided that the new bylaw would not come into effect until January 1, 1972, in order to give commands time to discuss the fraternal question at their conventions. In most cases, this would have been a straightforward procedure; however, with the matter of branch autonomy and lost revenue on the line, Nova Scotia Command bucked against the new bylaw.

"Some commands grumbled about it," said then-Dominion secretary Jean Lamy, "but Nova Scotia flatly refused." Dominion president Roche agreed that Bert Harris and Lamy should go to Halifax to sort things out. The command officials still refused to comply; in fact they were so stubborn that they wouldn't even call them a taxi.

The dispute simmered through 1972, until finally the newly elected president, Bob Smellie, began the necessary steps to suspend the command's charter. Faced with the prospect of being forced out of the Legion, Nova Scotia reluctantly complied.

By 1973, 48,000 fraternal affiliates were paying dues. Over time, the number of fraternals grew to more than 100,000.

Even before the additional per capita fee began to flow into the Legion's coffers from the fraternals, membership reached a new plateau in the early 1970s — topping 300,000 in 1970. At the Ottawa convention, Bob McChesney, who had taken over from Kohaly as membership chairman, reviewed what he called "the memorable membership decade of the '60s." With the backdrop of the 52,000-member increase of the previous 10 years,

McChesney repeated Kohaly's familiar refrain about the need for branches to work hard at keeping members active.

What was never broached in committee reports, nor on the convention floor, was the idea — dormant since 1931 — that the Legion open its doors to another entire classification of member: the sons and daughters of legionnaires. More than a few of those planning the Legion's future remembered what Sir Percy Lake had expressed in 1928, when the organization was only two years old: "We are pledged to hand down our ideals to our children. The best way to do it is to bring them into the Legion and interest them in our work." The question was how.

Although Smellie, McChesney and McDonald all believed that allowing legionnaires' children to join was the only logical way to keep the organization viable into the future, they realized that the push to make it happen would have to come from the grassroots. If branches and commands perceived that the concept was being forced on them from above there would be too much opposition to overcome. If commands balked at the idea, it might die on the vine. In addition, not everyone in a position of authority in the Legion was convinced that offspring should be allowed to join.

"I had my doubts that the organization could, or should continue without veterans," said longtime constitutional expert Charles Rhodes Smith.

Those in Kohaly's cabal, who stood united on the question of succession, knew that if influential voices like Rhodes Smith's spoke against the idea, it might well be doomed to failure. Slowly, though, the idea began to take root. Alberta-Northwest Territories Command is generally credited with being the first to openly debate the issue, although many members within Ontario Command also saw the potential of ensuring that the Legion would continue after the last veteran died. At the Dominion Command level, it once again fell to McDonald's organization and development committee to come up with a resolution on sons and daughters that would be palatable to a majority of convention delegates, and a strategy to ensure that the issue did not become divisive.

As it turned out, it was an issue that would dominate proceedings at the next four Dominion conventions.

Chapter 19

THE LIVING LEGACY

T he 24th Dominion convention in Regina, held May 21-25, 1972, drew the largest number of people ever — 1,587 delegates, 760 guests and 154 fraternals — and ushered in changes that significantly altered the Legion's makeup.

The organization and planning committee couched its recommendations — which included extension of ordinary membership and the creation of associate membership for sons and daughters — in the form of a motion for "progressive change." Even though this resolution itself would change nothing, it prompted vigorous debate.

"Let's face it," said one delegate speaking to the motion, "we're getting a little long in the tooth and in 10 or 15 years we'll have neither the stamina nor the inclination to work like we do now. Who's going to take over the responsibilities that our communities have come to depend on us to assume? Who's going to sponsor and coach the hockey teams, worry about helping retarded kids expand their horizons to their fullest potential, make sure the hospital has a resuscitator, start a youth band, acquire expertise in housing development so old people who have worked all their lives building this country can live in dignity and comfort? I've worked damned hard in this organization and I want to know it's going to go on after me."

As reasonable and articulate as that argument was, many delegates were opposed to the idea of change. A standing vote on the motion for progressive change proved inconclusive. The motion passed on a ballot vote, but it was clear that the membership changes would be anything but a cakewalk.

Nevertheless, the convention eventually supported the organization and development committee's recommendation that ordinary membership be extended to members of the Armed Forces, reservists with at least two years' experience and veterans with at least three months' active service in

Allied forces. A proposal to admit members of the RCMP with two years' service was tabled for further consideration.

Of course, the most contentious issue was whether to open the associate category to the children of life and ordinary members, and deceased ex-service personnel who were eligible for ordinary membership at the time of their death. Some delegates were vehement that the Legion should remain a veterans' organization, even if that meant winding down operations by the end of the century, as the last veterans became too old to carry on. Veterans' children, said one, were no more likely to relate to the Legion's concerns "than someone off the street." Another said that the legacy of peace veterans had fought for should be enough for the younger generation. More than one expressed the wish that the Legion should die with the last veteran.

Those who spoke in favor were just as passionate. "I hope," concluded one, "that we never have to have another war to qualify for membership in this organization."

Debate raged into a second day, a third and then a fourth. When the vote was finally called, the first two voice votes did not give chairman Chester Merriam a clear indication of the delegates' wishes; neither did a standing vote. Finally, the issue was determined by a ballot vote. Sons and daughters would be able to join the Legion as of January 1, 1974, although they could not vote or hold elective office.

"It took two years of selling to get them to accept the idea of associates," said Doug McDonald. "All things considered, it was an easier sell than the fraternals, but we just didn't know for sure going into it. It's hard to read the mood of a convention sometimes. Small, offshoot things can throw you off getting important things done. Somebody can say something that can change the entire course of debate on an issue and there's nothing you can do but watch the thing go down the drain. I think we laid the groundwork well by introducing the idea of associates at all levels before it came to the convention."

McDonald's committee also introduced changes to the elected officer structure. Following up on the changes introduced in 1970, the committee's report recommended altering the title of vice-president to executive vice-president and the title of executive officer to vice-president. It also recommended dropping the word "honorary" from the title of the Dominion treasurer.

Bob Smellie, 48, a member of Russell, Manitoba, Branch, was acclaimed president. A veteran of the Normandy landing, where he served with the Royal Winnipeg Rifles and was wounded, Smellie was a protégé of former Manitoba premier Duff Roblin — himself a former command first vice-president. Elected to the Manitoba legislature in 1958 as a member of Roblin's government, Smellie served as municipal affairs minister from 1963 to '66. He was Manitoba Command's chairman from 1965 until his election to Dominion Command in 1968.

Bob McChesney was elected executive vice-president by acclamation.

Seven legionnaires faced off for the four vice-president posts: incumbents Ed Coley, Jim Fagan and Dave Hunter; and newcomers McDonald, Paul Burden of Fredericton, Ray Tuokko of Kakabeka Falls, Ontario, and Jack Tattrie of Truro, Nova Scotia. McDonald joined Coley, Fagan and Hunter on the executive. Hunter would subsequently resign in 1973 and be replaced by Tuokko, an Ontario provincial civil servant, in a special vote by the Dominion Executive Council.

Incumbents Chester Merriam and James deLalanne were acclaimed as chairman and treasurer respectively.

"We thought we had planned for the smooth integration of associate members," said McDonald, "but we hadn't counted on the young people's lack of feeling for service groups." The Legion may have thought that sons and daughters would knock down branches' doors to get in, but only 2,411 people signed up during the first year after the historic vote. Pacific Command — one of those along with Alberta-Northwest Territories and Ontario to embrace the concept early on — led the way with 1,106. Prince Edward Island recruited just one.

The question of sons and daughters was not itself on the table for debate at the 1974 Dominion convention in St. John's, but the 1972 decision to admit them was reflected in other discussions. The organization and development committee, now chaired by vice-president Coley, stressed the need for branches to indoctrinate and train associates for the day when they could assume office. The question of extending membership to conscripts of the two world wars who refused to serve overseas was back again, directly as a result of the associate vote. Once again, delegates turned thumbs down on allowing them in, although it was now so close an issue that a standing vote was required.

Reporting on membership, McDonald said that 10,000 sons and daughters had joined, many in the closing months of 1973. Overall, membership had increased by 6.5 per cent, or 20,018, over the previous two years.

For the third consecutive convention, there was a change to the officer structure. This time, the Legion reverted to the title of first vice-president for the office previously known as executive vice-president.

Kirkland Lake, Ontario, native Bob McChesney was unchallenged for president. An RCAF veteran, he was a highly successful insurance underwriter. Although the Legion was only one of several community activities he was involved in, he had devoted enormous energy to working with Bob Kohaly on the membership campaign.

McDonald defeated Coley and Jim Fagan for first vice-president.

Eight men ran for the four vice-president slots. Coley and Tuokko were the only incumbents to return to the executive. Joining them were Rev. Bert Harris, a 57-year-old Anglican priest from Ocean Park, British Columbia, and Ron Bedgood, Halifax's police superintendent. Dominion treasurer deLalanne, along with Bill Janes and Fred Williams, both of the host city, were unsuccessful.

DeLalanne was replaced as treasurer by Austin Hunt, a chartered accountant from Regina, and Merriam was acclaimed for his seventh term as chairman.

Tragically, it would be the 64-year-old Merriam's last convention. Fifteen days after bringing the gavel down to close the proceedings in St. John's, he was killed in a car accident near his home in Tara, Ontario. Left without a chairman by the 1970 decision to eliminate the position of vice-chairman, the Dominion Executive Council voted to appoint vice-president Harris to fill out Merriam's term. Subsequently, the Executive Council voted to re-institute the vice-chairman post, and voted to appoint Ontario Command chairman Ron Watson to fill it until the next Dominion convention.

The recruitment of sons and daughters continued at a low-key pace, with the amount of effort invested a reflection of how enthusiastic individual branches were about the 1972 decision. Some branches eagerly sought out younger members; others simply ignored the new classification. More than half of the 1,862 branches encouraged associates to sit on committees, and 65 per cent involved sons and daughters in some branch program.

Beginning in November 1975, when the Legion launched a year-long celebration of its 50th anniversary, the 50,000 associate members who had joined became a national symbol of the Legion's renewal and its commitment to carry on. "We have faced up to realities and accepted the fact that in recent years we have lost most of those pioneers who were responsible for building the Legion on such a solid foundation," McChesney wrote in a special issue of *Legion Magazine*. "The assimilation of younger people into the Legion through our sons and daughters program will, I feel certain, ensure that our organization maintains its rightful place as a leader in the community for many years to come."

In March 1976, the magazine published an anonymous tribute to the Legion's first 50 years by a 30-year member and World War II vet that reinforced McChesney's message: "The Legion is now too big and too important to fade away with us... Sons and daughters have responded well (to recruiting) and indications are that they will be worthy successors to carry on the work of the Legion to ensure perpetuation for at least another two or three generations."

The same issue carried the results of a nationwide survey of members' attitudes toward associates. The answers indicated that there was no consensus on the worthiness of associates or their effectiveness to the organization. "They cannot possibly hold the convictions of their fathers, which is necessary to maintain a strong Legion," wrote one ordinary member who felt that admitting associates was a mistake.

While the majority disagreed, stating that the children of veterans were the logical ones to carry on the Legion's works, few felt that their entry into the organization had been handled properly. "Almost without exception the availability of sons and daughters has been greeted with cynical delight by the licensed branches who have seen them as nothing but a further source of potential drinkers," wrote one Pacific Command member. "A few branches have tried to make proper use of them, but from all I can understand, their efforts without exception have been in vain."

A fellow British Columbian disagreed: "Some branches have encouraged separate meetings and activities for sons and daughters. Others have integrated them into the normal committees. Either way, it can be said they have been handled properly. It has been reported that the separate group method has failed in some branches. This should not be a condemnation of the method until it is known whether this is because of lack of interest by the branch in sons' and daughters' activities or a subsidence of interest because of the inability of sons and daughters to be heard when presenting new or innovative ideas to the older and more staid members of the branch."

There seemed to be no agreement on how the new members should be integrated.

The associates who responded to the questionnaire showed little uniformity, either. Some were clearly frustrated that they were not allowed to vote or hold office. "If we're members we should be treated as members," wrote a Newfoundland associate. "Not having a vote makes one feel that he cannot participate fully in the aims of the Legion."

"I feel if I had the vote I would attend meetings and be able to contribute," wrote another from Pacific Command.

A Saskatchewan Command associate wrote: "I think if I'm going to volunteer my time and effort in different activities... then I would like to have a say about how it's being done and what is being done."

"If you can give your time and energy to an organization, it seems only fitting that you have some sort of a say in the running of that organization," echoed an associate from Quebec.

The feelings sounded similar to those expressed by the young men who returned from World War II, joined the Legion, and found themselves shut out of decision-making by World War I vets. But, of course, there was one major difference; while the World War II vets could, and did, start their own branches, the associates had no choice but wait for their elders to decide to extend their privileges.

By the time the golden anniversary convention was held in Winnipeg in June 1976, enough branches had expressed an interest in extending additional rights that Doug McDonald's membership committee put forward a motion to introduce greater command autonomy on introducing privileges. After some extended squabbling over the wording, delegates voted on this resolution: "Therefore be it resolved that provision be made in the general bylaws to authorize a provincial command by bylaw to regulate the rights, privileges and obligations of associate members who qualify as such under the sons and daughters rule, but not to make them eligible to vote or hold any elective office in the Legion."

Some delegates expressed concern over the motion, which was clearly intended to move associates one step closer to full privileges, others maintained that it was the only logical step if the Legion expected sons and daughters to succeed them. "If I hand over the torch I want it to be to someone ready, willing and able and presumably younger, and I don't know where I am going to find them unless we prepare them," said a delegate from Pacific Command.

After a decade of hard work, first as one of Bob Kohaly's foot soldiers on the membership committee and later as point-man for extending membership to fraternal affiliates and associates, McDonald was acclaimed president. At 50, the former navy man was a wealthy partner in a stainless steel manufacturing firm in Brantford, Ontario. Brusque and outspoken, he was a firm believer in Kohaly's approach of setting goals and encouraging consensus. Since joining the Legion in 1955, he had held virtually every office on the way up the ladder and built a huge network of contacts across the country.

There was an unprecedented four-way race to succeed McDonald as first vice-president. Ed Coley defeated Dave Hunter and fellow vice-presidents Ray Tuokko and Ron Bedgood.

Eight men contested the four vice-president positions. Tuokko and Bedgood were returned, and joined on the executive by Al Harvey of St. John's and Jack Chapman of Stettler, Alberta. Losing the race were Bob Jones of New Brunswick, Jim Doig of Manitoba-Northwestern Ontario, Jack Chamberlain of Quebec and Wylie Barrett of Prince Edward Island.

Austin Hunt was acclaimed for a second term as treasurer.

Ron Watson was unchallenged in a bid to become chairman. Quebec Command executive officer Bob Ford replaced Watson as vice-chairman, defeating Pat Watkins of Nova Scotia, and Tom Sinclair and John McLaughlin of Manitoba-Northwestern Ontario Command. A 42-year-old naval veteran of the Korean War, Ford became the first national executive member who had not served in either world war.

As he had when the question of admitting sons and daughters first arose, McDonald had put the ball back into the court of the commands. Not surprisingly, the issue of greater rights for associates dominated the provincial conventions in 1977.

Ontario Command traditionally holds its convention to coincide with the Victoria Day weekend, so the largest would be among the first to make its wishes heard. Thirty-nine speakers voiced their opinions in an hour-long debate on a motion to forward a resolution on associate voting rights to the Dominion convention. Feelings ran high on both sides, but delegates voted in favor of branch voting rights for sons and daughters.

Two weeks later, a large majority of delegates to the Alberta-Northwest Territories Command convention voted to recommend that associates be granted suffrage at the branch level. They also voted to recommend that associates be permitted to hold branch office after two years' membership, provided that associates did not exceed 50 per cent of the executive, and that they be eligible for election to any Legion office after five years' continuous membership.

Meeting at the same time, Manitoba-Northwestern Ontario delegates voted 154 to 99 to recommend full privileges for associates and to change the command bylaws to permit them to hold appointed positions, attend all meetings and serve on committees.

While there was unanimity about extending voting rights to associates, a split had developed between commands on whether to go further. This schism would dominate debate at the 27th Dominion convention in Edmonton in June 1978. Three resolutions on associate rights were up for discussion: one to extend full rights; one to vote and hold office only at the branch level; and another, limiting the new rights to branch-level suffrage. The powerful Ontario delegation supported the latter option, and had the backing of Nova Scotia, New Brunswick and Quebec. Pacific and Alberta-Northwest Territories led the fight for the second option, with the support of the other Western commands and Prince Edward Island.

Few supported the resolution to grant full rights at all levels, and it was soundly defeated with relatively little debate. Ontario Command assistant secretary Bing Forbes was the most vociferous and hyperbolic opponent of the motion to allow associates to hold branch office, saying that it would "cause hell at the branch level... (and) ultimately destroy the Legion and divide it."

Another angry delegate said: "If you vote no you're voting for the demise of the Legion."

A third added: "What you're saying is 'We want your money, your time, your effort, but you're still second-class'"

And still another said: "I don't want to go home and say, 'I'm sorry, we failed you again.'"

After the 30th speaker had been heard, a standing vote was called. Only 59 Ontario delegates broke ranks, and the command's 592 nay votes were the determining factor. The motion to give associates the right to vote and hold office at the branch level was defeated 1,107 to 1,068.

What otherwise might have been the key motion — to give associates the right to vote at the branch — was an anticlimax. It carried easily, but a large number of the delegates were left with the feeling that something had gone wrong.

Also anticlimactic was a vote on the once-controversial proposal to extend full membership privileges to wartime conscripts who were honorably discharged but did not serve overseas. Although the vote was relatively close — 1,208 to 915 — much of the steam had gone out of opposition to the "zombies."

The election of officers was particularly satisfying for Ed Coley, who was acclaimed president in his hometown. A naval pharmacist in World War II, he was employed as a sales representative for a large pharmaceutical company.

Al Harvey defeated two fellow vice-presidents, Ron Bedgood and Ray Tuokko, to become first vice-president.

Bedgood and Jack Chapman were returned for another term, and were joined on the executive by Dave Capperauld of Georgetown, Ontario, and Gaston Garceau of Hull, Quebec. Defeated in their bid for vice-president were Herman Keyes and Ray Harrison of Pacific Command, Harold Hague of Saskatchewan and Jim Doig of Manitoba-Northwestern Ontario.

Austin Hunt won a third term as treasurer by acclamation, incumbent chairman Ron Watson defeated Pat Watkins, and Bob Ford was unopposed to repeat as vice-chairman.

The membership committee reported that the total of life, ordinary, associate and honorary members had reached 419,474, an increase of almost 10 per cent over the previous two years. However, the number of ordinary members had declined for the first time since the 1950s. At 93,086, the number of associates surpassed the number of fraternal affiliates for the first time.

Although it passed some landmark decisions, the 1978 convention left some business unfinished. After the convention, several branches and commands sought clarification of the motion to permit associates to vote at the branch level. After studying the matter, Justice Gordon Blair, the Legion's constitution and laws committee chairman, ruled that the resolution passed in Edmonton allowed associates to:

- vote on any matter at branch meetings — including committee meetings if a member of that committee;

- make or second a motion;

- nominate a life or ordinary member for branch elective office;

- hold appointive office, including committee chairman;

- be a member of the branch executive in an appointive capacity if provincial command bylaws permit.

His ruling was endorsed in November 1978 by the Dominion Executive Council. Nova Scotia's representatives on Council voted against the ruling, contending that the convention "voted only to give them the right to vote."

As it had on the question of fraternal affiliates, Nova Scotia Command stood opposed to a Dominion Command decision. At its convention the following May the command voted to appeal the Executive Council's decision.

Ontario Command leaned further the other way. After leading the fight against full branch rights in Edmonton, the command voted 432 to 370 at its spring convention to recommend full rights at all levels to the 1980 Dominion convention. It also passed a motion to recommend extending associate membership to wives and widows of life and ordinary members.

Pacific Command joined Ontario in recommending that spouses be permitted to join as associates.

By the end of the year, the future of associates was clear. In November, the Executive Council disallowed Nova Scotia Command's appeal and determined to seek full rights for sons and daughters at the 1980 convention.

"The Dominion convention is often called the veterans' parliament," said former president and onetime Manitoba provincial cabinet minister

Bob Smellie. "Just like in real politics, decisions at the convention are made before things come to the floor for debate."

True to form, the final decision to provide equality to associates was a bloodless procedure. Only 14 delegates spoke on the motion — several on minor points of order. Vice-chairman Ford, who was in the chair at the time, called a standing vote, but the result was already obvious. After eight years of formal standing as members and at least a decade of lobbying behind the scenes, the sons and daughters were all the way in.

Chapter 20

ONCE MORE AROUND
THE PARK

In 1972, the Legion had every reason to feel pretty good about itself. Membership was well above 300,000, and promising to grow much larger, thanks to the decisions to allow veterans' children and members of the regular Forces to join. Yearly revenue stood at about $90,000, and the Centennial Fund was growing constantly larger. The new Pension Act had secured the provisions of the Veterans Charter, giving Canada the most generous ex-service legislation in the world. The typical Legion branch had between 100 and 500 members, owned a building worth more than $100,000, and contributed $1,000 to community projects, in addition to sports sponsorships and seniors' housing.

Many people might have been content with all that. Former president Bob Kohaly was looking for new challenges.

He found what he was looking for in an innocuous conversation at one of the annual Horizon conferences held in Ottawa for provincial presidents and secretaries. Nova Scotia Command president Ron Bedgood, Halifax's police superintendent, was expressing his dismay over the increase in crime and problems with the justice system. Law and order was on the minds of a lot of people; in the United States, President Richard Nixon had run for re-election on a platform of restoring morality. The rebellious decade of the '60s was over, and a backlash had begun.

As a criminal lawyer, Kohaly had seen society at its worst, and as a prominent citizen in a small prairie city near the American border he was aware that Canadians were sensitive about what they saw as the creeping malaise in society. Immediately, he recognized the potential for making the Legion the touchstone for people's concerns. As a national organization with roots in almost every Canadian community, the Legion could rally the citizenry to demand a better society. He eagerly accepted chairmanship of a new national committee to be called ACTION — A Commitment To Improve Our Nation.

His first move was to organize a meeting of 20 influential community leaders — including clergy, police chiefs and labor bosses — to hammer out some of the primary societal concerns. Meeting at Montebello, Quebec, between Ottawa and Montreal, the group drafted a policy paper listing 14 problem areas, everything from drug abuse to the environment. The next step would be selling it to the 1974 Dominion convention in St. John's.

In a speech that harkened back to his 1966 plea for a 50-cent per capita hike, Kohaly conjured up the words of former Dominion president John Anderson, who had died in 1970. Quoting Anderson's famous 1955 "crossroads" statement — the demand for legionnaires to look to their communities for future challenges — Kohaly said that the Legion had not fulfilled its promise. "We've been circling around those crossroads for a long time," he said. "(Meanwhile) there is an unrelenting deterioration of our way of life in Canada. How long are we going to keep circling?"

It was vintage Kohaly — passionate, stirring, fully committed — and his closing image was as persuasive as the down-and-out veteran who sealed the 50-cent increase eight years earlier. "Are you ready to head for the park bench?" he asked the delegates.

In response, the convention voted to support a plan for broad social action and to pay for it from Centennial Fund interest. The ACTION committee was given a mandate to seek outside expertise and initiate local programs in the areas of: law and order; drug use and abuse; capital punishment; the parole system; the quality of justice; protection of citizens' legislation; civil liberties versus national interests; decline of the family structure; freedom of the media; the work ethic; foreign influence; the environment; the Canadian image; and the price of Confederation.

As explained in the 50th anniversary issue of *Legion Magazine*, "The ACTION program's purpose is to act as a catalyst and an organizer. It will provide the impetus to bring people together to talk, a place to meet, and administrative support.

"The program will be implemented at the branch level, where the Legion is most in touch with the community, but most probably it will involve two or more branches working together, pooling their resources in an ACTION centre.

"Of all the Legion activities and programs, it provides the most hope for the future. At a time when the Legion is opening its doors to non-veterans and sons and daughters of Legion members the ACTION program is most likely to attract the young people with the values to carry on its aims and objects."

Using the approach that had worked so well during the 10-year membership push in the '60s, Kohaly asked each command to appoint regional and provincial chairmen to augment the national committee. Posters were designed and distributed to urge members to get involved at the local level. Kohaly himself stumped across the country, selling the ACTION program at provincial conventions in the summer of 1975.

At Ontario's convention in Kingston, the program picked up a valuable ally in Premier Bill Davis, who praised the Legion's initiative, saying: "Our task is to see that the freedom we enjoy is maintained and we are not compromised by violence... Collectively, we have become far too tolerant in accepting certain behavior and this is the first evidence of a society whose foundations are in danger."

Delivering the opening address at the Manitoba-Northwestern Ontario Command convention in Winnipeg, Kohaly told delegates that the ACTION program would help foster Canadian unity.

In July, he stopped in Saskatoon to describe the ACTION program to 500 newspaper editors at the Canadian Community Newspapers Association meeting. One of his goals was to convince the community papers to use the Legion as a resource to report on various community activities in the 14 target areas.

Legion Magazine, now being published by a separate company to preserve its second-class mailing privileges, gave the program a high profile with its own monthly column. In the initial column Kohaly asked members to "show that you give a damn; get involved."

In August, Kohaly reported that ACTION seminars had been held in several areas of the country. Prince Edward Island Command had staged seminars at every branch, including guests like a local chief of police and an RCMP inspector. A group of branches around Woodstock, New Brunswick, had formed an ACTION centre. A Saskatchewan branch had dropped ACTION brochures in each of the town's mailboxes.

In October, the provincial, regional and national ACTION committees met for two days in Ottawa to review their progress. Kohaly outlined the next stages of the program: "family-style" meetings that involved legionnaires, their families and friends; and community "public forums" with the media, professional people and youth groups. He said the biggest problem facing the program was moving it from the branch level out into the community. But there were other problems, as well. Quebec Command was refusing to support the program, citing the fact that the province faced more pressing concerns than those outlined by ACTION.

Quebec Command, it turned out, was not alone in having trouble identifying with the program. Charles Rhodes Smith, the Legion's longtime expert on legal matters, remembered: "I was at odds with Kohaly over his committee's interest in law and order. It was too hard for provincial presidents to set their own policy on these issues."

The more Kohaly and his committees pushed the program, the more resistance they got from legionnaires who were unsure what they were supposed to do. By the time of the 1976 Dominion convention it was clear that ACTION was in trouble. Delegates expressed their confusion about the program during debate on whether to extend funding for another two years. Some wanted to know what had been accomplished for the $108,000 that had been spent. Kohaly tried to defend the program, saying that its goals had to be somewhat vague, because "we simply don't have the expertise to take a position (on these social issues) one way or the other."

A delegate from Manitoba-Northwestern Ontario Command, asked: "How can you go out to the public and ask them to take a stand and we not have the guts to take a stand on these issues ourselves?"

Another said: "Get a program for or against the moral issues confronting our country and then go out and sell it to the nation."

Bob Ford, the ACTION committee chairman for Quebec Command, moved a motion to reduce the program's budget for 1977 to $10,000 from the proposed $68,600. He said that legionnaires should be given priority over the general public when targeting expenditures.

Fighting back, Kohaly responded that the Legion could care for veterans in addition to community work. Outgoing president Bob McChesney joined the debate, reminding delegates that they had supported the program enthusiastically just two years before. "We're just now starting to get results," he said. "Consider seriously what you're doing. I think it would be a grave error not to adopt the report, but it is your right to ask your incoming officers to consider new angles."

In the end, the convention voted to extend ACTION — with its original budget — for another two years, but only by a narrow margin. The program would have to continue without Kohaly's guidance, however; he was replaced as chairman of the national committee by McChesney. Shortly after the convention, the new president, Doug McDonald, and first vice-president Ed Coley met to work out new guidelines for the program. They determined that ACTION needed clearer definition, and set out five specific roles that the Legion would play:

- bring to public notice the concerns of communities across the country of which Legion branches are an integral part;
- provide Legion leadership, encouragement, organization and facilities to the citizens of the communities and give them the opportunity to become involved in the decision-making process;
- provide factual information on these concerns to ensure that decisions resulting from discussions are meaningful;
- determine the will of the people and ensure that their voice is heard at the appropriate level of authority;
- follow through with specific projects where justified.

In a *Legion Magazine* article entitled "A New Thrust For ACTION," McChesney stated: "I think we will be shortchanging ourselves and missing out on a fantastic, untapped potential for service if we choose to ignore or fail to try and really understand the worthiness of the ACTION program.

"Our future plan is to string together... activities taking place across the country and to coordinate and develop them into national activities. How many similar areas of concern will come to light? How many can we handle? Which ones will have priority? The truth is we don't know, but we intend to find out."

The Legion never really did find out. Without Kohaly to drive it, ACTION — as he had originally envisioned it — sputtered and died.

"It was nebulous," admitted McDonald, "too much so for members. I think it would have given the Legion a lot of prestige if it had matured... but it just wouldn't fly."

"I don't think it was ever really clearly thought out," said then-Dominion secretary Jean Lamy. "Its mandate was so broad that no two people saw it the same way."

The ACTION committee did not disappear, though. Instead, it shifted its focus to Canadian unity, a topic that was suddenly on everyone's agenda. With the stunning majority victory of the Parti Quebecois in the Quebec provincial election of November 15, 1976, the possibility of the province's separation from Canada became a primary issue with the Legion's leadership.

As a staunchly loyalist organization with deep English roots, the Legion had always had a somewhat prickly relationship with Quebec. After 50 years, only two French Canadians had held the post of Dominion president, and both Leo LaFleche and Redmond Roche had as many ties to the English tradition as they did to the French. In 1970, Roche and then Dominion treasurer James deLalanne, a fellow Montrealer, had tried to dissuade Jean Lamy from applying for the job of Dominion secretary, in the belief that legionnaires would not accept a francophone in the top administrative position. As late as 1976, the Dominion convention was still a unilingual affair. That year, when Quebec Command requested that the rules for the nomination and election of officers be read in French as well as English, some delegates demanded facetiously that Ukrainian and Polish translations be provided as well. "The first convention set up the Legion as a one-language organization," said one angry speaker.

For many legionnaires, the conscription issue and Quebec's refusal to vote with the rest of Canada in the 1942 plebiscite continued to rankle.

"As legionnaires we had to put aside our personal views and get behind Canadian unity," said McDonald. "With McChesney, Smellie and Kohaly behind me, we decided to go across the country to get everyone onside. There was a lot of hard swinging to do in the West and Nova Scotia."

"This task force was much more tightly focused than the original ACTION concept," recalled Lamy. "They had a very strong team and they spoke across the country in favor of unity. McChesney insisted on unanimous acceptance by every command, and once Ontario supported it the rest fell in line."

At Quebec Command's convention in May 1977 delegates took a strong pro-unity stand, earmarking $1 of a $3 per capita increase to fund the provincial ACTION committee's fight against separation. Outgoing command president Gaston Garceau told delegates: "The issue really is whether the province we leave our children will continue to be an example of tolerance and respect for the rights of others, as it has long been for the rest of the world, or a stifling, chauvinistic French ghetto."

Legion Magazine hired respected journalist Jean-Marc Poliquin to edit its French-language publication, *La revue Legion*, and began to publish articles that promoted the distinctiveness of French culture in Quebec, and the province's role in Confederation.

At the 1978 Dominion convention, Kohaly received a standing ovation during the unity task force's presentation when he told delegates:

"Each veteran and his or her family must reassess their efforts to hold the torch high... Extreme solutions on either side are not acceptable.

"If we choose to live together in harmony... it will indeed have been worthy of the sacrifice... This is our renewed gift to our nation."

As always, the Legion's leadership was cautious about appearing to involve itself in partisan politics, so it assumed a relatively low profile as the May 1980 referendum on sovereignty association approached. In June, two weeks after Rene Levesque's "Oui" side had been rebuffed by Quebeckers, ACTION committee chairman McDonald told delegates to the Dominion convention in Penticton that the Legion's campaign had been successful and congratulated Quebec Command for getting deeply involved. His report marked the official end of the ACTION program; delegates voted to change the committee's name to "leadership."

The fact is, by 1980 the Legion, and a great many legionnaires, had become preoccupied with a subject they could relate to directly: aging.

Branches and commands had conducted programs to assist aging veterans since the problem of "burn out" became evident in the early 1930s. Many had set aside time and energy to provide special care for aged veterans, whether they lived in their own houses, in seniors' residences, or chronic-care facilities. Overall, branches had invested more than $40 million in housing for seniors. Somehow, though, aging had always seemed to be the "other guy's" problem. But in the mid-'70s, with the average World War II vet well into his 50s, interest in aging became widespread and personal. In 1976, the Dominion Executive Council appointed a special committee to examine the problems encountered by aging veterans, and its report to the 1978 Dominion convention had far-reaching results.

Delegates endorsed a nationwide program on aging, and left the content up to Dominion Command. Ideas approved for consideration included the use of Legion scholarships to help those taking special courses in the care of the elderly, and consultation with university medical faculties to explore the benefits of supporting limited special research or planning projects in geriatrics or gerontology. The Executive Council issued a statement of general principles on aging: "Increasing numbers of older people in the population of Canada mean a greater need for special assistance with personal care, nutrition, house care, transportation, health and, of course, accommodation. The primary task of the Legion, or of any governmental or voluntary agency concerned with older people, should be to help them to continue their lives in their own homes and their own communities."

After further study and consultation, the Executive Council decided to grant three $20,000 fellowships, each for a doctor who would study geriatrics in 1980-81 and practise medicine in Canada. This grant was the third "gift to the nation" that had been budgeted for as part of the 50th anniversary celebrations. The other gifts were special lighting for the National War Memorial in Ottawa and a grant to the Canada Studies Foundation to prepare educational materials on the political and economic structure of Canada.

The council also directed *Legion Magazine* to commission articles by geriatric and gerontology experts, and established a standing committee on programs for aging veterans, which was later renamed the Legion seniors program.

Although the 1980 Dominion convention is best remembered for granting full rights to associate members, it was dominated by the issues of aging.

Delegates voted to spend $150,000 of the Centennial Fund's accrued interest to provide six additional fellowships in geriatrics in 1982 and '83 for doctors who, after their year's study, would teach and practise. The fellowships were targeted to spread across various regions of the country. About 300 delegates also took time off from business sessions to attend a special seminar on aging. Dr. Clyde Slade of the University of British Columbia's department of family practice described the geriatrics program funded by Vancouver's Mount Pleasant Branch, while Rein Selles, executive director of the Alberta Council on Aging, talked about the importance of volunteers in helping to define the needs of the elderly. Two experts on aging from the Department of Veterans Affairs explained how the department was focusing its activities on the specific concerns of aging veterans.

Several members of the new executive placed aging at the top of their priorities in office.

One of these was incoming president Al Harvey of St. John's. The first Newfoundlander to hold the office, Harvey, an electrical contractor, was a former president of the Legion's Imperials Section.

Dave Capperauld of Ontario defeated Ron Bedgood of Nova Scotia and Jack Chapman of Alberta for first vice-president. Bedgood returned for a fourth term as vice-president, joined by incumbent Gaston Garceau, Steve Dunsdon of Pacific Command, and Tony Stacey of Ontario. Of all the new executives, Stacey was the most committed to seniors' issues. A recognized authority on the problems of aging, he was chairman of Metro Toronto

Legion Village, served on the board of Toronto Legion Homes and was a trustee of Sunnybrook Medical Centre.

Old age was affecting the executive itself, and two sitting officers retired. Bob Jones of Saint John, the longtime chairman of the Centennial Fund investment committee, was acclaimed treasurer to replace Austin Hunt. Bob Ford moved up from vice-chairman to replace chairman Ron Watson. Pat Watkins of Nova Scotia defeated Jaimer Hall for vice-chairman.

While it was clear that aging would be the Legion's foremost interest as it entered the 1980s, considerable energy and money continued to be invested at the opposite end of the age spectrum — primarily in the traditional area of track and field. That the Legion was still involved in track at all in 1980 was a testament to its determination in the face of one of the biggest disappointments in the 1965 to '80 period.

With Geoffrey Dyson as sports program director in the mid-'60s, the Legion was the undisputed leader in training track and field coaches, and combined with the sponsorship of minor sports at the community level, the Legion was widely recognized throughout Canada as the most important booster of amateur athletics. In 1967, the track and field program expanded with the help of a grant of more than $44,000 from a private benefactor in Ottawa. The money was used to conduct winter indoor coaching clinics, which supplemented the summer coaches' camp and a rejuvenated athletes' clinic. By the time Dyson's contract expired in 1968, the Legion's program had provided instruction to about 1,300 coaches and involved about 60,000 young people. In addition to the clinics and camps, the Legion also published *Coaching Review* and *Track and Field Annual* — technical journals that were widely circulated.

"We had excellent cooperation from the government through this whole period," recalled then-Dominion secretary Don Thompson. "(Former president) Fred O'Brecht really worked hard to deliver a good program."

"O'Brecht didn't get the credit he deserved," agreed Bob Kohaly. "Sports was his sole interest, and he poured his heart and soul into the program."

In 1970, the government announced without warning that it was discontinuing its share of the funding of the Legion-led track initiative in favor of the newly created Canadian Track and Field Association.

"Fred was devastated," said Kohaly, "he had tears in his eyes when we had to make the decision to stop the program."

"We could see that the Canadian Track and Field Association could take over the program," said Thompson, "so we decided it would be best if we gracefully withdrew and left it where it belonged."

"It was a difficult decision," echoed Jean Lamy, then Dominion Command's director of administration. "Things that are going like that are hard to stop; they tend to have a life of their own."

Nevertheless, in the midst of a minor financial crunch and with the decision not to touch the Centennial Fund or its interest, the Legion had no choice but to get out of track and field on a national level. It was too well ingrained to die altogether, though. Many branches continued to sponsor track, as well as hockey, baseball and other sports, and Manitoba-Northwestern Ontario Command carried on with a program it began in 1962. That year, Winnipeg teacher George Phillips had contacted the Legion to help set up a summer track camp at the International Peace Garden on the Manitoba-U.S. border. Over the years the command continued to invest money and volunteer labor into the project, building a dorm and other facilities, and enabling the camp to expand into riding, sailing and other activities.

At the national level, track and field lay dormant for only a couple of years. Delegates to the 1974 convention voted to allow a study on the feasibility of launching a new track program, and a two-day pilot meet was staged in Waterloo, Ontario, in 1975. At the 1976 Dominion convention, delegates voted to fund an annual camp out of Centennial Fund interest. Dominion Command would pay for 60 per cent of the expenses, while the provincial commands would split the remainder.

"The Canadian Track and Field Association objected to the idea of a Legion meet at first," said Dave Capperauld, who became a solid supporter of the program during his eight years as a Dominion elected officer. The dispute was over the Legion's plan to run the camp for younger children, in the "bantam" and "midget" categories. The Canadian Track and Field Association, whose mandate is to prepare and fund athletes for international competition, wanted the camp to accommodate older kids in the "juvenile" category. Delegates at the 1976 convention objected to what they saw as pressure from the Track and Field Association and refused to give their permission to make the change, despite the track body's threat to not sanction the meet.

The first new national meet was held at Oromocto, New Brunswick, for five days in 1977. Riding the wave of interest in track and field from the 1976 Summer Olympic Games in Montreal, the meet was an enormous success. Enthusiasm among Legion officials was heightened by the fact that the meet came in $45,000 under budget. At the 1978 Dominion convention, delegates supported Dominion Command's plan to set its own age limits for the annual meet and adjusted the funding formula to a 70/30 split, with the bulk coming from Centennial Fund interest.

By 1980, the meet was attracting more than 300 athletes aged 12-16. Despite its initial reservations, the Canadian Track and Field Association had come to recognize the meet as one of the most important in Canada, and supplied coaches to conduct the clinics. Dominion Command's share of the budget for the camp had risen to $150,000. In an era when the Legion was putting more emphasis on community activity and Canadian unity, the track program covered both bases.

"The kids enjoy the camp and work hard at it," said Capperauld. "Perhaps more important, though, is the cultural exchange that takes place when you take kids from all over Canada and put them together in a situation like that for a week."

Section 5

1981 - 1995

CHANGING
WITH THE
TIMES

Chapter 21

KEEPING THE FLAME ALIVE

Entering the 1980s — 60 years after the disparate and disgruntled veterans of Vimy and the Somme began to agitate for better rights; 35 years after the World War II vets stormed back home full of vigor — the Legion was very much the embodiment of the ideals of the 60-year-olds who comprised its leadership. The issues of citizenship and tradition had always been important; now, with immigration on the rise, and the people belonging to the population bubble known as the Baby Boom taking the reins of power in government and business, the Legion began to think and act like a senior statesman.

Like a 60-year-old suddenly recognizing his own mortality, the Legion moved to put its legal affairs in order. After decades of living with its haphazard 1926 incorporation under the Companies Act and a set of bylaws that had been cobbled together as the years passed, the organization called on Parliament to amend the Act of Incorporation. The new act recognized the broadened membership, allowed for amalgamation of branches and disposal of branch holdings, and strengthened the copyright protection of the Legion's name and symbols.

The introduction of the bill amending the Act of Incorporation provided an opportunity for MPs to reflect on the Legion's accomplishments. NDP MP Stanley Knowles commented: "When all the nicest things have been said (about the Legion), they will all be deserved... There is no doubt that over the years the Legion has pressed, intelligently and with good background in terms of research, for legislation to take care of disabled veterans, older veterans, and of those who are in economic difficulties but do not have disabilities for which they could get pensions under the Pensions Act and they have stayed with the job... We are talking about an organization which has been working hard for over half a century..."

MP Len Hopkins categorized the Legion as an organization that "does not go around bragging about all the good work it does. Instead, its membership simply gets on with completing its many projects, be they of an individual nature, a community-oriented venture or national in scope."

Certainly, no one would argued with the validity of Hopkins' statement. In fact, the truth of what he said would come back to haunt the organization before the decade was over.

The occasion for the first of the Legion's "good works" of the 1980s was the marriage of Prince Charles and Lady Diana Spencer. In August 1981, the 10 provincial command presidents endorsed Dominion Command's decision that the Legion's wedding gift should be a contribution to the Terry Fox Youth Centre in Ottawa. Named for the courageous one-legged British Columbian whose attempt to raise funds and awareness for cancer research by running across the country inspired the entire nation, the centre was a project of the Council for Canadian Unity. The centre was designed to house 115 high school students, who would be brought to Ottawa to study and get to know peers from other parts of the country. Each year, the centre would accommodate more than 3,000 16- and 17-year-olds. Their curriculum at the centre would include Canadian history and geography, resources, the environment, law, and the economy. Of the overall cost of $1.6 million, the Legion decided to contribute $250,000 to furnish and equip the centre.

Fort William Branch in Thunder Bay, Ontario, was the first to rise to the challenge, contributing $1 for each branch and Ladies Auxiliary member — a total of $1,250. That was followed in short order by donations ranging from $7.50 from the 15-member Kandahar, Saskatchewan, Branch to $1,000 from the 43-member George Watters Post in Dayton, Ohio. Past president Ed Coley was especially keen on the idea of the centre, and eventually joined its board of directors. "It became a tremendous learning experience, not only for the youngsters, but for the teachers who worked there," said Coley in 1986. "The teachers were thrilled with the centre, and many said that their experience there would help them back in their own classrooms."

Track and field continued to be a major project, and a leading national expenditure. The cost of flying athletes and coaches to the annual meet and clinic rose sharply, forcing delegates to increase the Centennial Fund share of the event up to $175,000 in 1986. The actual cost of the 1987 camp was $325,746. In 1992, the cost dropped to $286,624, then rose slightly to $295,365 for 1993. That year, 324 athletes competed and practised under 22 coaches. In 1994, 332 athletes and 25 coaches attended at a cost of $294,756.

There were dividends to savor, too. Almost half of the 60 Canadian track and field athletes at the 1984 Summer Olympics were former participants in the Legion's track program.

In 1988, 12 years after the camp began, delegates voted to grant the track and field program an ongoing mandate, allowing long-term planning and obviating the need to seek funding at every convention.

Another project that continued apace in the 1980s was the Legion's support of the British Commonwealth Ex-Services League. In the years since Fred O'Brecht's 1966 pledge to Lord Louis Montbatten, the Legion's focus for contributions had become the veterans who lived in Caribbean region. In the fall of 1980 the Legion played host to the league's triennial conference in Ottawa. The Legion responded to Ex-Services League grand president Prince Philip's plea for donations by pledging $15,000 for each of the following three years. The conference gave Legion officials the opportunity to meet with their counterparts from the Caribbean nations and gain a better sense of the types of needs veterans there had. By 1982, the Legion's British Commonwealth Ex-Services League fund had grown to $222,394, thanks in large degree to its adoption as a special cause by Alberta-Northwest Territories Command, which contributed 70 per cent of that total.

Regular fact-finding missions to the Caribbean countries were launched, providing Legion officials with a firsthand view of what needed to be done and where past donations had been spent. Their reports were filled with stories of veterans living on meagre pensions in squalid conditions. Unfortunately, the efforts to direct funds to Caribbean vets were occasionally complicated by government instability in nations like Grenada.

Between 1982 and '84, the Legion donated $122,913 to projects in the Caribbean, dropping the fund's balance to just over $160,000. Donations from branches began to falter in the mid-'80s; just $3,864 was raised in 1983. The fund got a boost in 1986, when the $1-million worldwide Prince Philip Appeal was announced. Some $17,785 was raised from the floor of the 1986 Dominion convention. The raising of British Commonwealth Ex-Services League funds became a tradition at subsequent conventions, with donations rising steadily from $21,000 in 1990 to $41,000 in 1992 and $41,152 in 1994. Expenditures in these years fluctuated between $85,576 in 1991 to $171,199 in 1993. Among the projects undertaken were individual welfare grants, a chronic-care facility in Jamaica, and a new cenotaph in Grenada. In 1992, Ex-Services League secretary-general Mike Doyle told convention delegates that the Legion's funds were particularly appreciated by needy former Commonwealth soldiers living in countries where few social services exist and veterans' pensions are often unheard of. "We really need every penny and we spend every penny we get," he said. "Because you do so much (in the Caribbean), we in headquarters... have more money to spend elsewhere."

In 1986, the Dominion Executive Council voted to create a new program that was intended to spread the concept of remembrance to generations that were untouched by war. At its spring meeting the council decided to spend up to $60,000 to send 10 younger legionnaires — one from each command — to France for the 50th anniversary of the unveiling of the Vimy Memorial. One of the criteria to qualify for the trip was the ability to pass on the experience to even younger people; several of those on the first trip were teachers. This was intended as a pilot project for an ongoing program to be funded by interest from the Centennial Fund, but delegates to the 1986 convention had other ideas. They turned down the proposal over the objections of leadership, organization and planning committee chairman Dick Chapelhow.

Nevertheless, the pilot project went ahead using the Legion's general funds, and resulted in some powerful experiences for the 10 legionnaires under 30 who went along. "(The beach at Dieppe) is the most profound example of what wars were all about," said Laura Morrison, a teacher from Ponoka, Alberta, Branch. "These men, in a sense, walked valiantly straight into death. I think this is truly symbolic of the loyalty these men had and their efforts to maintain freedom for their country."

Danny Coughlin, another teacher, from Hartland, New Brunswick, Branch, said: "It has made me feel more like a Legion member and very proud to be a Canadian. History books cannot provide the feeling I got standing at the (Vimy) Memorial during the placing of the wreaths. When I return home, I hope I can find the proper words and explanations to describe this experience..."

Summing up the trip, then-Dominion president Tony Stacey commented: "If the Legion never sends another group of young people to visit the resting place of 100,000 Canadian citizens, there are 10 young people who have seen the sacrifice that was made and are enthusiastic to tell others their story. I believe we have achieved our goal."

The Legion did send more groups of young people. Renamed the Royal Canadian Legion Youth Leaders Pilgrimage of Remembrance after a three-year absence, the program continued in 1989 to take one youth leader from each command. Added on were veterans and their spouses, who paid their own way to go along as guides and touchstones to the past battles. In 1995, Dominion Command began to offer a cost-sharing program with provincial commands to allow former participants to travel inside their command and make presentations on remembrance.

As Canada's largest veterans' organization, the Legion was the natural gatekeeper of remembrance — a nationwide brotherhood that could protect the truth about the country's major conflicts. That was a respected position when it meant conveying funds to Caribbean veterans or ferrying young Canadians to foreign battlefields and cemeteries; it was not so widely respected when it came to correcting artists' views of the past.

The first controversy arose over a film called *The Kid Who Couldn't Miss*, which was made by Montreal-based director Paul Cowan in 1983. Cowan's central thesis, that society tends to glorify and justify war by creating heroes, might have escaped the ire of Canadian veterans; his assertion that World War I ace Billy Bishop faked the action that won him the Victoria Cross did not. Bishop, a Legion icon, was generally viewed as above criticism, so Cowan's creation of a scene in which Bishop's mechanic says that the flyer shot holes in his own plane to simulate the damage of an epic dogfight was particularly galling.

Adding to veterans' fury about the film was the fact that it was produced for the National Film Board of Canada, and — like most Canadian films of the time — partially financed by public funds. Two separate organizations, the Royal Canadian Air Force Association and the Royal Military College Club, sprang to Bishop's defence, spearheading a protest campaign that resulted in 3,000 letters. Many Canadians demanded that the film be either pulled from distribution or revised to remove the offending charge. Both Liberal Communications Minister Francis Fox and his Conservative successor, Marcel Masse, refused to get involved, citing the independence of the National Film Board, but the Senate subcommittee on veterans affairs agreed to examine the matter.

On November 28, 1985, Cowan and National Film Board commissioner François Macerola appeared before the subcommittee. While Cowan made no bones about having invented mechanic Walter Bourne's statement that Bishop faked the damage to his plane and made up the story of the triple-killing that resulted in his VC, Macerola was not as forthcoming. While he conceded that the film contained "some errors," he maintained, "We at the National Film Board were sure that the public would realize that this film was a docu-drama — even if we issued a press release saying it was a documentary..."

In the end, Macerola agreed that the film board would edit the film to insert a statement saying that it was "a docu-drama presenting a perspective on the nature of heroism and the legend of Billy Bishop."

The Legion, which had stayed in the background of the controversy for the most part, began to give it more coverage in 1986, when it was clear that the national media had largely ignored the issue. A *Legion Magazine* article speculated that the fuss over the film had given the National Film Board publicity "it couldn't possibly have bought." Refusing to be placated by the addition of a disclaimer, delegates to the 1986 Dominion convention voted to demand that the film be withdrawn from distribution. Their demand was ignored.

As important as the Bishop controversy seemed at the time, it was in fact only a foretaste of what was to arise in 1992 over a six-hour, $3.5-million television mini-series called *The Valour And The Horror*, which was co-produced by Galafilm, the CBC and the National Film Board. Directed by filmmaker Brian McKenna, who also co-wrote the script with the assistance of his journalist brother, Terry, the series concentrated on three key Canadian actions in World War II: the fall of Hong Kong, the bombing of Germany, and the drive to Falaise following the Normandy landing. It was the second segment, *Death By Moonlight* — and the McKennas' assertion that Canadian commanders willingly endorsed Bomber Command's policy of attacking civilian targets — that raised veterans' hackles and cast doubt on the veracity of the entire series.

The criticism began to flow from veterans soon after the programs aired on CBC — on three successive Sunday evenings in January 1992. Longtime *Legion Magazine* columnist Doug Fisher excoriated the McKennas and Galafilm in his monthly article. Dominion president Jack Jolleys sent strongly worded letters to CBC executives, media and other interested parties, describing the series as a "superficial, nasty little portrayal of Canada's World War II effort." The magazine published numerous letters, most of which echoed the sentiments expressed by W.W. Brown of Qualicum Beach, British Columbia: "Like (*The Kid Who Couldn't Miss*), which sought to prove Billy Bishop was a liar and a cheat, this series deserves only one resting place: a garbage can."

Once again, the Legion was not the only veterans' organization pushing to have authorities rectify the situation; in this case it was Cliff Chadderton, the high profile chief executive officer of the War Amputations of Canada and chairman of the National Council of Veteran Associations, who served as the point man. He was unrelenting in his demands to have the series withdrawn, a campaign that resulted in a hearing before the Senate subcommittee on veterans affairs and an independent review by the CBC's ombudsman. Nevertheless, the Legion's role as the primary representative for veterans put it front-and-centre in the public's mind when it focused on the controversy.

Unlike the storm over Bishop, though, the chain of events touched off by the official complaints reached far beyond a simple disclaimer added to a film. In a report released on the eve of Remembrance Day 1992, CBC ombudsman William Morgan ruled that the series was "flawed and fail(ed) to measure up to the CBC's demanding policies and standards." His report came at a stressful time for the CBC. Faced with mounting pressure from the Conservative government to cut costs, CBC employees had assumed something of a bunker mentality. When the corporation's president, Gérard Veilleux, commented on Morgan's report, expressing regret for "any distress the programs may have caused the audience," he drove a wedge between various factions within the broadcaster and eventually made his position at the CBC untenable.

Even senior broadcasters like former CBC news anchor Knowlton Nash, who felt the McKennas should have presented their series as a "point-of-view documentary," felt hard-pressed to side with the corporation's president's betrayal of established programming policies. Others at the CBC who had fewer ties to the establishment saw Veilleux's statement as a sop to groups like the Legion, who, in their view, saw history as sacred and closed to reinterpretation. The president of the Writers Guild of Canada demanded Veilleux's resignation, and a wide array of organizations representing the artistic community — including the Alliance of Canadian Television Radio Artists, the Association of Television Producers and Directors, the Canadian Association of Journalists, the Canadian Independent Film Caucus and the Quebec Federation of Journalists — denounced Veilleux's stand and Morgan's findings. Major newspapers like the *Globe and Mail* and the Montreal *Gazette* attacked the CBC president for his failure to stand by his news and current affairs department.

The fall of dominoes that led eventually to Veilleux's resignation in 1993 might just as easily have been initiated by any number of other events besides *The Valour And The Horror* debate, but as it was the incident went a long way towards souring the relationship between Canada's national media source and veterans in general, the Legion in particular. More importantly, a large number of Canadians who grew up believing in freedom of expression, and forgiving filmmakers their use of artistic licence, came to view organizations like the Legion as strident reactionaries out to muzzle the media.

If the Legion seemed out-of-step to many non-members over its stance on filmmakers like Cowan and the McKennas, its hard line on defence policy made it seem no less so as the Cold War ended and the decades-old barricades between East and West came down. No one but a veteran really understands the horrors of war, and the importance of avoiding armed conflict at almost any cost. In the 1980s, and into the '90s, the Legion reflected this reality by taking an uncompromising stand on the importance of maintaining a strong presence in Europe through NATO, and by supporting the United States' build-up of advanced nuclear weapons.

Sensing a change in the world's defensive policies as the '80s began, *Legion Magazine* launched an extensive review of the situation in seven key regions: China, Japan, the Soviet Union, Western Europe, Britain, the United States and Canada. Written by seasoned observers with long-term experience in their target countries or areas, the seven-part series provided a comprehensive overview of what would turn out to be one of the most dramatic eras in political and military history.

Against a rising tide of protest in Canada, the Legion was bullish on the tough anti-Soviet policies of U.S. President Ronald Reagan and British Prime Minister Margaret Thatcher. In 1983, Dominion president Dave Capperauld wrote to Prime Minister Pierre Trudeau supporting testing of the U.S. cruise missile over Alberta. In 1986, with Mikhail Gorbachev making peace overtures to the West, delegates to the Dominion convention voted down a resolution supporting the Canadian government's "leading role in promoting disarmament and world peace." Instead, they voted in favor of maintenance of adequate defence forces and the continuation of Canada's participation in NATO, NORAD and the United Nations. In addition, they directed the Dominion president to issue an official Legion defence policy.

At its fall 1986 meeting, the Dominion Executive Council presented a draft summary of the policy for discussion among provincial commands, and on December 12 it submitted an eight-page position paper to Defence Minister Perrin Beatty. The document stated that the Legion continued to strongly support the NATO objective of "undiminished security at lower levels of armament," and said that Canada must play an effective role in ensuring adequate western defence while advancing arms control measures. But, it stressed, arms control must not jeopardize Canadian sovereignty or security. "The Legion considers that any reduction in the Canadian Forces would be a serious error, since our forces are already inadequate for both national and international tasks." In addition to the policy paper, Dominion Command established an ad hoc committee on defence policy to advise the Executive Council and its Sub-Executive.

In response, Beatty invited legionnaires to provide views on Canada's defence in preparation for a planned government white paper. When the white paper was released in early June 1987, Dominion president Stacey applauded Beatty's strong proposal for a "three ocean navy" and urged the government to make the necessary funds available to support Beatty's plans.

Of course, events quickly overtook the white paper. Government restraint prevented implementation of many of Beatty's ambitious initiatives, and the minister himself was shuffled out of the portfolio before he could lobby within cabinet for support of his policies. On the global scale, things were also changing, and Gorbachev's increasingly open overtures to presidents Reagan and George Bush were making a hard-line policy of troop maintenance look outdated.

From 1988 onward, the chief of defence staff or his designated representative was a regular guest at Dominion conventions, but the message of increased spending cuts and shifting priorities moved consistently further from the Legion's concept of an ideal defence policy. In 1994, the defence committee discussed policy changes in light of a forthcoming government review, and, while acknowledging that the world had changed, reiterated the view that it was necessary for Canada to maintain troops that were adequately trained and equipped to meet defence needs at home and abroad. Delegates to the 1994 convention called for a swift review and reorganization of the defence department.

The Legion had somewhat better luck with a revived unity campaign, timed in this incarnation to coincide with the failure of the Meech Lake accord on constitutional reform. "Of all the battles our members have fought for Canada, from Vimy Ridge to the hills of Korea, on land, at sea and in the air, this may be the most important," stated Dominion president Gaston Garceau in a letter to Prime Minister Brian Mulroney. "...Should the Canadian fabric be rent by regional considerations... it will be an affront to the memories of those gallant people who died, and to the hundreds of thousands of their comrades who have survived."

Delegates to the 1990 Dominion convention endorsed the letter with a standing ovation. Introducing a resolution that the Legion use its energy to ensure that Canada remain united, Garceau reflected on the efforts of the ACTION task force on unity in 1978. "Many of the questions remain outstanding and in fact form the basis of the crisis facing Canada today," he said. "The situation in 1990, however, could be worse than ever before in Canadian history."

As in past campaigns of this type, the Legion took a diversified, regional approach to the task, asking commands to form unity committees across the country. In Alberta, the command presented the Legion's position to a provincial government committee on constitutional reform. New Brunswick Command planned a giant unity parade in Fredericton, with representation from community groups from across the province. Nova Scotia Command urged members to express their personal views on unity to local media and political representatives. Individual branches picked up the initiative, too. Col. R.H. Britton Branch in Gananoque, Ontario, worked with other concerned citizens to entertain 50 families from Quebec. North Bay, Ontario, Branch committed $15,000 to a unity campaign and held a news conference to explain the Legion's position to the local media.

At a meeting in the summer of 1991 to review the committees' progress, Dominion president Fred Williams reported: "We have made good progress since the Canadian unity program was launched earlier this year, but now is the time to increase our efforts. We are counting on our coordinators across the country to make sure this campaign continues until we have taken every possible initiative and made every possible effort to promote unity and ensure the Legion's contribution to the continued existence of one united Canada."

Late that year a series of public service announcements sponsored by the Legion to promote unity began airing on Canadian television stations. It was as vocal as the Legion had been about anything of a national scope since the flag debate in 1964. At the 1992 Dominion convention, Dominion president Jolleys delivered a straightforward message: "We are involved in a fight for national survival. It is a fight no less important than what many of us experienced during the past wars... The Legion's Canadian unity program is producing results; best efforts must continue to promote unity at every opportunity."

Officially, the Legion endorsed the Yes side in the October 1992 constitutional referendum, but there was no attempt by Dominion Command to compel legionnaires to vote as a block. In a followup survey article in *Legion Magazine* after the defeat of the Charlottetown Accord several provincial unity coordinators admitted to voting No along with the majority. Like many Canadians, most expressed a wish to forget the constitution and get on with the problem of eliminating Canada's crippling national deficit. In a telling move, the Dominion unity committee did not file a report to the 1994 convention, stating that it would continue to monitor the situation following the Quebec provincial election that was forthcoming. Delegates voted to continue to devote "all necessary resources" to ensure Canadian unity.

Chapter 22

NAVIGATING THE SLIPPERY SLOPE

Like an accountant watching the bottom line of a company's balance sheet to track its performance, legionnaires have traced the health of the organization by following membership statistics since sons and daughters were granted full rights in 1980. Some have continued to hold fast to the view that the Legion's decline is inevitable; the majority have looked for ways to keep membership numbers relatively stable.

In the wake of the landmark 1980 decision to allow associates to vote and hold office, it was time to take stock. The yardstick against which membership would be measured was the actuarial forecast that 80,000 of the life and ordinary members who belonged in 1980 would not live to celebrate the Legion's 60th anniversary in 1986. When the national membership committee met in March 1981, the balance looked pretty promising. Although the gradual slide in life and ordinary membership had continued, reaching 2,176 in 1980, some 10,708 new associates had joined. The year-end membership total was 437,379 — down a little from the mid-'70s peak, but a good plateau from which to build, reported chairman Dave Capperauld.

The committee set the 1981 goal at 450,000, and recommended several steps to help make the target a reality. Members agreed to step up recruiting among retired and active Armed Forces personnel, and called for vigilance toward branches that were charging higher dues to associate members. In May, the Dominion Executive Council responded by officially banning dues discrimination against associates.

Membership was also on the minds of delegates to provincial conventions in the summer of 1981. While Nova Scotia Command continued to buck against the new regulations — chasing Dominion president Al Harvey from its convention floor at one point — others were looking for additional changes. Quebec Command voted overwhelmingly to recommend extending associate membership to wives, widows and widowers of those eligible for ordinary membership. Manitoba-Northwestern Ontario Command would not go quite that far, electing instead to propose non-voting associate status for spouses and widows. In Prince Edward Island, the command took a giant step into the future by electing 35-year-old associate Al Parks to the post of chairman.

It turned out to be a banner year for membership, and with total Legion strength — including fraternal affiliates — at a record 562,578 it was not expected that legionnaires would look to open up the membership question again. But they did. In a surprise move, the 1,857 delegates at the 29th Dominion convention in Quebec City voted to extend full membership privileges to spouses, widows and widowers. Discussion on the non-concurred motion was not free from rancor. "My wife can rule me at home but by God she can't rule me at the Legion," fumed one delegate. "Is it possible that a German pilot could be the spouse of a female veteran and thus become a member?" theorized another.

Eventually, reason won out. "It took me 26 years to get to be president," said former Dominion president Bob McChesney. "I couldn't have done it without her."

"These are women who have worked for the Legion for 30 and 35 years and are denied the right given their own children," stated another delegate.

Forced to a ballot vote that included proxies, the associate category was extended by a margin of 2,332 to 1,718.

Another non-concurred motion — one to limit the term "comrade" to life or ordinary members — drew sharp responses before being defeated. "You have stripped the veteran of everything but the right to come into his own hall," said one angry delegate. Speaking against the motion, another countered: "It seems associates are at the bottom of the pile. If I were an associate I would be incensed. Comrade means those who are united for a common goal and objective."

First vice-president Capperauld was unopposed for the presidency. An RAF veteran of World War II, Capperauld had served on the Executive Council for more than a decade. A resident of Georgetown, Ontario, he worked as a structural steel checker on large construction projects.

All of the vice-presidents ran to replace Capperauld, with Steve Dunsdon of Summerland, British Columbia, emerging as the winner. Eight men then faced off for the four vice-president posts. Incumbents Gaston Garceau of Hull, Quebec, and Tony Stacey of West Hill, Ontario, were returned along with Don Hamilton of Moose Jaw and Dick Chapelhow of

Calgary. Defeated were Manitoba's Ron Highfield, Ontario's Ric Collins, Francis McNeill of Saint John, and Morgan McGaughey of Prince Edward Island.

Treasurer Bob Jones of Saint John and chairman Bob Ford, then of Burlington, Ontario, were acclaimed. Vice-chairman Pat Watkins of Springhill, Nova Scotia, defeated Fred Williams of St. John's and Elmer Simms of North Bay, Ontario.

Former president Redmond Roche paid tribute to retiring Dominion secretary Jean Lamy, saying: "He has served under six presidents, all difficult people, and he has survived." Replacing Lamy was former Dominion service officer Colin Graham, 63.

The period between the 1982 and '84 Dominion conventions was filled with growth unheard of since the heyday of Bob Kohaly's membership blitz in the 1960s. More than 30,000 associates signed on, easily outstripping the decline of 6,309 ordinary and life members. Total strength surpassed 600,000 for the first time, including 150,000 associates and 330,000 life and ordinary members.

After opening new membership categories at successive conventions, delegates to the 1984 national meeting in Winnipeg were content to concentrate on housekeeping details. The most contentious issue before them was a proposal to increase the per capita fee by $3 to $7.90 per annum. The ways and means committee had forecast deficits of $1.2 million for 1984, $773,500 in 1985 and $948,400 in 1986. After much debate, which saw Pacific Command strongly opposed to a 60 per cent increase in dues, Ontario Command carried the day with a compromise proposal of a $2 hike.

The only membership questions up for debate were clarification of what constituted a spouse eligible for associate membership, and the eligibility of associates for Legion honors and awards. Not open for discussion in Winnipeg was a so-called notice of intent that would come to dominate membership debates at provincial conventions in 1985. Developed by the leadership, organization and planning committee, the proposed resolution recommended consolidating the ordinary and associate-voting categories into one new category: "member."

Retired auctioneer and rancher Steve Dunsdon was acclaimed president. A Legion member since his discharge from the Royal Canadian Army Service Corps in 1945, he had served on the Dominion Executive Council since 1974.

Stacey defeated fellow vice-presidents Garceau and Hamilton for election as first vice-president. Both were subsequently re-elected in a vice-presidential race among 10 candidates. Incumbent Chapelhow was also returned. The newcomer was the popular Newfoundlander Fred Williams.

The sitting chairman, vice-chairman and treasurer were all acclaimed.

The convention approved a bylaw revision making the chairman and vice-chairman voting members of Sub-Executive.

Left to simmer at the convention's close was the leadership, organization and planning committee's notice of intent, which committee members hoped would speed assimilation of associates. The committee found little agreement across the country. Only Prince Edward Island, the first command to elect an associate to its executive, supported the motion. Others, like Manitoba-Northwestern Ontario Command, were vehemently opposed. Harold Bastable, a constant, vocal proponent of branch autonomy, thundered, "It's dough-heads who wrote (this motion), a figment of someone's imagination in Ottawa and absolute rubbish. I am wearing my medals and two years from now there will be a motion asking us not to wear (them) because we are discriminating." Not one of the associates at the convention voted in favor of the motion.

Opposition was so critical that the committee decided to reword the resolution. "Apparently somewhere along the line it was misconceived," said committee chairman Chapelhow. "It was not intended by this committee, myself or (former committee members) to try to change associates into ordinary members."

The new motion called for one badge for all voting members, and a single title: "legionnaire."

The committee's steering committee filed a gloomy report that stated there was little effort being made to encourage associates to become involved in Legion affairs. "What is most disturbing," it stated, "is the attitude that when the time comes the veteran will pass on and the younger member step into the breach. If we allow this sort of transition the Legion will suffer a drastic decline in membership and lose much of its viability. What many veterans have not accepted is that the time is now when these programs must be implemented and all voting members accepted as legionnaires."

Similar sentiments were expressed at several of the command conventions.

In Newfoundland, Colin Strong of Pleasantville Branch said: "The attitude of veterans towards associates is poor in many cases. We've got to relax a little bit. We've got to make associates welcome."

In Saskatchewan, former Dominion president Bob Smellie made an emotional pitch for associates. Using the example of three homegrown former presidents — Alex (Turkey) Ross, Mervyn Woods and Bob Kohaly — he said: "Look around and tell me who your president will be in 10 years... We have to start putting the pressure on... Go out and find another young Turkey Ross."

When Ron Anderson, an associate from Abbey Branch, declined a nomination for the post of vice-president citing a lack of experience, Dominion president Dunsdon commandeered the microphone. "This is a prime example of what we've been talking about. Why haven't we given associates what they need? We old bucks are a dying breed and we have to get moving on this."

In his official address to the convention, Dunsdon recalled the situation after World War II. "When I first joined my branch in 1946 it took three years to get one of us from the Second War on the executive. Now we're doing the same damn thing and it burns me up."

They were well-intentioned words; yet, by the end of the summer only two associates held executive posts: Prince Edward Island first vice-president Al Parks; and Ontario vice-chairman Ron Hummel.

Assessing the situation that fall, Kohaly was pessimistic. "Doug (McDonald), Bob (McChesney) and I have talked into the early hours despairing over the failure to bring in associates," he said. "I've reached the conclusion that it won't happen. The Legion hit a plateau in '72 and it's been going on ever since."

The revised leadership, organization and planning committee motion gained support at the Saskatchewan convention — the only convention that met after the resolution was re-drafted — but it proved little more popular than the original one. The most controversial topic at the 60th anniversary party that passed for the 1986 Dominion convention, the motion was soundly defeated. Nova Scotia Command chairman Wilfred Bisson represented the overwhelming mood of the record-setting 3,105 delegates when he asked rhetorically: "What's wrong with the way we are now?"

First vice-president Stacey capped a 40-year Legion career by being acclaimed president. Widely respected for his expertise in the field of aging, the retired refrigerator service owner had served overseas with the Royal Canadian Army Service Corps in World War II.

All four vice-presidents competed for first vice-president. Garceau won on the third ballot.

Neither Hamilton nor Chapelhow chose to seek a third term as vice-president, opening up the executive to three newcomers. As expected, incumbent Fred Williams was returned; he was joined by Hugh Greene of Ponoka, Alberta, Jack Jolleys of Cloverdale, British Columbia, and Jim Tyndall of Niagara Falls.

Treasurer Jones and chairman Ford were both acclaimed. Vice-chairman Watkins defeated Vern Burke of Corbeil, Ontario.

In his membership committee report, Williams caused uneasy laughter when he told delegates, "Statistics show that 25,000 veterans will die each year for the next 15 years, so I'll take the opportunity to say goodbye to some of you now." He projected that Legion strength would be down about 10,000 from the 1984 peak, although 7,000 more associates had joined in the previous two years. Ordinary membership stood at 292,446 for 1985 — a drop of 6,686; associate membership was 173,240.

After the convention, a *Legion Magazine* editorial entitled "The Future: Laying It On The Line" stated the various membership figures and asked: "What does it all mean? That 1984 was the high-water mark with a grand total of 602,489 — 488,541 members and 113,948 fraternal affiliates. That 1985 was the turning-point, the top step of a down escalator. That hard choices lie ahead... Canada's veteran population is 680,000, average age 66. In 1996 it'll be 388,000, average age 76, with an increased need for services and support."

The editorial quoted comments Stacey had made to New Brunswick Command's annual convention that year. "We will fail if we don't do more — and do it soon," he said. "We should get... younger members to the higher levels as soon as possible. Most of us who are leading now will, in 10 years' time, either have faded into history or will not be physically able to continue. It is our responsibility to give support and advice while we still have time.

"We must look further afield (for new members). But to whom? And where? When I remember the agonies the Legion went through at every previous attempt to accept a new type of membership, I hesitate to open this discussion... Every step has been hard, and the next one will be hardest of all... Do we open our doors to the great many Canadians who are not qualified for membership under the present rules, but who share our purposes and objectives? We have already had experience with this type of person. We all know many within our branches who would do as well as Legion members. This is a serious question, one that demands long and hard thoughtful debate.

"In the long run, you, the branch member, will ultimately decide, in your wisdom, the fate and course of our beloved organization."

The national membership committee decided to launch a renewed effort to sign up members of the Canadian Forces by recruiting on military bases, but found no solution to the problems of attracting associates and getting them to renew.

"We failed with the associates," said former Dominion president Harvey. "We took them in and we were ill-prepared... We're losing the veterans to regimental associations or whatever. We were all veterans. That bonded us together. There's nothing in common anymore. We were brutal and basic. Grade five was the basic qualification for World War II. Our sons and daughters are doctors and lawyers. You're not going to get them down there (at the branch) changing bingo cards."

The committee turned down a motion to extend associate status to members' grandchildren. But it was an idea that refused to die. Debated at most provincial conventions in 1987, the motion to allow grandchildren in was passed in Alberta-Northwest Territories and Saskatchewan commands. A recommendation to extend associate membership to the spouses of eligible sons and daughters was also passed in Saskatchewan and Newfoundland. Saskatchewan elected two associates — Ron Anderson and Ray Marjoram — to its executive, and in Prince Edward Island Al Parks became the first associate to attain the post of command president.

At the 1988 Dominion convention in Ottawa, the grandchildren question did not get a hearing, but delegates decided to allow spouses of associate-voting members to have equal rights. Despite concerns that the extension would hurt membership in the Ladies Auxiliary, the argument that small, rural branches needed the extra members to survive carried the day.

Ordinary membership was extended to Canadian Forces Reserve personnel who have served for at least one year instead of the two years previously needed to qualify.

The convention acclaimed first vice-president Garceau as Dominion president. A 68-year-old private bailiff with the Quebec Ministry of Justice in Hull, he was a 44-year legionnaire who had served as a ground crew instructor in the RCAF.

Vice-president Williams defeated fellow incumbents Tyndall and Jolleys for first vice-president. Both of the unsuccessful candidates were returned for a second term as vice-president. Greene was also re-elected. Bill Smith of Lucan, Ontario, was the sole new member of the executive.

Chairman Ford and treasurer Jones were both acclaimed for fifth terms. Vice-chairman Watkins staved off a challenge from Don Heyes of Winnipeg.

Significantly, no associates were nominated.

By 1989, the voices of alarm were starting to have a familiar ring. "From information accumulated over the past two years it is apparent that, generally speaking, we are failing to attract and hold the interest of our largest source of membership — the associate-voting members — in sufficient numbers to sustain the organization," outgoing Pacific Command president Derek Eyles told delegates at his provincial convention. In Ontario, president Joe Kobolak said in his wrap-up report: "(From) the increasing number of Legion funerals... it is very obvious we are losing a great number of veterans, which should alert and encourage us to make an effort to educate and prepare our younger members for the acceptance of Legion duties and responsibilities..."

Parks became the first associate elected to the Dominion Executive Council, but no associates moved up the provincial ladders to become the second associate president.

Once again, there was no unanimity on the question of extending rights. Ontario, Quebec, Manitoba-Northwestern Ontario, Alberta-Northwest Territories and Saskatchewan favored making grandchildren associates — seemingly ensuring their acceptance in 1990 — but Prince Edward Island and Nova Scotia were opposed. Several commands recommended extending associate status to brothers and sisters of ordinary and life members, while others wanted cadets in.

Despite the strong support for broadening membership to include grandchildren, the national membership committee did not concur with the resolution to the 1990 Dominion convention in Vancouver. "With the loss of over 6,000 ordinary members and the increase of over 11,000 associate members in 1989," it stated, "the Royal Canadian Legion could be in danger of losing its status with the government in dealing with issues relating to veterans, Canadian Armed Forces and National Defence... Current programs should be aimed at increasing ordinary membership by recruiting retired and active Armed Forces personnel."

The resolution sparked strong emotions on both sides of the issue, but those opposed had their way.

Membership was extended to give associate status to adults with three years service in the cadets, and ordinary status to those called for service in World War II but transferred to the RCMP for home service — a narrow category to be sure.

Sixty-eight-year-old Fred Williams became the second Newfoundlander to be Dominion president. A gregarious naval veteran, he had previously held the post of president of the Imperials section.

All four vice-presidents ran to succeed Williams as first vice-president, splitting the Ontario Command vote and allowing Jack Jolleys of Pacific Command to come up the middle.

Tyndall chose not to run again for vice-president, but the Ontario rivalry continued as Kobolak challenged Smith, along with nine others. Kobolak was the victor, as were incumbent Hugh Greene, Fred Winn of Abbotsford, British Columbia, and Bob Haley of Sydney Mines, Nova Scotia.

Once again, no associates were nominated.

The remaining members of the executive were returned by acclamation.

National unity and veterans' service issues dominated the provincial conventions in 1991, but the looming leadership crisis — which had been prophesied for so long it was beginning to sound like the storied wolf — was suddenly, tragically, a reality. On September 27, Williams became the first Dominion president, and only the third serving executive, to die in office. For only the second time in 65 years, the first vice-president had to step into the breach. But, unlike Alf Watts, who was 37 years old when he took over the presidential duties of the stricken Lionel Baxter, Jack Jolleys was 66. A former trades foreman with the Burnaby school board, he had been a legionnaire since 1947.

The decline in ordinary and life members was now outstripping the growth of associates. Between 1990 and '92, total voting strength in the Legion declined by 4,300. Membership committee chairman Kobolak struggled with the problem that had dogged his predecessors in the late 1950s. "Branches across the country were successful in recruiting over 30,000 new members in 1991," he stated in his report to the 1992 Dominion convention in Quebec City. "But getting them in the door is one thing — keeping them is another. There were more than 40,000 non-renewals... The question is why?" The answer was not forthcoming.

Perhaps in response to the bleak reality of mortality now facing them, delegates overturned the non-concurrence of Kobolak's committee to debate the question of allowing grandchildren in as associates. Former president McChesney put his weight behind the issue. "This resolution will merely add a succeeding generational link to the chain of Legion membership," he said. "There's a natural family connection."

Indeed, only the membership committee seemed to oppose the idea. No one spoke against the motion in 10 minutes of debate on the floor, and the motion carried easily.

History was also made in the voting for officers when Al Parks, the 46-year-old associate from Miscouche, Prince Edward Island, became the first non-veteran to hold the post of vice-president. Joining him on the roster were incumbents Haley and Kobolak, and newcomer Chuck Murphy, a non-veteran ordinary member from Port Moody, British Columbia. Haley and Kobolak had also competed for first vice-president, along with Winn and Greene. Greene won on the fourth ballot.

Jolleys was acclaimed to serve his first full term as president, and there was no opposition either for Jones, Ford or Watkins.

Parks' ascent to Sub-Executive wasn't the only significant change at the national decision-making level. After nearly 66 years, the Tuberculous Veterans Section vacated its seat on the Executive Council. Fewer than 1,000 chest-disabled veterans and associates remained as members of nine Tuberculous Veterans branches in six commands. With fewer than 25 TB-related pension claims a year, the section had already given up the requirement to maintain a designated service officer at Dominion Command, and now national president Ed Slater — the retired director of the Dominion Service Bureau — announced that the organization was winding down.

The imminent demise of the Tuberculous Veterans Section was no surprise; the radical decline of what had been the largest Legion branch as recently as 1983 was a shock. Financial problems forced Edmonton's Montgomery Branch to close its doors in early 1993. Once a booming operation with almost 7,000 members, it had seen its membership dwindle to 2,500 over a decade. The remaining members decided they were too old to continue to operate the building, and cited the lack of parking in downtown Edmonton as an insurmountable barrier to recruiting younger members.

Quebec Command was the only command to increase its membership in 1992. Overall, the final 1992 membership statistics showed a decrease of more than 8,400 members and affiliates. This combined with 6,000 members lost in 1991 and 2,000 lost in 1990 equals more than 16,000 members lost since 1989.

Despite plans to launch a national recruitment drive, there was not much improvement in the membership picture in 1993. While the voting strength increased slightly, from 465,092 for 1992 to 466,464 for 1993, the overall figure dropped by almost 6,000. Eighty-one per cent of the Legion's members were men. Almost 40 per cent of the membership were seniors, and one in eight legionnaires was over 75. Sixteen per cent were ages 55 to 64, and one-third were 30 to 49.

Membership was broadened again at the 1994 Dominion convention in Calgary. Associate membership was extended to the brothers and sisters of people who are or would have been eligible for ordinary membership, as well as to officers of the Navy League of Canada. Ordinary membership was opened to people who fought in the Vietnam War, provided that they were Canadian citizens at the time, and to members of the Royal Newfoundland Constabulary.

Seventy-year-old Hugh Greene was acclaimed president after almost 50 years of Legion service. A retired farmer and provincial civil servant from Ponoka, Alberta, Greene was an RCAF veteran.

Parks declined nomination to stand for first vice-president, leaving the field to his three fellow vice-presidents. Kobolak scored a second-ballot victory.

Eleven candidates ran for the four vice-president positions. Incumbents Parks, Murphy and Haley were all re-elected. Ralph Annis, a postwar RCAF member and former provincial command president from McAdam, New Brunswick, was elected for the first time.

Pat Watkins, 65, became the seventh chairman in Legion history, defeating Clarence King of Newfoundland and Bill Hine of Ontario to replace the retiring Bob Ford. King then defeated Hine for the post of vice-chairman. Treasurer Jones was acclaimed for an eighth term.

With five legionnaires who had not been to war — Watkins, Parks, Murphy, Annis and King — on the Sub-Executive, the torch was being passed at the elected level. The Dominion staff had already undergone similar changes. Post-war serviceman Fred Hannington had been appointed Dominion secretary in 1985, and the last veteran on staff, Service Bureau director Kerry Dunphy, had retired in 1990.

Chapter 23

"OUR LAST HURRAH"

I n 1975-76, the Legion had celebrated its 50th anniversary by distributing more than four million golden-yellow tulips across Canada. "The Legion hasn't had so much fun in years," wrote former president Alf Watts in an internal document. Six years later, with the memories of that celebration still fresh in their minds, the Dominion Executive Council decided to make the 60th anniversary even more memorable. Who better to organize it, the thinking went, than the same people who had done so well in '75.

The members of the Legion "mafia" had drifted away from the spotlight since the mid-'70s. Bob Kohaly, Bob McChesney, Doug McDonald and Bob Smellie had turned their attention back to their own businesses, and were all thriving. Except for occasional appearances at conventions, they had no presence on the national stage of the organization. Most associates were not even aware of the role the four had played in opening up the Legion to them.

Privately, Kohaly despaired for the organization's future. He saw the momentum his membership committee had built up draining away, and worried that the Legion had missed its opportunity to capitalize on the potential of the younger members. When the invitation was proffered to organize a diamond jubilee along with the other living former presidents, he and his old partners eagerly agreed to get back into harness.

"We knew we were the only ones who could do it," said McDonald. "We got together and planned the whole jubilee program over one weekend. The whole concept was to wake the membership up to the potential of the Legion... to let them know that the organization has it all: the members, the real estate, the funds, the communications. We always knew when we had a good idea, and we always came out unanimous."

The plan was to run a year-long celebration beginning in May 1985, culminating at the 1986 Dominion convention in Edmonton. The theme would be "Pride In Our Past — Faith In Our Future." McChesney was agreed upon as chairman of the organizing committee. Although the committee nominally included former presidents MacBeath, Roche, Coley, Harvey and Woods, it was set up the same way as Kohaly's old membership committee — with a core steering group (Kohaly, McChesney, Smellie and McDonald) to make the key decisions. Eventually, the committee was expanded to include representatives from each command, the Ladies Auxiliary and associates. Just as in the old days, each command was also asked to organize its own jubilee commitee to coordinate events.

The heart of the celebrations was to be another national tulip campaign, this time featuring blood red Darwin tulips. The goal would be to sell 10 bulbs for each Legion and Ladies Auxiliary member and fraternal affiliate — a total of six million. The bulbs would sell for $25 per hundred, of which $2.50 would go to the branch and $1 would go to the command for use in jubilee celebrations. Other elements would include: a calendar; a commemorative medal; a pictorial coffee-table book; a film that could be shown on TV; a nostalgic stage revue; a state dinner; an aural history; and production of Articles of Faith that would signify the commitment of sons and daughters to the perpetuation of the Legion's values and traditions.

At the 1984 Dominion convention, the committee previewed their arrangements. The Articles of Faith were being drafted by two people who had worked on the Canadian Charter of Rights and Freedoms. A Winnipeg company had been retained to shoot footage for inclusion in the TV film. Brantford, Ontario, photographer Jack Jarvie and Toronto writer Diana Swift were putting together the coffee-table book. An Ottawa theatre company, Staged Right, had written a musical show set in a British pub. Called *We'll Meet Again*, the show was designed so that branches or commands could purchase a kit for $50 and mount the play for local audiences.

The celebration was set to kick off May 8, 1985 — the 40th anniversary of VE-Day.

In November 1984, the steering committee appeared at the fall Executive Council meeting to provide an update. Kohaly reported that the Articles of Faith were completed, and would be made available to every branch and command. Watts made a special pitch to stir up interest in the aural history project and introduced Marcel Dirk, a young historian who had been hired to administer the project. Dirk explained that kits were available so branches could conduct interviews with members who had a long history in the Legion. "The aural history will be the legacy of Legion members not only to researchers and academics but one that a wide range of interested people across the country will use," he said. He explained that copies would be put on record at archives across the country for research purposes.

Kohaly explained that the steering committee hoped to enlist 10 leading Canadian corporations to contribute $30,000 each to become official jubilee patrons. Their sponsorship would be recognized in the stage show program, the pictorial book and at the state dinner.

Council granted approval for the steering committee to continue with plans for the state dinner, despite the concerns of two commands that the cost estimate of $200,000 was excessive. A committee request to transfer funds between jubilee programs was also approved.

The issue of funding for the diamond jubilee would become an ongoing sore point between the steering committee and Sub-Executive, which felt that there was not sufficient control over expenditures. The situation was exacerbated by the fact that the steering committee managed to attract just three corporate sponsors — Carling O'Keefe, Chrysler and Crown Life — and quickly ran up large bills.

There was also some discomfort on the part of Sub-Executive that the jubilee steering committee had retained the services of Continental Public Relations and budgeted $450,000 to promote the anniversary, conduct publicity seminars across Canada and gather news for *Legion Magazine* about celebrations at the branch level. It was the first time in 60 years that the Legion had looked outside for help in publicizing the organization. Kohaly defended the decision, saying that public relations has the highest priority in jubilee planning because of competition for the public's attention. "I see our message as being one of men and women — the backbone of Canada in time of need — who came out of World War I and II and Korea as citizen soldiers imbued with great values," he told a meeting of the national jubilee committee in December 1984. "These values we have left in our communities and we are willing to change our organization's character to see that they are carried on.... We may not be so vibrant on the 75th (anniversary)."

The tulip campaign was slow to catch on. By March 15 — halfway through the six-month blitz — only 157,550 bulbs, or three per cent of the target, had been ordered. "First indications were that all commands expected to go over their goals," said jubilee committee chairman McChesney, "but early returns don't reflect that attitude." A month later, with just 50 days remaining in the campaign, sales had doubled but a *Legion Magazine* editorial admitted: "Looking pragmatically, the numbers don't justify the (organizers') optimism." Against all odds, the campaign suddenly exploded. The trickle of orders became a deluge — reaching a staggering 1.5 million bulbs in one three-day period — and by June 12, with orders still flowing in, more than five million bulbs had been sold. A total of 5.7 million bulbs were sold in time for fall planting.

If the tulips were slow to bloom, there was no such reluctance shown in the acceptance of the jubilee medals or the Articles of Faith. Branches and commands seized on both as a way of celebrating the anniversary. The highlight of many of the provincial conventions held in 1985 was the signing of the Articles of Faith — usually an act that included veterans from both world wars and an associate member.

Signing the Articles of Faith was also a highlight of the Legion's state dinner held at Ottawa's Chateau Laurier on November 2. Among those whose signatures were recorded were: Governor General Jeanne Sauve, Chief Justice Brian Dickson, Veterans Affairs Minister George Hees and Victoria Cross holder John Foote. Other guests at the glittering affair included four other Canadian VCs — Cecil Merritt, David Currie, Smokey Smith and Fred Tilston — the Dutch ambassador, the command presidents and representatives of the Legion's jubilee corporate sponsors.

The elegance of the state dinner masked some problems that continued to dog the jubilee celebrations. Earlier in the day at an Executive Council meeting, McChesney had sought a vote of confidence to silence the rumblings from council. "We have tried to come up with imaginative things and enjoyed some success. Admittedly, everything did not go smoothly but, by the end of the jubilee, the Legion will be better identified as making a meaningful contribution to Canada."

McDonald reported that only 3,000 of 15,000 coffee-table books had been sold, but shifted some of the blame to Dominion Command for its refusal to stock and market the books. Watts announced he was resigning as chairman of the aural history project because of what he said was a conflict with his position as grand president. In fact, the program was having trouble gaining acceptance. Pacific Command had pulled out entirely, and Ontario was not fully involved. Former president Coley was appointed to take over the program.

But it was not slow book sales, reluctant commands or even the projected cost overrun of $500,000 that was the most controversial element of the diamond jubilee steering committee's plans. The biggest split between the "mafia" members and the current leadership was caused by what Kohaly called the "sunset provisions" of the Veterans Charter. At the Dominion Executive Council meeting in March 1986 he made his case for what he termed "our last hurrah." Hammering away at the idea that veterans are "citizens first, veterans second," he said that, through their wartime sacrifices, they had prepaid the nation for special economic consideration that should be due them at age 65 in cases of need. In addition to the existing system of old age security as a right and guaranteed income supplement as a need, he envisioned a third payment of perhaps $200 to $300 a month. Other provisions would maintain veterans in their own homes and guarantee housing and nursing care in their own communities.

By entrenching the sunset provisions in legislation, he argued, the government would be bound to provide for Canadian veterans to the last man and woman. His rationale for the provisions was that the increasing cost and bureaucracy involved in maintaining the existing Veterans Affairs infrastructure would lead a future government to cut back on service, to the detriment of those making claims. "The bureaucracy is growing while the veteran population shrinks," he told Dirk during his taping for the aural history. "The cost per veteran is growing."

While Council granted Kohaly the budget to explore how these provisions might be instituted and permission to approach Veterans Affairs and the National Council of Veterans Associations for cooperation, there was tremendous reluctance to pursue the matter. For one thing, Kohaly's plan would challenge the need for the Legion's service bureaus, since veterans would automatically qualify for some form of assistance. He knew it would be an uphill fight. "(first vice-president Tony) Stacey, (Dominion Service Bureau director Ed) Slater and (Dominion secretary Colin) Graham were all cool to the idea. Slater agreed with the need to reduce the bureaucracy, but he lost enthusiasm for the idea."

"Ed and I didn't understand the need for sunset provisions," agreed Graham. "I think it was a case that Kohaly was out of touch with how DVA (Veterans Affairs) had evolved. The Legion was still in the business of fighting for the provisions we always wanted."

While the staff had pragmatic differences with Kohaly, Sub-Executive's concerns were more focused on the optics of the sunset provisions.

"The media would've twisted the intention of the sunset provisions if the issue had come to convention floor for debate," said Steve Dunsdon, Dominion president during the jubilee celebrations.

In the end, Kohaly lost this fight. Although he had threatened to take the issue to the delegates at the Edmonton convention — in essence driving a wedge between the membership and the elected officers — he backed off. In an unusually subdued presentation to the convention, he announced that the sunset provisions would be reassessed by an ad hoc committee to be appointed by Sub-Executive.

Graham was right; Veterans Affairs *had* changed, and so had the Legion's relationship to it. In the early '80s, the Legion still made headlines with its unstinting support for ex-servicemen seeking compensation from the government. In one case, the national media reported on the Dominion Service Bureau's presentation of the case of Bjarnie Paulson, a 62-year-old World War II and Korea vet who claimed he developed basal cell carcinoma after exposure to damaged fire rods at the Chalk River nuclear reactor while he was an instructor in atomic warfare.

That kind of high-profile case was rare, though. For the most part, the Legion quietly presented briefs to committees or commissions looking into pension legislation. The Dominion Service Bureau continued to act on about 1,500 cases a year. However, the days of the protracted public battles over veterans' rights were pretty much done. The failure to head off Veterans Affairs' move to Charlottetown indicated that the Legion no longer had the power to influence political decisions the way it could in the 1940s or '50s.

Still, with 600,000 members and affiliates, the Legion represented one of the larger single-interest lobby groups in the country, and governments continued to respect its voting strength. In 1984, the newly elected Brian Mulroney showed his respect for it by making his first cabinet appointment 74-year-old George Hees to the Veterans Affairs portfolio. A faithful Conservative soldier for years, Hees was the perfect link to the past for the tyro Mulroney, looking to establish himself after his impressive defeat of Prime Minister John Turner. For the Legion, the appointment of the World War II vet and 40-year legionnaire filled a gap missing since the beloved Dan MacDonald's death.

Hees wasted little time in giving the Legion what it wanted. Promising "generosity, speed and courtesy" for veterans and their dependants, he initiated a series of measures, including: enshrinement in the Pension Act of annual disability pension adjustment by the greater of either the increase in the Consumer Price Index or the average wage of the composite group of civil servants; initiation of two-person entitlement boards, with any tie going to the applicant; continuation of disability pension at the married rate to a spouse for 12 months after death of the recipient; and expansion of the Pension Review Board.

"These first legislative initiatives show that (Hees' promises to treat veterans with generosity) are not just hollow words," stated a *Legion Magazine* editorial. "Indeed, coming at a time when the new government is acting swiftly to cut back federal spending and beginning an examination of social programs, the minister's ability to push this expansion of benefits through cabinet bodes well for the veteran population."

Hees also won kudos for his plan to consolidate district offices of the Veterans Service section of Veterans Affairs, the Canadian Pension Commission, the Bureau of Pensions Advocates and Veterans Land Administration in an effort to provide one-stop shopping. Lauded as well was the January 1986 announcement of a new name for the aging veterans' program. As the veterans independence program — widely touted by its acronym, VIP, for obvious reasons — Hees said it would increase efforts to keep veterans in their homes and independent as long as possible.

The only contentious issue — and it was hardly that compared to earlier pension battles — was extension of War Veterans Allowance eligibility to wartime volunteers who served a year or more but never went overseas. Widely promised by Conservative candidates in Ontario during the 1984 election campaign, eligibility for "CSOs" (Canada service only) had been requested by delegates to every Dominion convention since 1974. Calling it the Legion's top priority, Dominion president Stacey pressed the case for extended benefits again in March 1987 in a brief to the Commons standing committee on veterans affairs. Hees' reply was that the issue could not be given serious consideration until funds became available and after the future needs of other groups of veterans were provided for. In November 1987, Stacey appealed directly for support to every MP and senator: "...Our membership considers that if the government of Canada could find the money to defend our way of life in war, then it is duty-bound to recognize the outstanding debt by ensuring that these veterans and their dependants are not now in need. Volunteers whose duty was restricted to Canada freely offered their lives and the government has an obligation to them in a similar manner to those who served overseas. In fact, 10 per cent of the 44,000 total deaths during World War II occurred in Canada..."

The Legion's persistence paid off with a compromise. Hees used the 1988 Dominion convention — his last as Veterans Affairs minister — to announce that the federal government would spend an additional $200 million over five years under the VIP.

Hees accomplished much in his first four years at the helm of Veterans Affairs, and he left a much leaner, more efficient department

❦

behind when he retired. With him, however, went the sense that veterans had a sympathetic ear in government, and probably the last chance for the Legion to establish a close relationship with a Veterans Affairs minister. No matter how much Hees was, in reality, Mulroney's man, there remained the feeling among most legionnaires that he would always be theirs as well.

While Mulroney maintained Veterans Affairs as a separate portfolio during most of his second term — and Hees' successor, Gerry Merrithew, proved to be a popular minister — the eventual downgrading of the ministry was inevitable. In 1993, Mulroney doubled up on responsibilities, pairing Veterans Affairs and National Defence briefly under Kim Campbell. Although, during the 1993 election campaign, the Liberal party gave assurances that Veterans Affairs Canada (as it had been renamed) would revert to being represented by a separate minister, when Prime Minister Jean Chretien unveiled his new cabinet the department was under the direction of Defence Minister David Collenette, although junior minister Lawrence MacAulay was responsible for the department's management.

The Legion expressed its disappointment in a brief to the Commons standing committee on national defence and veterans affairs in February 1994. It had time to do little else; the Legion was asked to share a 15-minute timeslot with the Canadian Merchant Navy Prisoner of War Association. "That gives the Legion a second for every thousand veterans still alive," noted Dominion secretary Fred Hannington.

It has long been realized that one day the care of Canada's remaining veterans and their dependants would be handed over to some other federal agency — likely a branch of Human Resources and Labor Canada, which has jurisdiction over Old Age Security and other financial assistance programs. Whenever that occurs, it will not likely be at a time of the Legion's choosing. That was the reality Kohaly was hoping to avert with his sunset provisions. Whether his concern for the welfare of Canada's last veterans was justified is a question for the ages. Only the fate of the sunset provisions is clear. After some study by the ad hoc committee on veterans benefits, the term "sunset provisions" was dropped and its various components were broken up for future study.

The sunset provisions were not the only controversial product left at the conclusion of the 60th anniversary celebrations. There was also a deficit approaching $1 million on expenditures of $3.6 million and a lingering bitterness between members of the "mafia" and the current leadership. In a much-quoted speech, Bob Smellie summed up the diamond jubilee exerience by comparing it to baking a cake. His recipe:

flour (the provincial command representatives), fruit and nuts (the former Dominion presidents), three cups of sugar (Ladies Auxiliary representatives), three good eggs (associate representatives), butter (Continental Public Relations), baking powder (committee secretary Rod Johnston), one teaspoon of vinegar (Sub-Executive) and one cup of rum (the provincial jubilee committees). Blend in a mixer (Dominion Executive Council). Add more rum. Mix again. Divide into three pans — shallow (Dominion Command), medium (provincial commands) and deep (branches). Bake in an oven of controversy (jubilee medals, budget overruns, sunset provisions). Separate the layers with jubilee dinners.

The icing on this cake was Dame Vera Lynn, who had been hired for $45,000 plus expenses to take the delegates back to their glory days with a 45-minute selection of World War II songs.

Outgoing president Dunsdon called Lynn's fee outrageous and Smellie's speech "disgraceful... (Sub-Executive) had no control over the steering committee and got few reports from them. Continental Public Relations went hog wild spending money, with little to show for it. The film was a disaster and the pictorial history was a fiasco. I don't see the diamond jubilee expenditures as an investment."

Kohaly was considerably more sanguine. In his summary to the convention he capsulized the 60th anniversary year as "many high points, a few low points. We learned a lot. I wish we could start over with the knowledge we have now."

Chapter 24

A GROWING
INDEPENDENCE

While the hoopla surrounding the diamond anniversary celebrations dominated the Legion stage in the mid-'80s, the issue of aging continued to grow into the primary item on the organization's agenda — both at the national and the local level.

Since 1978, when the convention had endorsed a nationwide program on aging, the Legion had become the catalyst for a number of seminars and other activities to study the aging process. When the Legion got involved, the view of aging in Canada still revolved around the inevitable warehousing of people as they grew increasingly infirm. Most teaching hospitals did not offer special courses in geriatrics, and Canada had almost no geriatric specialists. The new concept of gerontology and geriatrics — that seniors could maintain their independence in familiar surroundings late into life provided that doctors treated specific ailments — had only recently arrived from Britain and Scandinavia. It was the foresight of people like former Dominion Service Bureau director Bert Hanmer and upcoming national leader Tony Stacey that turned the Legion's attention — and funds — to these new attitudes, and they quickly attracted proponents of the new philosophy in the health care community who were anxious to spread the gospel.

In August 1981, 30 influential legionnaires from across Canada attended a seniors program seminar, where they were told about the urgent need to change society's attitudes about aging and prepare for a future when a large number of Canadians would be in their late 60s and early 70s.

At the 1982 Dominion convention, delegates heard from Dr. John Bewick, one of the first recipients of the Legion Geriatric Fellowship. "I now realize that aging is not a disease," said Bewick of his studies in Scotland. "Your developing programs for the elderly are a reminder to us all of your tradition of service..."

"By 1990," added Stacey, "when one in three retired Canadians will be a veteran, his wife or his widow, the Legion Seniors Program must be

❦

strongly established everywhere to carry out the many tasks which will be demanded of it by you and me." Delegates voted to extended the fellowship program to June 30, 1987, at a cost of $90,000 per year from Centennial Fund interest, with provisions for increases due to rises in the cost of living.

In 1984, the Dominion convention confirmed a plan to expand the fellowship program by adding $15,000 a year for three years to include nurses.

By the mid-'80s, the field of geriatrics had changed significantly. Many of the doctors who had studied on the Legion fellowship were teaching; eight hospitals now offered courses in geriatrics, and Legion fellows no longer had to go abroad to complete their studies.

In 1986, the Legion again extended the fellowship program — to June 1990 — and agreed to contribute $25,000 to co-sponsor an annual conference on aging issues with Veterans Affairs and the National Advisory Council on Aging. Thirty-eight legionnaires were among the 88 delegates to the conference, which stressed the need for seniors to make their voices heard. "I am sure this conference will stand as a landmark," said Veterans Affairs Minister Hees. "Senior citizens already have more leadership experience than any other group in society. Your experience, together with the organization of the Royal Canadian Legion, is more than equal to the leadership challenge."

Stacey used the conference to trace the evolution of the Legion's program. "Since the Legion Seniors Program came into being in 1978, our concern was to ensure that as we grew older, adequate services would be in place to meet our many needs. With the exception of our war experience, we had no more in common than civilian seniors. Therefore, our interest in the needs of seniors became as wide and as varied as our membership."

Following the national model, three provincial commands — Nova Scotia, Pacific and Saskatchewan — made plans in 1987 to hold their own regional conferences on aging.

The federal government was increasing its involvement, too. In 1987, a Seniors Secretariat was established by the Mulroney government to act as a clearing house for information on gerontology and geriatrics, and to administer programs run by various special-interest groups. Hees was appointed minister of state for seniors, and brought as much enthusiasm to his new job as he had to Veterans Affairs. One idea that he imported from his years at Veterans Affairs was the Seniors Independence Program, aimed at providing funding for initiatives that would help keep older people in their own homes. Since the new federal body was looking for partnerships with existing projects, the Legion Seniors Program was an obvious place for it to invest. In 1989, the government offered the Legion almost $500,000 over three years to extend its program, hiring a project coordinator and designing community programs that could be administered through branches. The Legion's share of the cost for the extended program was about $230,000.

During the program's first two years it produced a directory of Legion housing across the country, a guidebook of seniors' programs, and kits to help branches access information. But the program's cost did not sit well with Ontario Command, which felt that the money might better be put to use for programs aimed solely at veterans. In a stormy session at the 1992 Dominion convention, Ontario delegates stood as a bloc against renewal of the program. Over the protests of vice-president Fred Winn, the program chairman, and vice-chairman Al Parks, Ontario used its voting strength to defeat the motion to commit $240,000 from general funds to extend it for another two years.

Despite the termination of the expanded national program, by the end of 1993 Legion seniors' programs accounted for about $4 million in national investment and some 365,000 hours of volunteer labor during the year. In addition, another $2.9 million were invested in medical and geriatric training, and Legion branches held about $167 million worth of community housing. The gerontology fellowships for doctors had been extended to the end of 1996, although the $60,000 annual payment now came from general funds and was divided among 12 physicians. Another $20,000 went to nurses, and $15,000 each to occupational therapists and physiotherapists.

Ontario's use of its massive size to kill the extended seniors' program was not without precedent, but it marked a growing independence among branches and commands. After 70 years, some elements no longer wanted to take — or sometimes even listen to — Dominion Command's counsel. In some respects, this reflected an organization-wide readiness to challenge authority. At a 1985 Executive Council meeting, Dominion president Steve Dunsdon had noted the increasing number of complaints against branch executives by members, and wondered rhetorically what it said about comradeship within the Legion. In 1993, at New Brunswick Command's convention, several officers noted the rise in bickering between members. The command's chairman of branch control and discipline, Dave Hogan, said: "I think the branches have lost touch with why we're here. There's a lot of backstabbing and a lot of infighting..."

In most circumstances, these internal conflicts stayed internal. The Legion was never known for washing its dirty laundry in public. Even the dispute over the change in status of fraternal affiliates in the early 1970s, which might have resulted in the suspension of an entire command, was kept within the confines of the organization. That tradition changed in the weeks following Remembrance Day 1993.

The trouble started innocently enough — with an invitation from Newton Branch in Surrey, British Columbia, to veterans to visit the branch. Three veterans who were members of the Sikh faith were asked to remove their turbans before entering. They refused, and were turned away.

The Legion tradition of removing your hat in clubrooms as a mark of respect for fallen comrades is well known and widespread. Just as well known is the fact that house rules are the purview of the branch, and that many branches make exceptions to the rule — from Stampede Days events in Calgary branches to visits from Santa Claus at Christmas parties. Also well known is the fact that the Canadian Forces permit Sikhs to wear turbans in messes, canteens, dining rooms and the like. So, when the Sikhs were denied access to Newton Branch, they accused the Legion of religious discrimination.

In an age charged with questions surrounding Canada's immigration policies — including the traditional belief in a multicultural mosaic as opposed to the American melting pot — and political correctness, the Surrey incident attracted media interest. Across the country, reporters called local Legion contacts for their response. The answers they got were varied. An official policy would not be forthcoming from Dominion Command until the Executive Council meeting scheduled for November 27 and 28.

At that meeting, Pacific Command president Mary Ann Burdett apologized for the actions of Newton Branch, saying: "It was never envisioned the house rules of any individual branch would impact on the image of The Royal Canadian Legion."

The council was unanimous in its agreement to adopt a new bylaw concerning the wearing of head coverings on Legion premises. The new bylaw stated: "Branch bylaws or house rules shall include a provision for the wearing of head-dress in the premises, and, when doing so, must provide that religious head-dress of the Jewish and Sikh faiths is not considered to constitute head-dress in the traditional sense. Therefore, once a person who is required to wear a head-dress for these faiths has been accepted as a

Legion branch member, or invited as a guest to the Legion branch, he is to be authorized admission to all areas of that branch that are normally opened to the general membership or invited guests."

Although effective immediately, the amendment would be put before the 1994 Dominion convention for review.

As soon as the new bylaw was announced, legionnaires began expressing their feelings in a relative torrent of letters to *Legion Magazine*:

"I strongly support (the Executive Council's) position... Should the Newton Branch action... be upheld at the national convention in May, I will perceive this as a matter of racial and religious prejudice and will cancel my membership in The Royal Canadian Legion," read one representative letter.

"These guys (the Sikhs) have got to realize that they are now living in Canada. In no way should we change our rules for them or anyone else," wrote an Ontario reader at the opposite side of the issue.

The Executive Council ruling did nothing to stop public debate in other forums, either. On *Morningside*, CBC Radio's national showcase, two legionnaires appeared to discuss the issue, but the interview quickly turned to name calling and the questioning of the turban as a legitimate religious symbol. In other arenas, outspoken veterans even questioned the legitimacy of Sikhism itself, thus aligning themselves with various extremist "experts" who cloaked racism in the guise of religious scholarship. The issue was becoming a public relations nightmare, and it was obvious that it was going to boil over at the convention if something was not done.

At its February 1994 meeting, the Executive Council discussed the controversy again. Dominion president Jack Jolleys attempted to clarify the rationale for the new bylaw, citing advice from human rights officials that rejecting or failing to comply with it could be considered institutional discrimination. "The Canadian Human Rights Commission has confirmed that the turban is accepted and has the status of a religious symbol or tradition," he said. "It is therefore not... feasible to attempt to avoid the issue by using the argument that a turban is not a religious symbol."

Chairman Bob Ford said: "I'm hoping that I can get enough (information) that when the matter comes to the floor, I can cut discussion off right away on two grounds: one, it's detrimental to the Legion if we are liable,... and secondly, if the matter is in conflict with the laws of Canada it cannot be debated by the Legion... I hope that we can have as little debate as possible."

His hope was not to be realized.

Despite Jolleys' admonition that "the whole country is watching us," legionnaires proceeded to vent their anger over the bylaw on national TV and radio.

Ford prefaced debate on the bylaw by warning that *Robert's Rules Of Order* — which guide Legion meetings in instances not covered by the Legion's own rules — state that an organization should not vote on matters where the outcome contravenes the law. Nevertheless, he said he felt compelled by the wishes of the convention to allow the debate. The discussion that followed was emotional.

"The Legion is my temple," argued one delegate, his voice shaking with anger. "A Legion is not just a canteen or a hall. It is a temple in every sense of the word."

"They're trying to take the 'Christ' out of Christmas," shouted one woman.

Six hundred and twenty-nine delegates voted to retain the bylaw — against 1,959 opposed — but after the vote reporters could not find anyone who would admit to supporting the Executive Council. Meanwhile, there was no shortage of legionnaires prepared to gloat about the result for the benefit of cameras and microphones.

The fallout from the vote was not long in coming. Following a recess, Ford told the convention that by going against *Robert's Rules* he had compromised himself as chairman, and with that he handed the meeting over to vice-chairman Pat Watkins, closed his briefcase, stood and walked off the stage. His resignation stunned the convention and was the focus of national news coverage, despite the fact that he was widely rumored to be considering retirement after 18 years at Dominion Command.

Not since the 1964 debate over the maple leaf flag had the Legion attracted this much media attention for something not related to remembrance. The day after the vote, several delegates compounded the problem by accusing the media of making the Legion look bad. Some called for censure of the *Globe and Mail* and CBC-TV.

It is true that the media played up the racism angle, focusing on the remarks of those delegates who sounded most reactionary. What most media overlooked was the fact that many delegates had voted in favor of maintaining branch autonomy, not to bar Sikhs from branches. Several weeks after the convention, Dominion Command attempted to put the entire incident into perspective in a letter to all branches:

"It is wrong to say that the convention 'banned turbans.' The delegates did not vote to ban religious head-dress from branches. The vote was to rescind a national general bylaw that imposed a dress regulation on branches. This decision took the responsibility for branch head-dress rules back into the hands of the branches.

"The responsibility now is for branches to comply with Canadian and provincial human rights codes and decisions or face the consequences, which... will depend on the decisions of the provincial human rights commissions and the courts...

"Convention delegates may not have been wrong to return the responsibility for branch dress to the branches, but the membership and leadership will be wrong if they permit discrimination in their branches on the basis of religious head-dress."

Chapter 25

THE LEGION AT 70

A s divisive and potentially destructive as the turban controversy was, it embodied several themes that have dominated the Legion's history: the desire for branch autonomy; the acceptance of renegades within the organization; and respect for tradition. The organization was founded by diverse elements to fight for a common goal, and that feisty quality — that willingness to stand firm against government authorities — has always been present. It is not really surprising that delegates to the 1994 convention took the stand they did against the threats of Canada's various provincial and federal human rights authorities; it is the same stance they have taken against various bureaucracies since the years before the Great Depression.

In judging the Legion's effectiveness over 70 years you must begin with the issue of veterans' rights, and in that area of endeavor there is no question that the organization has exceeded its original expectations. It is widely recognized that Canada has the best record of treatment for its ex-servicemen and women, and the most generous veterans' legislation in the world.

To be fair, that is partially because of Canada's own history. Because the country was less than 50 years old when the first casualties of World War I started coming home, and had relatively little experience with warfare as a sovereign nation, the government went looking for guidance where it could find it. The Great War Veterans Association's early work consulting on a veterans' resettlement program set the precedent for the work done on behalf of the government in later years by former and future Legion leaders like Basil Price and Mervyn Woods. As well, the Canadian veteran has benefited from the presence in high places of men like Chubby Power and George Hees, who had firsthand experience and empathy with veterans.

That said, the development of the core of expertise that has existed in the Dominion Command Service Bureau since the late '20s went a long way toward ensuring that successive governments lived up to the pledge made by Prime Minister Sir Robert Borden in 1917. The work of legionnaires like Robbie Robinson, Kerry Dunphy and Ed Slater often went unnoticed, but thousands of veterans and their dependants were better off for the knowledge these service officers collected and the skills they brought to the job.

The Legion's record in the non-veteran field is only slightly less solid. From its early calls for socialized medicine, a public broadcasting system and a distinctively Canadian constitution, the organization has lived up to the prediction made by the Great War Veterans Association's magazine in 1924 that, next to service work for veterans, "the major work... will be nation building." The Legion slipped in the early '60s by battling Lester Pearson on the flag issue, but redeemed itself in the public eye with its tough stance on national unity.

At the community level, the Legion's twin legacies are Canada's strong amateur sports networks and the forward-looking stance on aging. In both areas, the organization was well ahead of the federal government in recognizing the importance of giving support and direction at the poles of the age spectrum.

If there has been a major failing, it is the Legion's inability to have the public connect it to these achievements. Instead, the average Canadian continues to think of the Legion in terms of old soldiers reminiscing over beer, or gathering on Remembrance Day. It is a problem the organization has wrestled with since Dominion president John Anderson turned it toward community work in the mid-'50s. It is a problem the diamond jubilee steering committee spent hundreds of thousands of dollars trying to overcome in the '80s. At the heart of the problem is a riddle: How do you publicize your own selflessness? It is a problem that makes the misunderstanding over the turban issue, and the harsh words of a few renegades, that much more damaging. At this point, with membership aging and declining, it is unlikely that the Legion will now ever be in a position to change the public's perception.

A more pressing issue today is survival itself. It is difficult to imagine the death of an organization that was so entwined with the country as the Legion, but perhaps no more difficult than it might have been to imagine the rapid decline of Edmonton's once-mighty Montgomery Branch.

If there is one constant in the '90s, it is change — particularly among Canada's most-entrenched institutions. The first half of the decade has witnessed the near-destruction of one of the country's dominant political parties, the bankruptcy of several prominent retailers, and the end of the provincial telephone companies' century-old monopoly. The decline of the Legion would not be nearly as surprising. Certainly, unless there is a radical and sudden increase in enlistment, the organization will see its membership drop by at least one-third over the coming decade as those legionnaires now older than 65 die or become inactive. The most important issue, then, is how the remaining members will choose to carry on. Will they decide to increase community spending, effectively winding up the organization's existence? Or, will the remaining 350,000 legionnaires re-dedicate themselves and decide to live on? Either way, leadership will be critical.

In the '80s, as time slipped by and only a small handful of associate members moved up the chain of authority, several prominent legionnaires fretted over who would lead the organization into the next century. The most commonly heard concern was that there did not appear to be another Alex Walker, Alf Watts, Mervyn Woods or Bob Kohaly on the horizon. Some people decried the traditional "ladder" system that saw future leaders move through the ranks at branch, district, zone, command and Dominion levels. Yet, several of the Legion's best leaders — Watts and Woods most prominent among them — did not come up this way. Who, as Walker ended his third term as Dominion president, could have foreseen the rapid rise of a World War II veteran? Who would have guessed that Watts and Woods would prove to be such dogged fighters for veterans' rights? Somewhere among the close to 80,000 Legion members under the age of 40 there may well be a leader with the kind of vision that Alex Ross and Kohaly brought to the job.

Even if that person never appears — if the Legion were to simply continue pouring dollars and hours of volunteer labor into amateur sports and seniors' housing and charitable work — the organization could continue for years as Canada's largest service organization. At about 30,000 and 17,000 members respectively, other leading clubs like Rotary and the Kinsmen do not even come close. Is that enough? A number of veterans still believe it is not. Nothing that has happened since 1972 has changed their minds about the suitability of associate members to carry on in their absence. Once the last veteran is gone, they ask, what use is the Legion?

True, once the last old soldier has died, there will be nothing left of veterans but memories. The question the Legion will have to ask itself as that day approaches is, will memories last without the organization? Who, without the Legion's stubborn presence, will — at the going down of the sun and in the morning — remember them?

Bibliography

Bowering, Clifford. *Service: the Story of the Canadian Legion, 1925-1960*, Ottawa: Dominion Command, Canadian Legion, 1960.

Capperauld, Dave. Interview with Marcel Dirk, Diamond Jubilee Aural History Project.

Coley, Ed. Interview with Marcel Dirk, Diamond Jubilee Aural History Project.

Dunsdon, Steve. Interview with Marcel Dirk, Diamond Jubilee Aural History Project.

Graham, Colin. Interview with Marcel Dirk, Diamond Jubilee Aural History Project.

Harvey, Al. Interview with Marcel Dirk, Diamond Jubilee Aural History Project.

Kohaly, Robert. Interview with Marcel Dirk, Diamond Jubilee Aural History Project.

Lamy, Jean. Interview with Marcel Dirk, Diamond Jubilee Aural History Project.

Matheson, John Ross. "Flag Debate" in the *Canadian Encyclopedia*, Edmonton: Hurtig Publishers Inc., 1985.

McDonald, Douglas. Interview with Marcel Dirk, Diamond Jubilee Aural History Project.

Morton, Desmond. *When Your Number's Up: the Canadian Soldier in the First World War*, Toronto: Random House of Canada Ltd., 1993.

Rhodes Smith, Charles. Interview with Marcel Dirk, Diamond Jubilee Aural History Project.

Roche, Redmond. Interview with Marcel Dirk, Diamond Jubilee Aural History Project.

258

Smellie, Robert. Interview with Marcel Dirk, Diamond Jubilee Aural History Project.

Smith, Gene. *The Ends of Greatness: Haig, Pétain, Rathenau and Eden — Victims of History*, New York: Crown Publishers Inc., 1990.

Stacey, Charles P. "World War II" in the *Canadian Encyclopedia*, Edmonton: Hurtig Publishers Inc., 1985.

Terraine, John. *Ordeal of Victory*, Philadelphia and New York: J.B. Lippincott Co., 1963.

Thompson, Donald. Interview with Marcel Dirk, Diamond Jubilee Aural History Project.

Watts, Alfred. Interview with Marcel Dirk, Diamond Jubilee Aural History Project.

Woods, Mervyn. Interview with Marcel Dirk, Diamond Jubilee Aural History Project.

Appendix

GRAND PRESIDENTS

Field Marshal Earl Haig of Bemersyde, KT, GCB, OM, GCVO, KICE
1925-1928

General Sir Arthur Currie, GCMG, KCB
1929-1933

Lieutenant-General Sir Percy Lake, KCB, KCMG
1934-1940

Lieutenant-General Sir Richard Turner, VC, KCB, KCMG, DSO, VD
1942-1948

General H.D.G. Crerar, CH, CB, DSO, ADC
1948-1965

Major-General The Honourable George R. Pearkes, VC, CB, DSO, MC, CD
1966-1976

Brigadier-General J.A. de Lalanne, CBE, MC, OSt.J, ED, BA, CA
1977-1984

His Honour Judge Alfred Watts, AFC, ED, QC
1984-1991

The Honourable J. Gilles Lamontagne, CP, OC, CD, BA
1991-1994

The Honourable D. Gordon Blair, BA, LLB, BCL
1994-present

DOMINION PRESIDENTS

Lieutenant-General Sir Percy Lake
British Columbia, 1925-1927

**Lieutenant-General
Sir Arthur Currie**
Quebec, 1928

**Lieutenant-Colonel
Leo R. LaFleche**
Ontario, 1929-1930

Major John S. Roper
Nova Scotia, 1931-1933

Brigadier-General Alex Ross
Saskatchewan, 1934-1937

Lieutenant-Colonel W.W. Foster
British Columbia, 1938-1939

Alex Walker
Alberta, 1940-1945

Major-General C.B. Price
Quebec, 1946-1947

Lieutenant-Colonel L.D.M. Baxter
Manitoba, 1948-1949

Group Captain Alfred Watts
British Columbia, 1950-1951

Dr. C.B. Lumsden
Nova Scotia, 1952-1953

Very Reverend John O. Anderson
Manitoba, 1954-1955

D.L. Burgess
Ontario, 1956-1959

Mervyn Woods
Saskatchewan, 1960-1961

Judge C.C. Sparling
Manitoba, 1962-1963

F.T. O'Brecht
Ontario, 1964-1965

R.E. MacBeath
New Brunswick, 1966-1967

Robert Kohaly
Saskatchewan, 1968-1969

J. Redmond Roche
Quebec, 1970-1971

Robert G. Smellie
Manitoba, 1972-1973

Robert D. McChesney
Ontario, 1974-1975

Douglas McDonald
Ontario, 1976-1977

Edward C. Coley
Alberta, 1978-1979

Al Harvey
Newfoundland, 1980-1981

Dave Capperauld
Ontario, 1982-1983

Steve Dunsdon
British Columbia, 1984-1985

Anthony Stacey
Ontario, 1986-1987

Gaston Garceau
Quebec, 1988-1989

Fred Williams
Newfoundland, 1990-1991

Jack Jolleys
British Columbia, 1992-1993

Hugh M. Greene
Alberta, 1994-present

DOMINION SECRETARIES

John Reginald Bowler
1930-1942

J.C.G. Herwig
1943-1949

T.D. Anderson
1949-1959

Donald M. Thompson
1959-1970

John E. Lamy
1971-1982

Colin H. Graham
1982-1985

Fred G. Hannington
1985-present

SUB-EXECUTIVE COMMITTEE
PRESIDENTS AND VICE-PRESIDENTS

1925-1927
Lieutenant-General Sir Percy Lake

Brigadier-General F.S. Meighan

Lieutenant-Colonel
Leo Richer LaFleche (1927)

Lieutenant-Colonel Jim McAra
(1927)

1928
Lieutenant-General
Sir Arthur Currie

Lieutenant-Colonel
Leo Richer LaFleche

Major John S. Roper

1929-1930
Lieutenant-Colonel
Leo Richer LaFleche

Major John S. Roper

Brigadier General Alex Ross

1931-1933
Major John S. Roper

Brigadier-General Alex Ross

Lieutenant-Colonel W.W. Foster

1934-1936
Brigadier-General Alex Ross

Lieutenant-Colonel W.W. Foster

Lieutenant-Colonel
George A. Drew

1936-1937
Brigadier-General Alex Ross

Lieutenant-Colonel W.W. Foster

Lieutenant-Colonel B.W. Roscoe

1938-1939
Lieutenant-Colonel W.W. Foster

Colonel C. Basil Price

Alex Walker

1940-1943
Alex Walker

Lieutenant-Colonel W.C.
Nicholson

Major J.D. Winslow

1944-1945
Alex Walker

William Walker

Edward James Struthers

1946-1947
Major-General C.B. Price
Lieutenant-Colonel L.D.M. Baxter
Captain Allan Piper
Group Captain Alfred Watts

1948-1949
Lieutenant-Colonel L.D.M. Baxter
Group Captain Alfred Watts
E.S. Evans
W.A.T. Anglin

1950-1951
Group Captain Alfred Watts
Dr. C.B. Lumsden
Joseph K. Kennedy
Very Reverend John O. Anderson

1952-1953
Dr. C.B. Lumsden
Very Reverend John O. Anderson
Edward S. Evans
George E. Gleave

1954-1955
Very Reverend John O. Anderson
George E. Gleave
H.W. Sutherland
Donald S. McTavish

1956-1957
D.L. Burgess
H.W. Sutherland
Donald S. McTavish
C.C. Sparling

1958-1959
D.L. Burgess
Mervyn Woods
C.C. Sparling
F.T. O'Brecht

1960-1961
Mervyn Woods
C.C. Sparling
F.T. O'Brecht
R.E. MacBeath

1962-1963
Judge C.C. Sparling
F.T. O'Brecht
R.E. MacBeath
Robert Kohaly

1964-1965
F.T. O'Brecht
R.E. MacBeath
Robert Kohaly
J. Redmond Roche

1966-1967
R.E. MacBeath
Robert Kohaly
J. Redmond Roche
A.H. Adams

1968-1969
Robert Kohaly
J. Redmond Roche
A.H. Adams
Robert G. Smellie

1970-1971
J. Redmond Roche
Robert G. Smellie
Robert D. McChesney
David Hunter
Ed Coley
James Fagan

1972-1973
Robert G. Smellie
Robert D. McChesney
Ed Coley
David Hunter
James Fagan
Doug McDonald

1974-1975
Robert D. McChesney
Douglas McDonald
Ron Bedgood
Ray Tuokko
Ed Coley
Reverend H.E. Harris

1976-1977
Douglas McDonald
Ed Coley
Ray Tuokko
Jack Chapman
Ron Bedgood
Al Harvey

1978-1979
Ed Coley
Al Harvey
Ron Bedgood
Dave Capperauld
Jack Chapman
Gaston Garceau

1980-1981
Al Harvey
Dave Capperauld
Ron Bedgood
Steve Dunsdon
Gaston Garceau
Anthony Stacey

1982-1983
Dave Capperauld
Steve Dunsdon
Gaston Garceau
Anthony Stacey
Dick Chapelow
Don Hamilton

1984-1985
Steve Dunsdon
Anthony Stacey
Don Hamilton
Dick Chapelow
Fred Williams
Gaston Garceau

1986-1987
Anthony Stacey
Gaston Garceau
Hugh Greene
Fred Williams
Jack Jolleys
James Tyndall

1988-1989
Gaston Garceau
Fred williams
Hugh Greene
Jack Jolleys
Bill Smith
James Tyndall

1990-1991
Fred Williams
Jack Jolleys
Hugh Greene
Robert Haley
Joe Kobolak
Fred Winn

1992-1993
Jack Jolleys
Hugh Greene
Joe Kobolak
Chuck Murphy
Robert Haley
Allan Parks

1994-1995
Hugh Greene
Joe Kobolak
Chuck Murphy
Robert Haley
Allan Parks
Ralph Annis

SUB-EXECUTIVE COMMITTEE
TREASURERS, CHAIRMEN AND VICE-CHAIRMEN

1925-1926
Lieutenant-Colonel
Leo R. LaFleche
A.E. Moore
Lieutenant-Colonel
J. Keiller Mackay

1927
J.A. MacIssac
A.E. Moore
Major John S. Roper

1928-1933
J.A. MacIssac
A.E. Moore
E.W. Cornell

1934-1935
Major Milton F. Gregg
A.E. Moore
E.W. Cornell

1936-1937
Major Milton F. Gregg
A.E. Moore

1938-1939
Lieutenant-Colonel
Milton F. Gregg
A.E. Moore

1940-1945
Captain G.H. Rochester
A.E. Moore

1946-1949
Captain G.H. Rochester
A.E. Moore
Lieutenant-Colonel
Lucien Lalonde

1950-1951
Group Captain H.R. Stewart
Erle R. Burgess

1952-1953
Group Captain H.R. Stewart
Erle R. Burgess
Captain A.G. Munich

1954-1957
Group Captain H.R. Stewart
Erle R. Burgess
Alan MacDonald

1958-1959
Group Captain H.R. Stewart
Erle R. Burgess
Donald S. McTavish

1960-1961
Group Captain H.R. Stewart
Erle R. Burgess
Jean Miquelon

1962-1967
Group Captain H.R. Stewart
Chester M. Merriam
The Honourable Myles Murray

1968-1969
Brigadier-General James A. de
Lalanne
Chester M. Merriam
The Honourable Myles Murray

1970-1973
Brigadier-General
James A. de Lalanne
Chester M. Merriam

1974-1975
H. Austin Hunt
Chester M. Merriam

1976-1979
H. Austin Hunt
Ron Watson
Bob Ford

1980-1993
Robert G. Jones
Bob Ford
Patrick Watkins

1994-1995
Robert G. Jones
Patrick Watkins
Clarence King

Dates to Remember

1909
- Last Post Fund organized.

1914
- World War I begins (July 28).

1915
- John McCrae writes *In Flanders' Fields* (May 3), first published in *Punch*, Dec. 8, 1915.
- Prime Minister Sir Robert Borden creates the Military Hospitals Commission to care for returning veterans (June).

1916
- Percy Lake takes command of the British forces in Mesopotamia.
- The government appoints the Board of Pension Commissioners.

1917
- Canada's four divisions, fighting together for the first time, record a major victory at Vimy Ridge (April 9).
- Representatives of 147 veterans associations meet in Winnipeg to form the Great War Veterans Association (GWVA) (April 10).
- Parliament passes a bill to create a program to resettle veterans on land in the West.
- The GWVA launches a national magazine, *The Veteran* (December).

1918
- Moina Michael, a New York City YMCA canteen employee, suggests using the poppy as a symbol of remembrance.
- The federal cabinet summons an advisory committee from the GWVA to advise it on how best to absorb returning soldiers into civilian life.
- World War I ends (Nov. 11).

1919
- The Soldiers' Settlement Board is established.
- The basic rate for a 100% war disability is established as equivalent to an average unskilled laborer's wage.

1920
- Poppy replicas are used widely in the United States on Decoration Day.

1921
- The GWVA's dominion executive committee adopts the poppy as the organization's flower of remembrance (July 5).
- GWVA representatives attend the founding conference of the British Empire Service League (BESL) in South Africa.
- Grant MacNeil is appointed secretary of the GWVA.

1922
- James Layton Ralston heads a Royal Commission on Pensions and Re-establishment.
- The Department of Soldiers Civil Re-establishment creates Vetcraft Shops to manufacture poppy emblems.
- A group of hospitalized veterans form the Tuberculous Veterans Association.
- The federal government initiates annual contributions to the Last Post Fund.
- The GWVA invites five other veterans groups to form the Dominion Veterans Alliance in an effort to lobby for joint concerns.

1923
- The GWVA issues a declaration of principles that calls for veterans' unity.
- BESL head Earl Haig proposes that the organization hold its next conference in Canada to help promote unity.

1924
- The GWVA issues an official invitation for the BESL council to visit Canada.

1925
- At its annual conference, the GWVA passes a resolution supporting the union of all Canadian veterans groups (June).

- Earl Haig addresses 3,000 veterans in Ottawa and asks them to put aside their differences (June).
- Haig appoints Sir Richard Turner VC to organize and chair a veterans unity conference set for Nov. 25 in Winnipeg.
- Delegates from 10 organizations and 50 independent regimental societies and clubs gather in Winnipeg's Marlborough Hotel. Sir Percy Lake heads a 21-man committee to draft a constitution for the Canadian Legion of the British Empire Service League. Delegates elect Lake as first Dominion president.
- Two major veterans groups — the Amputations Association and the Army and Navy Veterans — decline the offer to join the Legion.

1926
- Saskatchewan becomes the first province to ratify the Legion's constitution and form a command (Feb. 17).
- The 14-member Spokane, Washington, unit of the British War Veterans Association becomes the first American post of the Canadian Legion (March).
- Lake and seven other members of the Dominion Executive Council (DEC) create the

Dominion Command Service Bureau to take over from the GWVA's legislative and adjustment bureau in Ottawa; Thomas Lapp is named acting director. *The Veteran* is reconstituted as *The Legionary*, effective May 1. The sub-committee decides to call the Legion's local bodies 'branches' (April).

- The DEC selects a design by George Inglis as the official Legion badge. The first copy is struck from Manitoba gold and presented to Gov. Gen. Viscount Byng (May 29).

- Secretary of state George Perley issues letters patent under the Companies Act granting a national charter to the Legion (July 17).

- The 4,000-member Tuberculous Veterans Association disbands and becomes the Tuberculous Veterans Section of the Legion (Oct. 1).

1927
- The Legion holds its first convention, in Winnipeg. Treasurer Leo LaFleche reports a surplus of $10,000. Delegates vote to have the Legion remain the sole distributor of poppies manufactured by Vetcraft Industries. Lake is re-elected president; he accepts on the condition that he can designate many duties to LaFleche. 'Comrade' is adopted

as the official term of address for legionnaires (Jan. 24-29).

- Against Legion protests, the government sets Armistice Day for Nov. 7; many branches hold services on Nov. 11 regardless.

- The Imperial Veterans of Canada join the Legion.

- In Toronto, the poppy campaign raises $40,000.

- Thirty Canadian veterans travel to France and Belgium for the first conducted tour of the battlefields and cemeteries.

1928
- Earl Haig dies at age 67 (January).

- The Liberal government appoints a special committee to examine pensions, disability treatment, land settlement programs and civil service jobs for veterans.

- Legion membership reaches 50,000.

- Delegates to the second convention, in Saint John, elect Sir Arthur Currie president. The post of vice-chairman is eliminated. Strong support is given to a resolution in favor of a national broadcasting system for Canada. Dominion Command is requested to study the feasibility of organizing a pilgrimage to coincide with the dedication of a monument at

Vimy Ridge. Outgoing president Lake asks Legion members to consider admitting sons and daughters as members (June).

1929
- Dominion chairman Jack Moore initiates the Foster Fathers' Program.
- An ailing Currie submits his resignation as president. Delegates to the convention in Regina elect LaFleche. The issue of bringing sons and daughters into the Legion is raised again, but postponed without a decision (November).

1930
- Parliament passes the War Veterans Allowance Act.
- The government establishes a pension appeal court; LaFleche is named one of three members.
- Winnipeg veteran Reg Bowler is named the Legion's first general secretary.
- Legion branches begin to operate 'mulligan kitchens' to feed hungry Canadians.

1931
- LaFleche resigns as president to become deputy minister of National Defence.
- Delegates to the convention in Niagara Falls elect John Roper president. The issue of membership for sons and daughters is raised, and postponed, once

more; it will not reappear for 38 years.
- Parliament amends the Armistice Day Act to entrench Nov. 11 as the day of national remembrance.

1932
- Believing they can win more rights on their own, some Canadian veterans begin to form splinter groups; *The Legionary* blames the disenchantment on "blatherskites and oldtime barrack-room lawyers."
- The Depression hits *The Legionary* hard; circulation falls to 11,000, and the subscription rate is dropped from $1 to 75¢. John Hundevad is named editor, replacing Thomas Lapp (September).

1933
- The government creates the Canadian Pensions Commission.
- As president, Roper takes a hard line against the government's unemployment policies.
- *The Legionary* warns that "war clouds are darkening the international horizon" and decries the wretched condition of Canada's armed forces.
- Legion grand president Currie dies in Montreal at 57. His funeral draws one of the largest contingents of military personnel ever gathered on Canadian soil (Dec. 5).

✤

1934

- Meeting in Ottawa, more than 1,500 delegates elect Brig.-Gen. Alex Ross as president, who issues a call for legionnaires to "branch out boldly into a new and wider sphere" and not count on government help. The convention votes to resurrect plans to organize a Vimy Memorial pilgrimage (March).

- Dick Hale, former president of the Tuberculous Veterans Association, is appointed the Legion's first chief pensions officer.

- The government gives in to pressure from the Legion to reorganize the Canadian Pension Commission, and establishes a royal commission under Judge J.D. Hyndman to study the unemployment problem.

1935

- The Legion presents a brief to the Hyndman Commission calling for full employment of veterans (March 15).

- Hyndman recommends special treatment for unemployed veterans, establishment of a Veterans Assistance Commission, and formation of a Corps of Commissionaires (June).

- Prime Minister Mackenzie King names three legionnaires to his cabinet (October).

- Legion membership stands at 160,000.

1936

- In Vancouver, convention delegates establish a $250,000 endowment fund to continue the work of the Dominion Service Bureau. Ross is re-elected president (March).

- Some 6,300 veterans and their family members sail from Montreal on five ships bound for France. Another 4,000 pilgrimage participants join them at the Vimy Memorial for the unveiling of Walter Allward's 42-metre twin towers (July 26).

1937

- *Salute to Valor*, a filmed record of the Vimy pilgrimage, has its premiere at Shea's Hippodrome Theatre in Toronto (July 9).

- Dominion president Ross leads a delegation to Germany and places a wreath at the tomb of World War I ace Manfred von Richtofen.

- The Rattray Commission recommends making unemployed veterans the responsibility of the federal government, and establishes the Corps of Commissionaires.

1938

- Legion membership surpasses 175,000.

- The seventh convention elects Vancouver police chief W.W. Foster president. Delegates vote to establish a permanent Dominion Command committee on education (January).

- The Legion files a brief with the Rowell-Sirois Commission on Dominion-Provincial Relations calling for a strong central government and repatriation of a Canadian constitution with some form of amending formula.

- During the Munich Crisis, Foster offers to put the Legion's resources at the country's disposal (September).

1939

- In a two-week period, more than 10,000 Canadian veterans under the age of 60 answer the Legion's call for prospective volunteers.

- The Ontario government assigns Legion members to guard hydroelectric facilities (April).

- Ten thousand legionnaires turn out in Ottawa for the unveiling of the National War Memorial (May 21).

- Three days after war is declared, Foster calls on all veterans to get involved to the best of their ability; the average age of legionnaires is 49 (Sept. 13).

- The government issues a charter for the Canadian Legion War Services Inc. (CLWS); Ralph Webb of Winnipeg is appointed general manager. The Canadian Legion Educational Service (CLES), an extension of the Dominion Command education committee, is created under the auspices of the CLWS.

- The CLWS opens its first recreation hut at Camp Barriefield, Ont., (December).

1940

- Dominion convention delegates in Montreal demand the government immediately conscript able Canadians. Former sergeant Alex Walker becomes the first non-commissioned officer to be president (May).

- Walker meets with Prime Minister King and asks for "complete and unrestricted mobilization" (June).

- A Legion brief recommends that the government avoid the mistakes made with returning World War I veterans and institute effective rehabilitation plans.

- The government announces plans to create a veterans welfare division within the Department of Pensions and National Health.

❦

1941

- The Legion makes rehabilitation recommendations to a Commons committee on pensions.
- The Legion heads a joint appeal for funds for overseas troops; incorporating the Salvation Army, Knights of Columbus, YMCA, YWCA and others, the fund is soon oversubscribed by $1 million.
- The Legion releases a manifesto entitled *Call for Total War* (Oct. 21).

1942

- Dominion education officer John MacNeil becomes the first Legion staff member to die in battle.
- General secretary Reg Bowler drowns in the Ottawa River (March).
- In the aftermath of a national plebiscite on conscription, Walker says King's lack of action is creating disunity.
- Delegates to the ninth convention re-elect Walker and every other incumbent officer — a first. Another first is the presence of M.G. Ford, the first World War II veteran to vote at a Legion convention. George Herwig is appointed general secretary (May).

- Walker tells the prime minister to "heed the lesson of Dieppe" and invoke conscription (August).

1943

- Parliament passes three key pieces of rehabilitation legislation: the Civil Reinstatement Act, the Post-Discharge Reestablishment Order and the Veterans Land Act.
- The Legion urges King to establish a federal department to represent veterans.

1944

- The government announces plans to form the Department of Veterans Affairs (January).
- Parliament passes the Gratuities Act in response to Legion requests.
- Delegates to the convention in Vancouver welcome news that Allied forces have landed in France. Walker is re-elected for an unprecedented third term. Allan Piper, a double amputee, becomes the first World War II veteran elected to the DEC (June).
- Legionnaires boo Defence Minister Andrew McNaughton for defending King's policy of "conscription if necessary, but not necessarily conscription" (Nov. 6).

- King gives in to pressure and announces that 16,000 home-service draftees will be sent overseas (Nov. 22).

1945
- Walker returns from an overseas tour with recommendations that King address the employment concerns of Canadian service people (April).
- The Legion advocates a "first in, first out" de-mobilization policy.
- The CLWS turns over $1.1 million to the government's Canteen Fund.

1946
- Four hundred World War II veterans register at the convention in Quebec City. Maj.-Gen. Basil Price is elected president. Delegates reinstate the position of vice-chairman after an 18-year absence. A motion to extend membership to conscripts who fought overseas is defeated (May).
- The CLES wraps up its work and enumerates its achievements: 60 elementary, high school and technical courses administered to more than 200,000 people; more than two million textbooks distributed.
- Returning veterans swell the ranks of Legion branches, but not without some problems.

- Operation Fitness is launched to bring the fitness level of Canadian children up to world standards.

1947
- The Legion studies housing shortages and lobbies the government for assistance for veterans.
- Allan Piper resigns as Dominion second vice-president to become the Legion's deputy chief pension officer.

1948
- Delegates at the convention in Saskatoon press for higher disability pensions and war veterans allowances. The beret is adopted as official Legion head-dress. Lionel Baxter is elected president. Sir Richard Turner resigns as grand president after 23 years of Legion involvement (May).
- Baxter suffers a heart attack; his duties are assumed temporarily by first vice Alf Watts.

1949
- Legion officials visit Newfoundland to discuss possible amalgamation.
- General secretary Herwig dies at age 59; T.D. Anderson is named to replace him.
- The GWVA of Newfoundland votes to surrender its charter to the Legion (Oct. 12).

1950

- Legion branches and commands raise more than $60,000 for flood relief in Manitoba.

- Delegates to the convention in Winnipeg adopt a standard Legion uniform: beret, blue blazer and grey slacks or skirt. Overseas conscripts are granted membership after a 90-minute debate. Alf Watts, 39, becomes the first World War II vet to be elected president. With the Korean War three months old, delegates call for "total preparedness of Canadian troops."

- Dominion chairman Jack Moore dies at age 68, three weeks after being elected to his 14th consecutive term; Erle Burgess assumes post.

- DEC requests pension increase of 33.3 percent and other changes to legislation (Nov. 10).

1951

- Chief pension officer Dick Hale dies at age 63 (March).

- The Legion launches a harsh attack against government proposals to change the way pensions are assigned (May 17).

- Watts travels to all provincial conventions to rally support against the government's proposals.

- Don Thompson is appointed to head Dominion Service Bureau.

- A sports medal is created to encourage sports at the community level.

- The government introduces legislation to increase pensions by 33.3 percent and withdraws controversial means-test provisions (Nov.16).

1952

- Bill Lumsden becomes the first former private to be elected president. The organization and development committee recommends that the Legion "give serious consideration to a revaluation and reconsideration of its aims, objects and methods of operation" (May).

- The Legion's service work is re-emphasized across the country.

1953

- Ontario Hydro Branch sponsors the Canadian Olympic Training Plan (COTP), forerunner of the Legion's track and field program.

1954

- Legion membership is 190,000; two-thirds are World War I vets.

- Very Rev. John Anderson is elected president at the convention in Toronto.

1955
- The first national membership committee is formed.
- Anderson writes in *The Legionary* that the organization is "at the crossroads," spurring members to increase the focus on community efforts.

1956
- Convention delegates vote to seek support from each command for the COTP. With no serving executives available to step up, delegates elect David Burgess. A two-year membership drive is launched (June).
- The Legion recommends plans for a national war memorial to honor Canadian casualties in World War II and Korea.

1957
- The COTP is renamed the Canadian Legion Sports Training Program; $20,000 is allocated to run clinics.

1958
- Legion membership reaches 237,000.
- The British Empire Service League votes to change its name to the British Commonwealth Ex-Services League (BCEL).
- Burgess is re-elected for a second term. Convention delegates in Edmonton vote to change the organization's name to the Canadian Legion. Delegates voice their support for a Canadian Red Ensign flag that combines a Union Jack and a maple leaf.
- DEC asks Alan Beddoe to design a new Legion badge; an acrimonious debate ensues.

1959
- DEC commissions Clifford Bowering to write *Service*, a history of the Canadian Legion's first 35 years.
- Legion housing projects are valued at more than $3 million.
- Twenty-six of 30 Canadian track and field athletes at the Pan-American Games are graduates of the Legion's program.

1960
- The Queen grants permission to re-title the organization The Royal Canadian Legion.
- Dominion secretary T.D. Anderson resigns to become chairman of the Canadian Pension Commission; he is replaced by Don Thompson. Murray MacFarlane replaces Thompson as Service Bureau director.
- Convention delegates in Windsor vote in favor of the traditional Red Ensign as Canada's flag. Mervyn Woods is elected president.

1961

- Legion membership surpasses 250,000.
- Woods faces criticism of proposed new Legion badge at provincial conventions.

1962

- The federal government grants $50,000 to help finance the Legion's track program.
- Clare Sparling is acclaimed president in Halifax. Chester Merriam is elected chairman. Third vice Bob Kohaly is appointed to lead a 10-year membership drive. Delegates ask the government to adopt the Red Ensign as Canada's flag. A committee is formed to develop projects for Canada's centennial. The new Legion badge is approved.
- Seventy-nine Canadians fly to Holland for the first post-World War II pilgrimage (September).

1963

- Geoffrey Dyson is hired as the Legion's national sports director. The Legion grants $125,000 for its fitness program.
- A battle begins to brew over newly elected Prime Minister Lester Pearson's plans to adopt a new Canadian flag.

1964

- Convention delegates in Winnipeg boo the prime minister when he announces plans to introduce a new Canadian flag. Fred O'Brecht is elected president. The Legion decries government plans to transfer administration of some veterans hospitals to civilian hands.
- Legionnaires voice their opposition to Pearson's flag design during an extended debate.

1965

- The Centennial Fund campaign is initiated to raise $1 million (April 9).
- The government appoints Mervyn Woods to examine the work of the Canadian Pension Commission.

1966

- The Legion presents a 136-page brief to the Woods Commission
- A record-setting 1,063 delegates to the convention in Montreal demand that the government adjust the basic pension rate. The Legion pledges support to veterans in developing Commonwealth countries. Ron MacBeath is acclaimed president.
- The Centennial Fund is officially created (Oct. 21).
- Membership stands at 280,000.

1967

- Legion branches and commands launch centennial projects.
- The track and field program expands with a private endowment of $44,000.

1968

- The Woods Commission files its report; the Legion cooperates with other veterans groups to push for government acceptance of the report.
- Convention delegates acclaim Kohaly president in Penticton.
- The Centennial Fund stands at $1,011,404.

1969

- The joint veterans group continues to press for acceptance of the Woods Report.
- Changes in postal rates create a 1,400 percent increase in mailing *Legion Magazine*; significant changes to the publication's design and structure follow.

1970

- Dominion secretary Don Thompson resigns to become chairman of the War Veterans Allowance Board.
- The government withdraws its support of the Legion's track and field program; the national program is suspended until 1976.

- Redmond Roche is acclaimed president. Convention delegates in Ottawa vote 1,357-1,320 to force fraternal members to pay dues. For the second time, the post of vice-chairman is eliminated.
- Membership surpasses 300,000.

1971

- The new Pension Act becomes law (March 30).
- Jean Lamy becomes Dominion secretary (April 1).
- Commands begin to discuss the idea of extending membership to sons and daughters.
- Computerization is introduced to the Legion's membership processing system.

1972

- The government introduces annual cost-of-living adjustments to pensions and allowances (May).
- Delegates to the convention in Regina elect Bob Smellie as president. Membership is extended to armed forces personnel. Entry for sons and daughters is set for Jan. 1, 1974 with limitations.
- A combined veterans group recommends a new formula for determining the basic pension rate.
- The Early Bird membership campaign is introduced.

1973

- Vice-president Dave Hunter resigns; DEC replaces him with Ray Tuokko.

1974

- Convention delegates in St. John's vote to study funding a revamped national track and field program out of Centennial Fund interest. Bob McChesney is acclaimed president. The Legion determines to promote citizenship with a committee named ACTION — A Commitment To Improve Our Nation.

- Dominion chairman Chester Merriam dies in an automobile accident 15 days after being elected for his seventh term. DEC votes to appoint vice-president Bert Harris as interim chairman; the post of vice-chairman is reinstituted and filled by Ron Watson.

- Associate membership stands at 10,000.

1975

- ACTION chairman Kohaly promotes the program at provincial conventions.

- A year-long 50th anniversary celebration is launched (November).

- The Legion illuminates the National War Memorial as the first of three golden anniversary gifts to the nation.

1976

- The Legion launches Operation Service to inform all Canadian veterans of potential benefits (April 9).

- Doug McDonald becomes president. Watson is acclaimed chairman. The convention in Winnipeg votes to extend ACTION for two years, but doubts are expressed about its effectiveness.

- The government announces plans to move the Department of Veterans Affairs to Charlottetown (Oct. 28).

- DEC appoints a special committee to study the problems encountered by aging veterans.

1977

- The ACTION committee shifts its focus to national unity.

- The issue of greater rights for associate members dominates provincial conventions.

- Quebec Command takes a strong pro-unity stance (May).

1978

- The Legion protests the relocation of DVA.

- Convention delegates in Edmonton vote 1,107-1,068 to allow associates to vote and hold office at branch level. Membership is extended to wartime conscripts. Ed Coley is elected president.

- Total membership reaches
419,474, but the number of
ordinary members declines for
the first time since the 1950s.
- The Legion Seniors Program is
launched.

1979
- DEC grants three $20,000 fellow-
ships in geriatrics.
- Ontario Command votes to
support full rights for associates
(May).

1980
- Convention delegates in
Penticton, B.C., vote to extend
membership privileges to sons
and daughters. Delegates focus
on issues related to aging.
Al Harvey becomes the first
Newfoundlander to be elected
president. Bob Ford replaces
retiring chairman Watson.
- The Legion hosts the BCEL
conference in Ottawa and
pledges additional funds.

1981
- The Legion pledges $250,000 to
the Terry Fox Youth Centre as a
wedding gift to the Prince of
Wales.
- DEC bans dues discrimination
against associates (May).
- Allan Parks is the first associate
elected to provincial office in
Prince Edward Island (June).

1982
- Dominion secretary Jean Lamy
retires; he is replaced by
Colin Graham.
- In Quebec City, convention
delegates extend membership
rights to spouses, widows and
widowers. Dave Capperauld is
acclaimed president. The term
'comrade' is reconfirmed for
all members. A committee is
formed to plan celebrations for
the Legion's 60th anniversary.
- The National War Memorial is
altered to reflect the sacrifices
in World War II and Korea.

1983
- Total Legion strength surpasses
600,000 for the first time.
- The Diamond Jubilee committee
settles on a theme: "Pride In
Our Past — Faith In Our
Future." Numerous projects
are announced.

1984
- At the Winnipeg convention,
Steve Dunsdon is acclaimed
president. The gerontology
fellowship program is extended
to include nurses.
- An aural history project is
launched to capture the memories of legionnaires across
Canada.
- The Let Us Help You campaign
renews the objectives of
Operation Service.

1985

- A notice of intent to consolidate the ordinary and associate-voting categories into one called 'legionnaire' is hotly debated at provincial conventions; it receives little support. The highlight of most conventions is the signing of the Legion's Articles of Faith.
- Fred Hannington is appointed Dominion secretary.
- Almost six million Darwin tulip bulbs are sold to bloom during the diamond jubilee year.
- A state dinner kicks off the Legion's anniversary (Nov. 2).

1986

- A record-setting 3,105 delegates celebrate the Legion's 60th anniversary. Dame Vera Lynn caps the Edmonton convention with a nostalgic performance of wartime songs. Tony Stacey is acclaimed president.
- Ten young legionnaires are sent to Europe to help spread the concept of remembrance.
- The Legion protests against the distribution of *The Kid Who Couldn't Miss*, a film that questions the war record of Billy Bishop.
- A Legion-sponsored conference studies aging issues.
- DEC files a position paper with Defence Minister Perrin Beatty supporting maintenance of adequate defence forces (Dec. 12).

1987

- The Legion presses the case for extended War Veterans Allowance benefits (March).
- Allan Parks becomes the first associate to become provincial president (P.E.I. June).
- Alberta-Northwest Territories and Saskatchewan commands vote to extend membership privileges to grandchildren.

1988

- In Ottawa, Gaston Garceau is acclaimed president. The track and field program is given an ongoing mandate.
- The Prince Phillip Appeal for the BCEL reaches its goal of $1 million.

1989

- Parks becomes the first associate on DEC.
- The annual youth pilgrimage is reinstated.
- The government grants the Legion $500,000 over three years to extend its seniors program.
- The Legion Still Cares program is initiated to contact all veterans and dependents without benefits.

1990

- Convention delegates in Vancouver vote in favor of a renewed national unity campaign. Fred Williams is elected president.
- The Legion presents a brief to a Senate sub-committee studying the impact of the federal budget on incomes and the purchasing power of seniors.

1991

- Canadian unity dominates the agendas at provincial conventions.
- The president, Williams, dies; Jack Jolleys becomes president (Sept. 27).
- The Legion's Canadian unity public service announcements air on national television (December).

1992

- The Legion joins other veterans groups to protest the CBC television programs *The Valour And The Horror.*
- Delegates in Quebec City vote to extend membership to grandchildren. Jolleys is elected for a full term. Parks becomes the first associate elected to Dominion office.

- The Tuberculous Veterans Section vacates its seat on DEC and begins to wind up its operations.
- The Legion backs the 'yes' side for the national referendum on constitutional reform.

1993

- The Legion's voting membership stands at 466,464. The total strength stands at 572,281.
- Ten World War I vets — one from each command — are transported to Ottawa for Remembrance Day to mark the 75th anniversary of the end of the war (Nov. 11).
- A controversy over branch autonomy begins when Newton Branch in Surrey, B.C., bars three Sikhs from entering its premises without removing their turbans (Nov. 11).
- DEC passes a bylaw to permit the wearing of religious headdress by members and invited guests on branch premises.

1994
- Meeting in Calgary, delegates reject the proposed head-dress bylaw. The convention elects Hugh Greene as president.
  Pat Watkins replaces the retiring Bob Ford as chairman. Membership is broadened to include siblings of people eligible for ordinary membership.

- The Canadian Unity committee is reactivated.
- The government introduces fundamental changes to the disability pension system.

Index

✦

✦